The STRATEGY Dialogues

"When an author can make something as practical as it is entertaining, you have something special! John Hillen makes strategy actionable and understandable in a way that everyone will be able to navigate, grasp and put into practice."

Patrick Lencioni
New York Times bestselling author of 13 books, including
The Five Dysfunctions of a Team, with over 8 million copies sold worldwide

"We hear the word 'strategy' everywhere, but it rarely rises above a buzzword. Relying on decades of experience in business, academia, and public life, John Hillen masterfully breaks down the fundamentals of what strategy is and how to use it to make your company and life more effective and meaningful."

Arthur C. Brooks
Harvard Professor and #1 New York Times bestselling author

"John Hillen has reproduced a masterclass on how to think and act strategically in book form. His imaginary students come to appreciate that developing their businesses is all about asking the right questions rather than applying rigid formulas."

Professor Sir Lawrence Freedman
Author of Strategy: A History

"As a CEO, strategy is important for setting the long-term vision and direction for the company. Adapting to changing market conditions and rethinking strategy at the right time is also critical. John's creative approach in this book helps readers virtually engage to learn the difficult tenets of strategic thinking."

Carey A. Smith
Chair, President and Chief Executive Officer, Parsons Corporation (NYSE: PSN)

"While after I read most strategy books, I wish I hadn't because they make no contribution to the theory and practice of strategy, I felt the opposite after reading The Strategy Dialogues. John Hillen makes a valuable contribution by helping readers appreciate the importance of the dialogue process in creating great strategy and providing practical advice on how to conduct a productive strategy dialogue."

Roger L. Martin
Former Dean of the Rotman School of Management
and Thinkers50 #1 Management Thinker in the World

A Primer on Business Strategy and Strategic Management

John Hillen

With illustrations by Amber Anderson

Concise books for smart learners

Our mission at econcise publishing
is to create concise, approachable and affordable books
that help people grow and thrive in business and life.

If you're interested in staying informed about current developments
in the field and getting more information about new books for smart
learners, you are welcome to visit *www.econcise.com/newsletter* and
subscribe to our newsletter.

Hardcover ISBN: 978-3-903386-31-0
Paperback ISBN: 978-3-903386-28-0
ePub ISBN: 978-3-903386-29-7
Kindle ISBN: 978-3-903386-30-3

Cover design and illustrations: Amber Anderson, https://amberanderson.co.uk/
Copy editor: Harriet Power

First published 2025 by **econcise**
© 2025 econcise GmbH
Am Sonnengrund 14
A-9062 Moosburg (Austria)

Contents

*To my many strategy students and clients over the years,
who taught me that an involved dialogue was the best way
to grasp strategic concepts and acquire a strategic mindset.*

Preface

"I would not give a fig for the simplicity that lies on this side of complexity,
but for the simplicity that lies on the other side of complexity,
I would give my life."

—Oliver Wendell Holmes

Over the years, I have taught, written, and consulted on strategy (as well as executing my own strategy as a CEO of several public and private firms). During that time, I have continually been asked a variation of this question: "Tell me *the one* book, article, or podcast I should read or listen to, to get strategy." Or, "You're the expert, Hillen—give me *the one* read to get up to speed on this mysterious discipline."

I understand why people ask me these questions. At some point in their careers, every executive and leader is exhorted to "think strategically." But most executives have little practice at it—they have likely succeeded thus far by executing managerial tasks or employing their technical and tactical skills to solve the problems at hand. So, they have often not had much practice in their careers at being strategic.

Some executives intuit that strategy is not a natural competency for most managers and leaders. One famous study found that only four percent of the executive population naturally explains decisions and seeks to convince people by using strategic logic.[1] Despite all that, the people who ask me for *the one* strategy article or *the one* strategy book are utterly aware that they want, perhaps need, to access this skill and wield its power.

I lose points with them when I hem and haw a bit instead of having a simple, ready answer. "Well, there's not really *one* book or *a* book ...", "Strategy is a big topic; it depends on which aspect of it you are most interested in learning about ...", and so on. Usually, I'm left with the choice of recommending something from among many (there are some excellent one-volume books, after all) or recommending a mini library

---

1 Rooke, D., and Torbert, W. (2005). Transformations of leadership. *Harvard Business Review, 83*(4), 66–76.

of books, articles, videos, and podcasts to give aspiring strategists a more fulsome perspective.

I know some other strategists who send people huge decks of diagrams intended to represent strategic tools or frameworks, which strategists use to organize their thinking. One of these monster decks floating around is called *100 Models and Diagrams for Strategic Management*. It is a 100-page PowerPoint deck, and each page has a different and often complex strategic concept captured in the matrices or diagrams we strategists love to use. It's a cool deck for us strategy geeks. Still, absent any further explanation for the recipient, I cannot see how it can do anything but confuse and perhaps even harm the person looking for "the one thing" to "get" strategy. It feels akin to giving a race car to someone who has never driven before—and then telling them to drive it in a competitive race!

Often, these questioners have their own answer after my hemming and hawing. Could they sit in on my classes? Or eavesdrop on one of my strategy workshops in the corporate world? Over the years, in both those settings, I've developed a good track record and a winning methodology—based on teaching basic strategic concepts through dialogue and interaction. When I integrated that method into my MBA classes, I won the Outstanding Professor award every year I taught the core strategy course. My business clients loved the exercises and the interactions that led them to understand and frame their own strategic possibilities—much more than they liked me walking into their conference room and telling them what strategy to adopt. The dialectical approach to learning strategic management and developing a strategic mindset worked. But I could only have so many people audit a class or spy on a workshop.

I wrote this book to solve this dilemma and answer these questions— but only partially. *The Strategy Dialogues* is not meant to replace business school textbooks or the big books written by business strategy gurus. Instead, it is meant to be an accessible supplement for either. This book is for anybody seeking the basics of business strategy and strategic management, be they an executive on the job or a business school student seeking to master a core discipline of the business world.

The Strategy Dialogues is meant to help on three levels. First, it is a primer for what I consider to be essential knowledge about business strategy and strategic management. The book offers the foundational ideas and frameworks strategists use for analysis and insight—business strategy's canon of ideas. Of course, any such list is subjective; I have chosen the ideas and strategic tools I consider to be the "greatest hits" of the strategy revolution over the past fifty years. I curated this selection with the experience of what I have seen work with students, clients, and my own companies. The things that made the light bulb of understanding go off and spark a key insight or help deliver an outcome. What got them to "Ah ha! I get it!"

I avoid what might be termed "theological arguments" that are popular among academic strategists. These are not entirely of the "How many angels can dance on the head of a pin?" variety—but in learning strategy basics, they can often distract rather than inform. One of these debates in which I am deeply interested is about how many schools of strategic thought there are—the positioning school versus the design school versus the planning school versus the ... you get it. I love this intricate debate, and I have found practical utility in all the schools of thought—who wouldn't want all the clubs you can carry in your bag? Nonetheless, as important as that debate may be at some level, it is an argument beyond the scope of a primer.

Second, because many readers will want to go deeper—in general and on specific topics—the book can act as an essential reference guide for books, articles, and other easily accessible resources I have assembled at the end of each chapter. I've limited this to what I consider to be the helpful basics and relatively general frameworks. Executives or students who want to go even deeper or into more specialized and arcane strategic territory will have no shortage of thinkers or material. I will compile some of those other resources on the book's website. The fundamental strategy frameworks and concepts covered in this book are more than enough to tackle ninety percent of strategic challenges.

Third, and most importantly, I've chosen to present the material through invented dialogues between people trying to understand and solve strategic problems using fundamental strategy methodologies. You, the reader, get to eavesdrop on those dialogues.

As I mentioned, I've found that this is the easiest and best way for people to learn the sometimes ephemeral concepts of strategy and strategic thinking. This isn't a new approach, of course. For millennia, dialogues between people with different perspectives have been used to help humans sort through the complexities of complicated ideas and seek higher truths. In the Western tradition, we often trace this to Plato's famous Socratic dialogues concerning the most important questions of philosophy, politics, and ethics. The method was repeated by Saint Augustine, Galileo, David Hume and many other philosophers and thinkers over the years—not to mention playwrights. The method predates those examples and crosses every culture. Many foundational religious texts—*The Bhagavad Gita*, *The Bible*, *The Dîgha-Nikâya* (*The Dialogues of the Buddha*), and Confucian texts—use dialogue to illuminate complex ideas and concepts. When humans encounter alien or obscure concepts, they talk it through, apply it to real situations, get guidance and provocation from a teacher and each other, and work it through together.

This is not a so-called business novel. Instead, it lets you be a fly on the wall in a strategy workshop, where you can overhear an imagined but typical dialogue between people as the strategy process unfolds. In each dialogue, the participants come to understand strategic management concepts and how to apply them to their enterprise. I have had hundreds of these dialogues with clients, my executives, partners, investors, and students over the years when I have been in a position to help them come to their own understanding of how strategy works and how they can use it in their organization. Understanding is a *process*—this is how I've often seen executives "get it."

Naturally, I've used my judgment to determine what and what not to talk about in the strategy dialogues. I'm pretty well trained in strategy—by some of the best minds of our time—and I've practiced it in military, political, policy, and business settings, often at the highest levels or in high-stakes environments. I have taught strategy to hundreds and hundreds of students and executives. I think I have a unique perspective, and many people have told me throughout my career that I have a knack for explaining complicated things in simple but not simplistic terms. I hope you'll find this the case and this book helps you to think strategically. You'll be the judge!

List of Characters

Conrad Orosco and **Jada Akilah** are strategy consultants.

Kurt Amery is a partner in *Argo Ventures*, an investment firm that invests in well-performing small/medium-sized businesses searching for opportunities to break out, scale, and move to the next level of market penetration and success.

Derrick Jouet is the CEO of *Creativia Playsets*, a company that makes playsets that combine physical and virtual experiences for children of all ages. Creativia is struggling to fully understand the competitive dynamics of its market space.

Liz Fiscella is the founder and CEO of *Healthy Family Foodstuffs (HFF)*, a small chain of grocery stores that offer affordable and healthy foods oriented toward growing families. Liz and her team at HFF are confused about which element of their business to use as a foundation to invest and expand.

Steve Adlar is the CEO of *Secure Home Suite*, a company that makes office suite software for mobile and small home-based businesses. Secure Home Suite is baffled about choosing between moves that will expand their current business to more customers and moves that will give them access to new and different customers.

Ian Driscoll is the CEO of *Coactum Financial Technologies*, a software company that automatically matches financial trades for various financial instruments, reducing the time and cost of normal brokered transactions. Ian and Coactum have a successful strategy but are searching for a more profitable business model.

Suzie Nguyen is the founder of *Andromeda eGaming*, an electronic gaming company that uses AI to give each player a different gaming experience every time they play. Andromeda has developed some other products and services related to its game production and is looking for a method to weigh up the various strategies it might need for different business units within the company—and whether mergers, acquisitions, or divestments should be considered.

Alexis Chapman is the CEO of *Celar Logistics*, a regional delivery service focused on last-mile and rural-area delivery. Celar has a strategy to expand but is uncertain about the best method for turning that strategy into a detailed plan and how to track its execution.

The Dilemma:
Good Businesses Treading Water

"A course more promising
Than a wild dedication of yourselves
To unpathed waters, undreamed shores ..."

—William Shakespeare, *A Winter's Tale*, Act 4, Scene 4

Kurt Amery, partner at Argo Ventures, glided into the lobby of his building from the elevators and enthusiastically greeted his guests.

"Conrad, Jada!" he said with a smile. "I am so thrilled to meet you, and thanks for coming on short notice."

"Our pleasure," said Jada Akilah, the younger of the two partners. "Your call intrigued us; we rarely hear directly from professional investing companies."

Kurt guided them to the elevator. "That surprises me," he said as they stepped in. "Why do you think that is the case?"

"A few reasons, I think," said Conrad Orosco. "First, given the investment cycles and performance expectations that investing houses have for their portfolio businesses, they often want a fairly quick fix, and some measurable results in short order. There's nothing wrong with that, of course. It's just that working through strategic changes can be a bit more time-consuming and doesn't necessarily produce instant results."

Kurt nodded as they stopped on his floor and proceeded to his office. "Yes, well, that sounds like my industry—we like to see changes drop better numbers right to the bottom line. Who wouldn't?"

"Right, who wouldn't?" agreed Jada. "But not only does a new strategy often need some time to work, it needs some time to be formulated— perhaps even experimented with and tested ... and then reformulated. Your type aren't known for patience," she said with a twinkle in her eye. "Fair?"

"Semi-fair," said Kurt with a smile. "Though, if we hold a company in our portfolio for five to seven years, in today's dynamic marketplace, that should be enough time to shift strategy or change direction in a company, yes?"

"Hmm, yes," agreed Conrad as he and Jada sat with Kurt at his office table. "But even if an investor is patient enough to let the strategy process unfold, among the things a new strategy might require is an investment—putting even *more* money into a company you've already taken some pains to acquire."

Kurt looked thoughtful. "Okay, that's also a semi-fair critique. If another round of investment is required in a portfolio company to unlock its full value, we can see and judge that pretty conventionally—various return on investment formulas, break-even analyses ... all that. If the analytical model is good, and the assumptions are sound, we can do that math." He smiled. "We are good at math, after all."

"No doubt," said Jada. "But a good grasp of math and returns formulas often leads to our third reason why professional investment companies do not usually engage us."

"I'm all ears," said Kurt, his pen poised over his pad.

"Easily observable metrics-based improvements," said Jada. "That is a language more natural to professional investors. Things like a more cost-effective supply chain, a more efficient balance sheet, process improvements, or even more experienced leadership. These are the kinds of improvements that we tend to see investment firms working on with their portfolio companies."

"And," added Conrad, "at the risk of repeating myself, nothing wrong with that. All good stuff—who doesn't want a company to be better, healthier, and more efficient? It's just, well ..."

"It's just ...?" inquired Kurt.

"It's not strategy," finished Conrad.

"Exactly!" cried Kurt.

"Exactly?" asked Jada. "You agree with us?"

"Of course I do," laughed Kurt. "That's why I invited you here. We need to do something more than our usual improvement playbook for some of our companies. Look, I get it that most investment firms focus on giving their portfolio companies more efficient capital and financial structures. That is their expertise for the most part—financial wizardry. Others, Danaher comes to mind, help them to improve their operational performance. Or help them to onboard more experienced management teams or processes. All those things are great, but I think some of our companies need a strategy injection."

Conrad looked hard at Kurt. "Okay, and if such an injection existed, what would you perceive differently about the patient after it? What would it do for them?"

"Well," answered Kurt. "It wouldn't just make them modestly better at what they do now, but it would help them frame new directions in which to go—new markets, new customers, new products and services, new partnerships—things with more growth potential. They must position themselves for sustained and future advantage, not just squeeze more juice out of their current orange."

Conrad and Jada looked at each other. They could see that Kurt understood more than many of their potential clients. They were always wary of business executives who had been rewarded throughout their careers for hammering more productivity out of an enterprise. Many of those people wanted to hire them. However, those executives often failed to understand that perhaps the most fundamental insight of business strategy is that strategy is about changing and positioning for future advantage, *not* being better at what you do now.[1]

"Ah ..." sighed Conrad. "It sounds like you do understand the potential of a good strategy. This will make it harder to talk you out of engaging us."

Kurt laughed. "Yes, you've not succeeded so far."

"Let me take another shot at losing this potential engagement for us," smiled Jada. "So, you, the financial sponsor, seem to understand the possible benefits of the strategy process. *But* ... are your portfolio companies open to the hard thinking and even harder work that goes into using strategy to reposition in the market? We can help lead them toward water, but will the companies want to drink?"

"I think so, for sure," said Kurt enthusiastically. "At Argo Ventures, a handful of amazing companies have hit a plateau—they perform well and understand their markets. They are success stories."

"But ...?" pushed Jada.

"They are a bit stuck," admitted Kurt. "All of them can see significantly more potential for their businesses if they push into new markets, customers, geographies, adjacent businesses, partnerships—and more. They are looking for ways to think through all that—understand how to analyze the choices, weigh the trade-offs and risks, allocate their resources, set new objectives, and measure progress and success. This is what we need help with."

"Much of that will come out of the strategic process, for sure," said Conrad. "But let me take one last shot at talking you out of this."

"Fire away," said Kurt, jutting his chin out.

"Are your executives looking for an easy answer to these future strategy questions? A formula that tells them what to do? 'Make this product and launch it here, acquire this competitor and do this, expand to Europe' and so on? We don't provide a new strategy under the Christmas tree that a company can unwrap and execute."

> *A strategy helps a company frame new directions in which to go—new markets, new customers, new products and services, new partnerships—things with more growth potential. It aims to position a company for sustained and future advantage.*

Kurt looked a little disappointed. "Yes, I heard that from some references I checked out. They said that you two should charge by the question, rather than by the answer, since you ask lots of the former and provide few of the latter."

"Well … we like the so-called answers," said Jada, "to come from your people, not us."

Conrad leaned forward. "Look, Kurt, based on this conversation, you understand a bit about strategy. However, we think the best way to learn it is to understand that it is a thought process and a way of thinking about things rather than a specific outcome. You can certainly get clearly defined outcomes from a good strategy, but I think of those outcomes as more of a by-product. The driver of strategic results is having a sound strategic process. We can help your team through that."

"I'm with you," said Kurt. "If I wanted shrink-wrapped new strategies for everyone, I could hire a famous consulting firm to do all the analysis and hand my portfolio companies their new strategies, or at least some strategic options and the analysis behind them. But I want our leaders to go through that process themselves—to learn to think strategically, not just to have a new strategy."

"Ah, that's good ... very good, Kurt," said Conrad. "In our opinion, some people don't understand that strategists are not in the coming-up-with-good-ideas game," he sighed. "They are in the how-to-think-a-certain-way game. Which then could lead to good ideas."

"So, this is your way of saying 'no guaranteed results'?" Kurt laughed.

Conrad smiled. Jada stood up and put out her hand. "No," she said. "This is our way of saying we would love to sit down with your company leaders and start a strategic dialogue that, if conducted in the right way, might lead to different results."

Kurt stood up and shook her hand. "I'll take that deal. Can you start next week?"

Note for the Prologue

1   See Porter, M. E. (1996). What is strategy? *Harvard Business Review, 74*(6), 61–78.

Chapter 1

What Are We Talking About Here Anyway? A Dialogue on Strategy

"Hope is not a strategy."

—*Attributed to legendary football coach* VINCE LOMBARDI

Several of the executives running some of the companies in Argo Ventures' portfolio have gathered with Conrad and Jada to kick off their strategic process. Before they can start framing out their strategic ideas, however, the initial dialogue reveals that even experienced corporate leaders can carry lifelong misconceptions of what strategy is (and is not). The leaders in the room come to see that while visions, missions, values, goals, tactics, company activities, and other elements of corporate existence are parts of a strategy, they are not a strategy themselves. The group works on understanding those elements of a strategy statement that give a firm a game plan to position itself for sustained advantage in the future, as market circumstances change. Having explored what goes into a strategy, some of the leaders are skeptical about the commitment they can give to strategic management, versus the daily challenge of running operations in their firms. They come to understand the many benefits to them as leaders from having a clear and concise strategy that can give renewed purpose and direction to everyone in their enterprise.

What strategy is ... and is not

"Do you agree you should have a strategy?" asked Conrad. "You sound like you're saying you're too busy for it."

Conrad had an extensive reservoir of patience. But forty-five minutes into his meeting with a handful of the CEOs funded by Argo Ventures, Kurt Amery's investment group, he was now drawing deeply on it to dampen people's growing aggravation.

"Absolutely, yes," said Steve Adlar, the CEO of Secure Home Suite, a software company that makes office suite applications for mobile and small home-based businesses. "But I'm telling you, we already have one. This year's strategy is to increase our market share of the mobile and home-based business market from eight to eleven percent."

Conrad had heard Steve's commitment to market-share goals before. In a previous session, he and Jada had also heard Steve complain about night calls from staff in India. It seemed like every week the software boss was woken in the night to an urgent demand from developers in Bangalore requiring him to clarify orders on the next steps in a complex project.

"So why do people phone you at all hours?" asked Conrad. "Why can't they just consult that strategy of yours—let it be their guide?"

Steve blew out a lungful of air. He scanned the floor-to-ceiling windows as if looking out at the blue sky; as if he would see an answer painted there. He realized the calls at night were just a hint: he didn't have a system to guide his business when he wasn't at his desk.

As Conrad and Steve went back and forth, Kurt Amery followed every word. Kurt was not dissatisfied with Steve's performance. He knew Steve ran a tight ship. But he wasn't sure how well that ship would manage in the future. Was Steve sailing without an essential navigation instrument?

He also sensed that the chiefs of his other businesses were doing the same. Although each executive was meeting profit and return goals, their markets were changing with breathtaking speed. They might all be missing something to sustain their success or beat their rivals to future markets.

None of these businesses, Kurt realized, had faced up to a shared weakness. Each company's performance could gyrate or vanish as quickly as a fashion fad in a changing market if they weren't ready for the future. If Steve was at a loss for a critical navigation instrument, the other chiefs likely were as well.

Liz Fiscella, founder of Healthy Family Foodstuffs, was also present. Kurt looked over to her. He wondered what instrument would guide her company over the horizon. What was she going to do when currents swept her into unfamiliar waters?

"So let's go over this thing again," said Kurt, who was now scanning the ceiling thoughtfully. He looked at Conrad. "I called you because the heads of my businesses need to plan better and act ahead of events, so they can shape the future … not just react to it and be shaped by it."

"Just so," said Conrad, who liked seeing business chiefs like Steve wrestle with thorny questions to ensure everyone arrived at answers they trusted. "So, let's keep your premise and return to what Steve says is his strategy. Would a strategy to boost market share by a certain percentage guide the company to better plan and act ahead?"

"That strategy has worked wonders," Steve said, albeit now unsure of himself. "It has guided us like a lighthouse. We've made significant progress with everyone pointing at that single dot of light."

"That's a good thing," said Conrad. "Your lighthouse provides a clear signal for everyone. You can measure people's success in approaching it. But that light is not a strategy. It's a goal—a key component of a strategy, perhaps even its starting point, but not a strategy itself."

Conrad had a knack for timing the back-and-forth conversation to coax strong-willed business chiefs to see the limitations of their thinking. He let his words sink in.

A goal is a key component of a strategy, perhaps even its starting point, but it is not a strategy itself.

"Liz, what about you?" Conrad asked. "You are your company's founder—you must have it in your bones. What's your strategy?"

"Gosh, I've been living it for fifteen years, so it's always top of mind," said Liz. "Healthy Family Foodstuffs aims to bring affordable and healthy food choices to busy families. We don't want people to take the junk-food shortcut just because they are short on time or money. 'We make healthy easy' is our tagline."

"Inspiring—and needed!" Conrad said. He got up to write it on a whiteboard. "It's a powerful vision, no doubt about it." Then he hesitated, marker held out as if expecting Liz to say more. "But ..."

"But?" said Liz, her head tilting, eyes wide. "But?"

"But it's not a strategy?" chimed in Jada Akilah, who had entered the room during the discussion. "It is indeed an inspiring and guiding vision—critical to defining your purpose ... but not a strategy."

Jada set a box of croissants on the table. She could tell the group needed something to sweeten the atmosphere.

Jada, Conrad's longtime business partner, had a shared mastery of strategic thinking. The two were clearly so comfortable with each other that they finished each other's sentences as if they had rehearsed many times.

"A vision informs and helps set boundaries for a strategy," added Jada. "But it's not a strategy itself."

The croissants replenished everyone's patience and goodwill. "Ah ha," said Liz Fiscella, wiping her fingers. "Well, at least I've got the vision thing down."

Kurt could see that his business chiefs did not have a crisp idea of what "strategy" meant. Conrad and Jada were now testing that understanding.

"What about my business?" said a woman at the table named Alexis. "It's called Celar Logistics." She explained: "We employ locals to do the so-called last mile of delivery in a long supply chain. However, with the pandemic, the work-from-home phenomenon, and the rise of Amazon, the business has changed. Everybody is delivering right to the door, even on low-density or rural routes. So our strategy is to constantly renegotiate competitive rates for the most profitable routes with the major shippers further up the supply chain."

"That sounds pretty crucial to your business model," said Conrad. He wrote it on the board.

"It's a great strategy when it works!" chimed in Kurt. "If Celar locks in those route rates and then increases its efficiency on them, it's all extra profit to the bottom line."

"True," said Jada. "But that is just a tactic, correct?"

She drew blank stares from Alexis and Kurt.

"It's a business move—a critical tactic, no doubt, but just one," Jada continued. "However, a strategy is a *series* of connected tactical moves that, when linked together, exploit your overall strengths to attack an opportunity in the market."

> *A strategy is a series of connected tactical moves that, when linked together, exploit strengths to attack an opportunity in the market.*

"Well, couldn't locking in better rates for our key routes be the most fundamental piece of the strategy for the company?" argued Alexis.

"Indeed, it could be the centerpiece of a strategy," said Conrad. "But, no matter how well you do it, it is a tactic," he continued. "It's just a piece of the strategy. You will want to tie other business moves you might make to it to sustain whatever advantage you gained in that rate negotiation."

"Okay," said Kurt. "Take another of our businesses, Andromeda eGaming. I just received their strategy. It was printed on a set of cards: Innovation, Agility, and Design. That is what Andromeda will be known for."

Jada gave him a sympathetic smile. "No again. Those are values, not a strategy—values you definitely want associated with your brand, but …"

"Okay, fair enough," said Kurt. "Let me try another one of our companies, Creativia Playsets." Creativia's strategy, he explained, was to provide children of all ages with creative playsets that allow them to combine the physical and the virtual worlds to foster their imagination and ingenuity.

Conrad wrote it on the board, eyed carefully by Kurt, who had an inkling he was still off the mark.

"A great mission statement," said Conrad, "but not a strategy."

Kurt sighed. "Okay, what about to increase profit and shareholder value? I mean, that's the payoff for an investor like me. A knockout strategy in my mind!"

"But, like market share, that's a goal, not a strategy," said Steve. "Hey, I'm starting to get it!"

"Aha," said Jada. "Wanna give defining your strategy another try, Steve?"

"Well, I certainly know what we are spending most of our time on," he said with his brow furrowed. He explained that the large companies offering office suite software and productivity apps were starting to move downstream into his company's territory—the small home-based and mobile business market. As a result, Secure Home Suite's strategy was to produce and update their customized small-business applications and the middleware that links apps together faster than anyone else.

"We've done process mapping, adopted agile software methodologies, and used some technology consultants in pursuit of this strategy," he added. "We will be faster—maybe even cheaper than the other guys."

Kurt could see that Jada and Conrad were still not buying it. He chuckled under his breath, eager to get to the bottom of this issue.

"A laudable project, no doubt, but it's not really a strategy … per se," said Jada. "Instead, it's a productivity improvement. Doing something better, cheaper, and faster than competitors. It's laudable—it could even be a key enabler of your strategy, but it's not strategy itself."

Conrad explained that a famous strategy professor named Michael Porter had shown how strategy is different from improving operationally. Porter's major point was that if a company wanted to position itself for sustainable competitive advantage, it wasn't enough to do the same things as its rivals but simply faster or cheaper. Instead, a firm should want to do those things differently so that, in the minds of its customers, that firm is distinct from its rivals.[1]

"Ah," said Steve, "but isn't it distinctive to have a quick turnaround on products and upgrades or to be cheaper than the big guys?"

"It could be," said Conrad. "But is it sustainable?" He noted that Porter's research showed that competition catches up over time to improvements in speed, operational effectiveness, or price advantage.

"Okay, I get it," said Steve. "But I think our applications are different—simplified, not weighed down by the attempt to do too much. Maybe we should emphasize that."

Conrad rested his chin in his hand and said, "I'm not sure we'd know which is best. I think Porter would tell you to stick with whatever makes you most distinctive and gives you a unique and advantageous position in the market."

The group in the room sat back and took that in. Jada looked around at their faces.

"How about this," she interjected. "Let's park that concept for now and take stock of where we are." She moved over to the board. "Look at some of the components you have up here. We have objectives, we have activities, we have some sense of competitive advantage, we have some operational improvements, and we have some compelling visions and mission statements. That's good stuff, and if we add in a few more details, stir it the right way, and bake it, we might have a short statement of an overall strategy."

If a company wants to position itself for sustainable competitive advantage, it isn't enough to do the same things as its rivals but simply faster or cheaper. Instead, a firm should want to do those things differently so that the firm is distinctive from its rivals.

"So, what does that look like when it comes out of the oven, then?" asked Liz.

"Well, it looks like a full game plan and road map for getting your company to what you would consider the next level," said Jada. She explained that a good strategy statement captures the company's vision and mission. But it only starts to become a strategy—a game plan—when it spells out specific objectives, articulates the scope of a firm's activities, and identifies the company's comparative advantage over rivals.

"If you put enough detail in there," she said, "it will tell everyone what you are trying to accomplish, where and how you do it, and why customers will pick you over the next guy. In its fullest form, it gives you a game plan for taking your company into the future."

"Man, sounds like a big document," said Kurt.

Conrad replied, "It can be—as a full strategic plan with all the detail in it. Ultimately, when you put together the elements of a strategy that you've all mentioned so far—your goals, the kinds of activities you do and don't do and why, and the relative advantage you are seeking over your competitors—then what emerges is a full blueprint for moving your company to a different, better, more advantaged position."

"Excellent," said Alexis. "I am all about getting that blueprint and executing. Is that a today thing?"

Jada laughed. "Whoa, whoa—a full strategic plan is definitely not a 'today thing'—but we can start to zero in on its essence. I think our 'today thing' is understanding what goes into a strategy and how it is derived."

"Let's do an exercise to get going," said Conrad, standing up and moving to the whiteboard. "Let's try and construct a simple strategy statement. You want your leaders to be able to express its essential components as clearly and concisely as possible. Two strategy professors named Collis and Rukstad once said a good enterprise should be able to say its strategic statement in thirty-five words or less!"[2]

> When you put together the elements of a strategy—your goals, the activities you do and don't do and why, and the relative advantage you are seeking over your competitors—then what emerges is a blueprint for moving your company to a different, better, more advantaged position.

"Wow, we should try that," said Liz. "What's the formula?"

Conrad explained that there are three key areas to articulate in a strategy and he gave the group five questions to answer. He wrote on the board:

```
┌─────────────────────────────────────────────┐
│                                             │
│        A STRATEGY STATEMENT                 │
│        ─────────────────────                │
│                                             │
│   OBJECTIVES: What are we trying to         │
│   ─────────   accomplish?                   │
│                                             │
│   SCOPE: Who are the customers we serve?    │
│   ─────   In what markets?                  │
│           With what kind of products or     │
│           services?                         │
│                                             │
│   ADVANTAGE: What unique value do we        │
│   ─────────  deliver?                       │
│                                             │
└─────────────────────────────────────────────┘
```

"That's a serious word-smithing drill to get that down to thirty-five words, I'd imagine," said Liz. "If I had to do it off the top of my head I would say that 'We are hoping to double our store footprint in the next five years by focusing on families on a budget seeking healthy food options. Our customers will pick us because we have the supply chain to give them healthy food but in bulk and at lower prices. Our value proposition is kind of between a Costco, a Whole Foods, an Aldi, and a Trader Joe's!'"

"That's not bad at all!" encouraged Jada. "It strikes me that you all are very much in touch with the essential purpose of your companies, the nature of the markets you are in, the customers you serve, the things you do—and don't do—and the value you bring to the table. Like Liz just did, I bet each of you can pretty quickly craft a brief strategy statement."

"And it doesn't have to follow that exact formula," said Conrad. "Another simple framework for understanding what goes into a strategy was offered by A.G. Lafley, a former CEO, and Roger Martin, a strategy professor, in a book the two wrote called *Playing to Win*. They maintain you can see the essence of your strategy in five similar questions."[3] Conrad took up a marker and drew a cascading series of boxes on another part of the board.

Kurt looked up at what Conrad had drawn. "Seems like a similar concept, but in this one I feel like the questions take you toward more detail on what you might need to get the strategy done."

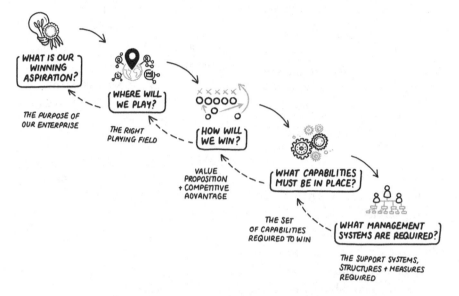

The essence of your strategy in five different questions

Figure 1.1 Strategic Questions framework from *Playing to Win* by Lafley and Martin

(Source: Figure 1-1 from Lafley, A. G., & Martin, R. L. (2013). *Playing to Win: How Strategy Really Works*. Boston, MA: Harvard Business Review Press, p. 15. Reprinted with kind permission by Harvard Business Publishing)

Jada nodded. "Yes, I think that's right. The basic elements are the same. Every strategy ultimately addresses what you are trying to get done, how you will do it and in what kind of environment, how you will keep score, the resources you need to get it done, and how it comes together. These frameworks are both good, as they serve to get your strategic-thinking juices flowing in the right way by emphasizing the essential elements of a strategy."

Bringing all the pieces together

Jada, Conrad, and Kurt huddled in Kurt's office during the break.

"Whew," said Kurt, "we pretty much dove right into it back there."

"Yeah," agreed Conrad, "deep end of the pool swimming—sometimes the best way to start."

"Well, I remember reading a piece you two wrote in *Forbes* where I first heard of you—one where you said strategy was a thought process and not the annual business plan. I guess this is part of the thought process."

Jada laughed. "Knowing what we are talking about when we say 'strategy'? Yeah, I would say that is pretty much part of the process."

"As you can see, Kurt, she's the sarcastic one on the team," smiled Conrad as the three of them returned to the conference room.

> Every strategy ultimately addresses what you are trying to get done, how you will do it and in what kind of environment, how you will keep score, the resources you need to get it done, and how it comes together.

When they all got seated again, Conrad was pleased to see that several of the executives had doodled draft strategy statements following one of the models he and Jada had written up on the board.

Liz raised her hand before anyone said anything. "Hey, before we kick back off, can I share an observation and get your thoughts?"

"For sure," said Conrad. "We don't have a set agenda, we just want to have a dialogue about what you think strategy means and how you know it when you see it."

Liz nodded. "This is something I was chatting about with Steve and Alexis during the break. All the companies in Kurt's portfolio seem to have a firm sense of purpose—we know why we exist and what we hope to do. I'm on the boards of several nonprofit organizations in my community, and they are even more mission-driven, as you can imagine. Especially as they don't have the profit motive of a company. But I feel that the companies in this room are really mission-driven too. You told me that a mission is not a strategy. So, where does that fit into these strategic formulas you've given us? They feel a bit dry to me without mission and purpose."

"Totally fair, Liz," said Conrad as Jada jumped up and started to draw something on the whiteboard. "At the center of a strategy should always be a strong sense of organizational purpose—why you exist. As Cynthia Montgomery, another strategy professor, framed it, your strategy should tell you, the firm, what you want to be, not simply the kind of plans you have to make progress in the future.[4] She might agree with you that a plan with just goals, activities, and how you leverage your relative advantage might not really capture purpose."

"So," chimed in Steve, "where do things like vision, mission, and our values come in? We spend a lot of time on those things as leaders—put them on our badges, write them up on our websites and breakroom walls—all that."

Jada was almost done drawing a diagram, and she started answering while drawing. "We think that a company's vision, mission, and values *inform* the strategy and the strategic process. How could they not? They are the essential foundation and answer some key questions for stakeholders. But they are upstream from strategy, so to speak, as you can see from the way I am drawing it here."

Alexis volunteered, "I once heard that a way to separate these things is that the vision tells you the *Why*, the mission tells you the *What*, and the strategy itself tells you the *How*.[5] That's not a bad way to think about it?"

> At the center of a strategy should always be a strong sense of organizational purpose— why you exist.

"Hmm, I kind of always think about vision and mission together, almost interchangeable," offered Kurt.

"I can see where you're coming from, Kurt, but let's pull on the thread Alexis gave us there," rejoined Conrad. "It is worth pulling them apart to separate *Why* and *What* and *How*. Here is the way I like to think about it." He moved to a different section of the whiteboard and wrote:

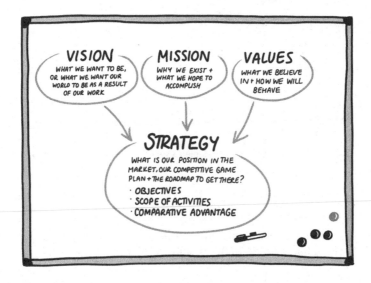

"As the diagram shows, the strategy really fills in that *How* piece. How we accomplish that mission and attain that vision."

Heads started nodding around the room, and Jada took advantage of the moment. "Here is a graphic way of seeing the relationship between these elements that all underpin or provide detail to a good strategy," she said.

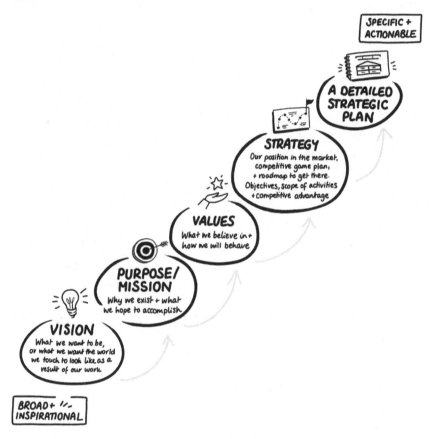

Figure 1.2 The hierarchy of the elements shaping and informing a strategy

Jada explained at the board, "You can see here, coming back to Liz's earlier point, that vision, mission, and values are always a starting point of sorts. They are aspirational and broad—and often without detail. If you didn't know what Tesla actually produces as a company, you might not be able to guess it from their vision statement: 'To accelerate the world's transition to sustainable energy.' Similarly with Nike and other companies with broad visions. Nowhere in their visions do they say 'cars' in the case of Tesla or 'athletic wear' in the case of Nike."

"And then it gets more detailed as it flows down to a strategy and strategic plan?" asked Kurt.

Jada nodded. "Yes, the mission will put a little more meat on the bones and the values will capture much of the culture, systems of belief, and patterns of behavior. But the strategic details are derived later in the process —*informed* by the core purpose and values—but containing details and plans that will change over time in a way that core purpose will not."[6]

Liz Fiscella looked a bit confused. "I dunno," she said. "I get the overall idea—but at a practical level, that seems like quite a leap from mission, vision, and values right into strategies to gain advantage and then detailed plans to pull that off."

"Yes!" said Conrad. "I agree. But down the road in this process we will fill in that 'leap' with lots of analysis and data so that it isn't purely an aspirational leap of faith consistent with a broad vision. In the meantime, there is another tool you can use if you need it."

He went to the board and wrote a bubble in the middle of the diagram:

Strategic theme or intent

"This is a kind of theme or intent that really cements principles and boundaries for the company."

Alexis jumped in, "Is this something similar to what we called in the Air Force 'the commander's intent'? It was useful there because in situations where we needed to improvise from the original plan, we could always go back and look at the intent of the boss and make a better judgment about what to do to be consistent with that intent."

"Great point, Alexis," said Jada, "and you've hit on one of the benefits of having a strategy bolstered by a compelling vision, mission, and values— and perhaps reinforced by a clear strategic intent from the leadership. It gives people a sense of organizational direction even when the details of a business plan may be missing or may not fit the situation. Let me give you an example. Anybody shopped at an IKEA—or been in one?"

Everyone in the room nodded.

"Well," said Jada, "as they rapidly expanded in their early days, the company didn't even really have a policy handbook for new store managers. Instead, they had a little book written by their iconic founder, Ingvar Kamprad, called *The Testament of a Furniture Dealer*. It was a huge statement of the vision, mission, and values of IKEA and also the themes of how he wanted the company to operate, like 'offering a wide range of well-designed, functional home furnishing products at prices so low that as many people as possible will be able to afford them.'"[7] He even appended an IKEA dictionary to his testament so everyone spoke the same language. However, the new managers largely had to figure out the policy and business details—the finances and the processes. Even so, with the guidance of this powerful expression of Ingvar's vision and values for the company, and his strategic intent of delivering furniture in a more accessible way to more of the market, IKEA managers pretty much had what they needed to formulate and execute a strategy within certain boundaries."

Steve broke in with, "Sounds like Ingvar figured out a way to be everywhere at once! The boss was always in the room even when he wasn't in the room."

"Just so, Steve," said Conrad. "The guidance in the book certainly missed out on a ton of details that a strategic plan would contain, stuff that would be a really useful playbook for a new store manager. On the other hand, his testament was crystal clear about the strategic direction he wanted IKEA and all its stores to take so it could achieve its mission and live by its values. His strategic vision for IKEA was so powerful and distinctive that it signposted a clear trajectory for the company. And it served up one great benefit of having a strong strategy: the strategy can be the boss when the boss is not around."

A clear strategy can act like a boss when the boss is not around.

"Useful," chimed in Alexis. "My operations go around the clock, and I'd rather not have to wake up to take a question from one of my managers in the middle of the night. If that manager can look at my strategy and my intent—or even our vision, mission, and values—they can likely make the right call on whatever issue is facing their team without having to get more guidance from me or someone else."

"I like it," said Jada, who moved over to an unused patch of whiteboard and started a list:

Benefits of having a clear strategy:

1. Can be the boss when the boss is not around.

"Wait, before we go further on that, I'm still feeling in my gut like something is missing," said Liz. "Even if we have a clear direction and intent, that is still pretty broad guidance to get to what you say will ultimately be a detailed game plan to move in a new direction."

"Of course," reassured Conrad. "There is more, you're just ahead of the game. For instance, going into the analysis of various strategic choices and options would not only be all this guidance," he said as he pointed to the bottom left of the diagram, "but we would also consider all sorts of analysis about external market issues and internal resourcing. There is a lot of work to do before you get left with a sound strategy that can ultimately become a plan."

Liz looked half-satisfied. Jada picked up the challenge. "Liz, let me ask you this. Would you ever formulate a set of business objectives for your company that completely ignored what was happening in your market?"

"No," scoffed Liz. "Of course not; few industries are more competitive than grocery. I'm always thinking about competitors and suppliers and much more."

"Uh huh," nodded Jada. "How about this: would anyone here ever make a big business plan to change something fundamental in the way you do things that didn't consider what kind of company you were and what resources you had?"

"Of course not," Steve offered. "Even if you are pushing big changes, you have to understand the company you are and the things you have to work with."

While Steve spoke, Conrad added more pieces to the middle of the board.

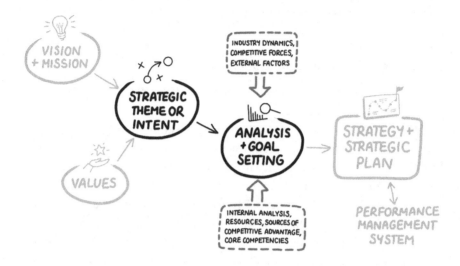

Figure 1.3 How the strategy pieces fit together

Kurt spoke up. "Okay, so it looks like before you can even get to those basic objectives that might be the first part of your strategy statement, leaders and their teams have to do some basic analysis of the external forces shaping their world and also some reflection on what kind of enterprise they really are, and what capabilities they have at their command."

"Exactly," said Conrad. "Then they can have a more informed process for coming up with even broad goals and objectives."

"So, this is a pretty involved process," sighed Alexis. "That's a lot of work to pack into thirty-five words."

"Well, it can or it can't be," replied Conrad. "I sense that you all have most of the answers ready at the front of your minds. You know your markets, you know your customers, you know your own companies. And it doesn't need to be done exactly left to right as on the diagram. As some strategic thinkers have pointed out, it's not necessarily about the sequence—success is more rooted in each piece being robust and well thought out.[8] In any case, a thinking process like the one on the board is necessary to work out when a seemingly good idea or strategic option may not be a good strategy."

"Come again?" said Liz. "A good idea could be a bad strategy?"

"For sure. Think about it this way," said Conrad. "I bet any bright person on your team can develop a good idea or strategic option that might meet a need in your market. But that does not necessarily make it a good idea for *your* firm; you might be uniquely ill-positioned or ill-equipped to pull it off. Even if it was a market need and meeting that need was a good fit for your company, that does not necessarily make it a good business decision or even an activity that advances your strategic objectives. Look at Amazon Destinations, Quibi, or CNN+. These were all undertaken with a pressing market need in mind that somebody should fill ... but resulted in disasters for the companies that launched them. So, strategists have processes that use frameworks for analysis, such as the ones represented in the diagram, about when you might consider external trends and internal dynamics."

"Even more work than I thought!" said Alexis, throwing up her hands. "It feels like I'm already chained to the wheel sixteen hours a day."

"I hear you," said Jada, who'd often heard this lament from business executives. "But there are a lot of benefits that having a strategy, or at least a sound strategic process, can bring your firm—and your own personal leadership life."

What does having a strategy do for you?

Kurt huddled with Jada and Conrad in the hall during another break. "This is a great conversation; I hope my company leaders are willing to tuck into this."

Jada looked at Kurt and replied, "Your companies and their leaders are pretty interested and seem open-minded—but it's early days. I'm not sure that, at this point, we've convinced them that they should be spending much time on this rather than simply minding the shop floor."

Kurt nodded. "Yeah. But I really want us to charge ahead of the pack and not be left behind."

Conrad watched the group down the hall start filtering back into the conference room. "Well, then, we need to convince them their job is not to run the businesses as they are, but to create the businesses they ain't. It's about the future, yes?"

"And what's more," said Jada, "as Ingvar Kamprad showed at IKEA, a clear strategy can lighten the leadership load, among other things."

"Hmm," Kurt looked at her. "Is that the sales pitch—it makes their job easier? I'm all for reducing stress, but as the owner, I'm mostly interested in performance."

"Yep—we get it," replied Jada. "But better performance is a pretty typical by-product of a sound strategy and a good leadership team. Shoot, that's why you undertake it in the first place—to move the enterprise to a more advantageous position for the future. That sustained advantage should make for great performance."

"Okay," said Kurt. "I think I follow you—but I'm not really the audience. Let's jump in and see where we go."

Conrad opened the session. "Okay gang, I know lunch is looming ahead of us; let's close out a really good discussion this morning with some thoughts on what you might or might not get out of framing a new strategy to position yourself for advantage in the future. Before we get back to Jada's list of possible benefits, let's get your thoughts on what might be giving you pause about our discussion of investing in the strategic process."

Steve raised his hand and said, "Alexis was reading my mind when she said just how busy she was with the business itself, there are so many day-to-day and week-to-week issues to deal with. We both run kind of 24–7ish enterprises. I don't know when I would have time for all this."

"Okay," Conrad nodded as Jada wrote "**Too busy**" on the board.

"I think I get everything you said," Liz said. "And I find it fascinating. But we're just a specialty grocer—a small local chain—and this seems very much meant for big companies that have the resources to do it and a large scope of activities to make it worthwhile."

"**Big-company drill**," wrote Jada on the board.

"It seems pretty academic to me," said Alexis. "It feels very classroom, textbook, formula, and whiteboard-oriented. I am just not seeing in my mind's eye how it would make an actual difference in my business."

"Yeah," agreed Liz. "I've been sitting here thinking for the past hour about what would be different in my stores or in my business plan based on this conversation. Not sure I can think of anything yet."

"**Too theoretical**," wrote Jada.

"Okay, fair enough—those are common laments about doing strategy—especially with hard-working executives," said Conrad. "But let's play a game with Jada's list and see if we can get you thinking about working *on* the business rather than just *in* the business. In other words, you are planning the business of the future and how it becomes that—you're not just focused on today's issues, finances, and operations."

He moved over to Jada's list and grabbed a marker. "Okay, I'm going to add some things to the list; tell us if it helps or hurts your workload and/or your plans for the firm. We're talking about having a good strategy here—a coordinated game plan for the company and a road map to move to a better position in the market where we can thrive in the future."

Jada picked up, "We've already agreed that it's handy to have some kind of guidance, like a strategy, that can give managers or employees clear direction—even if not detailed instruction—about how your company operates and what it values, yes?"

Everyone in the room nodded.

"Okay, let's add some things that people have told us they got out of a good strategic process that led to a sound strategy. Somebody yell out when it is something you don't want for your enterprise."

Conrad then started adding lines to the list:

Benefits of having a clear strategy:

1. Can be the boss when the boss is not around.
2. Can pull your company toward an identifiable place—and purpose.
3. Can support the vision and mission, making both possible by identifying the right goals and activities to achieve them.
4. Can help you maintain the continuity of core values and core purpose but identify changing external and internal dynamics that allow for new activities that support your mission.
5. Can help create a distinct set of operational and support activities—and link them together coherently.
6. Can help make priorities, identify trade-offs, recognize dependencies, sequence actions, and allocate resources.

7. Can let everyone know what the firm is not in the business of doing.
8. Gives you a way to "keep score" on how the company is doing.
9. Leaves no doubt as to who is responsible for what and how the company sources the resources to get it done.
10. Can help keep you ahead of the competition.
11. Can help you create more value for your employees, customers, and shareholders.
12. Can help you more efficiently allocate the firm's limited time and resources (and your time and energy!).
13. Can tame crisis management or uncoordinated activity.
14. Can help you communicate more effectively with stakeholders about all the company's activities and impact.
15. Can help you sustain your market advantage.
16. Can help you change when you need to.

Silence greeted Conrad as his marker squeaked across the board.

"Okay, we get it," said Steve. "It's all good stuff. At least at my company, I feel that we do a bunch of this already."

"No doubt, no doubt," agreed Jada. "We're not saying that having a strategy is a silver bullet or that these good things can only happen when you're officially working on a strategy. But, just like a brand, you have a strategy whether you are thinking about it or not. If I were in your shoes, I'd want to address that with some intentionality rather than only having a strategy by default. We call that a realized strategy and everybody has one—it's what actually happens in your organization.[9] But you have a choice here: have your people not just work toward the next product launch at Secure Home Suite, but toward a different future for the whole company in what you described as a rapidly changing market."

> A good strategic leader is working on the business—tomorrow's direction—rather than just in the business—today's details.

"Make a new plan, Stan!" broke in Kurt. "Just like the song says."

"That's a good note to end today on, Kurt; thanks for that," said Conrad. "I think all of you seek to change your firms and go to the next level.

In that case, as Kurt reminds us, the singer Paul Simon was correct in saying you need a new plan. Doing some strategic thinking and going through the strategic process will help produce that plan and enhance your chances of getting that sustained advantage."

"Before we close," said Jada as she leaned forward, "I would add a leadership point to this argument about the sheer cost-benefit utility of spending time on the strategy process. Harvard professor Cynthia Montgomery reminded us that 'all leaders must accept and own strategy as the heart of their responsibilities.'[10] It's in your job description as company leaders. Your employees, customers, shareholders, and any other stakeholders expect you to provide direction for the firm—and the rationale behind that direction. I mean, who else in the firm should be responsible for it?"

Heads nodded around the room.

"How about this," said Conrad, looking at Kurt. "Let's reassemble in a few days, and instead of jumping right into some analysis that will help us frame some basic courses of action for our respective companies, let's talk briefly about what it means to think strategically. According to all the headhunters I speak to, this is an executive competency that everybody says they want in a leader, but nobody seems able to describe it to me. So, let's spend some time on that to set ourselves up for success when we start pulling in the details for our analysis and decision-making."

Strategy is not a distraction from a leader's work; it is at the heart of their responsibilities and perhaps their most important work.

Kurt looked around the room. "Sounds great to me. I'm going to bring in a few other portfolio CEOs while these guys do their strategic statement homework. I'll send out a note and look forward to seeing everyone then."

Conrad and Jada's key takeaways

A strategy is *not*:
- Grand statements or aspirations.
- Goals.
- Operational effectiveness or technical advantage.
- Non-competitive positioning in the market.

A strategy *is*:
- A game plan of coordinated activities to gain and sustain superior performance relative to competitors.
- Aimed at giving a firm a unique or differentiated strategic position within an industry.
- A blueprint for progress that spells out specific goals, the scope of activities, the competitive advantage, and the way the firm will bring it together.

A strategy answers fundamental questions such as:
- *Objectives:* What are we trying to accomplish? Our winning aspiration?
- *Scope:* Who are the customers we serve? In what markets? With what kind of products or services? What is our playing field?
- *Advantage:* What unique value do we deliver? How do we win? What capabilities and systems are needed?

Strategy is not so much what to think (an answer from a formula) as a way to think (a thought process using questions, frameworks, insights, and choices).

Works cited and recommendations for further study

Books

De Kluyver, C. A., and Pierce, J. A. (2013). *Strategic Management: An Executive Perspective.* New York, NY: Business Expert Press.

Editors of Harvard Business Review (2005). *Harvard Business Essentials: Strategy: Create and Implement the Best Strategy for Your Business.* Boston, MA: Harvard Business Review Press.

Evans, V. (2020). *Key Strategy Tools: 88 Tools for Every Manager to Build a Winning Strategy.* 2nd ed. Harlow, England: FT Publishing International.

Kiechel, W. (2010). *Lords of Strategy: The Secret Intellectual History of the New Corporate World.* Boston, MA: Harvard Business Review Press.

Lafley, A. G., and Martin, R. L. (2013). *Playing to Win: How Strategy Really Works.* Boston, MA: Harvard Business Review Press.

Lenox, M., and Harris, J. D. (n.d.). *The Strategist's Toolkit.* Darden Business Publishing Storefront.

Mintzberg, H. (1998). *Strategy Safari: A Guided Tour through the Wilds of Strategic Management.* New York, NY: Free Press.

Reeves, M., Haanaes, K., and Sinha, J. (2015). *Your Strategy Needs a Strategy.* Boston, MA: Harvard Business School Press.

Rumelt, R. P. (2011). *Good Strategy, Bad Strategy: The Difference and Why It Matters.* New York, NY: Crown Business.

Various authors in Harvard Business Review (2009). *HBR's 10 Must Reads on Strategy,* Volume Collection. Boston, MA: Harvard Business Review Press.

Various authors in Harvard Business Review (2020). *HBR's 10 Must Reads on Strategy 2,* Volume Collection. Boston, MA: Harvard Business Review Press.

Articles

Casadesus-Masanell, R., Nanda, A., and Rivkin, J. (2020). Crafting strategy. *Harvard Business School Module Note 720-407,* April 2020 (revised January 2021).

Cespedes, F. V. (2015). Well said: Why articulating your strategy can set you apart. *AFP Exchange* (Association for Finance Professionals), *35*(2), 49–51.

Christensen, C. M., Allworth, J., and Dillon, K. (2013). Is your strategy what you say it is? *Rotman Management Magazine,* August 1.

Collins, J., and Porras, J. I. (1996). Building your company's vision. *Harvard Business Review, 74*(5), 65–76.

Collis, D. J., and Rukstad, M. G. (2008). Can you say what your strategy is? *Harvard Business Review, 86*(4), 82–90.

Hambrick, D. C., and Fredrickson, J. W. (2001). Are you sure you have a strategy? *The Academy of Management Executive, 15*(4), 48–59.

Martin, R. L. (2010). Five questions to build a strategy. *Harvard Business Review, 88*(5), 3–8.

Montgomery, C. (2008). Putting leadership back into strategy. *Harvard Business Review, 86*(1), 54–60.

Porter, M. E. (1996). What is strategy? *Harvard Business Review, 74*(6), 61–78.

Reeves, M., Love, C., and Tillmanns, P. (2012). Your strategy needs a strategy. *Harvard Business Review, 90*(9), 76–83.

Vermeulen, F. (2017). Many strategies fail because they're not actually strategies. *Harvard Business Review.* https://hbr.org/2017/11/many-strategies-fail-because-they-re-not-actually-strategies, published November 8, 2017, accessed September 15, 2024.

Watkins, M. D. (2007). Demystifying strategy: The what, who, how, and why. *Harvard Business Review.* https://hbr.org/2007/09/demystifying-strategy-the-what, published September 10, 2007, accessed September 15, 2024.

Notes for Chapter 1

1 Porter, M. E. (1996). What is strategy? *Harvard Business Review, 74*(6), 61–78.
2 Collis, D. J., and Rukstad, M. G. (2008). Can you say what your strategy is? *Harvard Business Review, 86*(4), 82–90.
3 Lafley, A. G., and Martin, R. L. (2013). *Playing to Win: How Strategy Really Works.* Boston, MA: Harvard Business Review Press.
4 Montgomery, C. (2008). Putting leadership back into strategy. *Harvard Business Review, 86*(1), 54–60.
5 Watkins, M. D. (2007). Demystifying strategy: The what, who, how, and why. *Harvard Business Review.* https://hbr.org/2007/09/demystifying-strategy-the-what, published September 10, 2007, accessed September 15, 2024.
6 Collins, J., and Porras, J. I. (1996). Building your company's vision. *Harvard Business Review, 74*(5), 65–76.
7 Kamprad, I. (1976). *The Testament of a Furniture Dealer Including a Little IKEA Dictionary by Ingvar Kamprad.* Inter IKEA Systems.
8 Hambrick, D. C., and Fredrickson, J. W. (2001). Are you sure you have a strategy? *The Academy of Management Executive, 15*(4), 48–59.
9 See Mintzberg, H., and Waters, J. A. (1985). Of strategies, deliberate and emergent. *Strategic Management Journal, 6*(3), 257–272.
10 Montgomery, C. (2012). *The Strategist: Be the Leader Your Business Needs.* New York, NY: Harper Collins, p. 13.

Chapter 2

Looking at the World in a Different Way: A Dialogue on Strategic Thinking

> "If chess has any relationship to film-making, it would be in the way it helps
> you develop patience and discipline in choosing between alternatives
> at a time when an impulsive decision seems very attractive."

—*Filmmaker* STANLEY KUBRICK

....

Several more leaders, in whose companies Argo Ventures is invested, meet Conrad and Jada to talk about thinking differently during the strategic management process. Being high achievers who have built thriving enterprises, they struggle to understand the difference between using a strategic logic and an operational logic, the latter being rooted in known data and tasks accomplishment. Conrad and Jada walk the group through a series of conversations about building their strategic-thinking muscles—a competency required of every senior executive. Thinking long-term, not short-term. Thinking broadly and about the unknown future, rather than with a narrow focus on the known present and past. Reasoning through analogies rather than just deduction. Thinking in systems and seeing patterns and connections in the market—pulling things together. Not just using analysis to break down problems to their most solvable level. The team learns some ways to get more comfortable with uncertainty and ambiguity, and some methods to creatively wrestle with possibilities and weigh courses of action.

....

Thinking strategically

Alexis Chapman from Celar Logistics wasn't looking so confident the next time she sat with Jada and Conrad. Her understanding of strategy had fallen apart after the discussion the earlier week.

"After processing what we talked about," she said, "I'm a little dazed to tell the truth. I got lost in a hall of mirrors about what it means to have a strategy. If a desirable end result of spelling out one's strategy—its objectives, its scope of activities, and its comparative advantage over others—is a different place in the market, doesn't that require a certain way to think about that market, and the others in it, and one's own company and where it sits in there ... and then how to move to a better place for the future—and even then, what does *better* mean—what does *place* mean?! Jeez, as I started thinking through the implications of us just batting around what strategy is, I got confused about what we need to do—and know."

"Yeah, I hear you, Alexis," sympathized Jada. "The bad news, although I hope you come not to think of it that way, is that your instincts are right—it is not a small task to formulate and execute a new strategy. We have to start by thinking *differently* than most executives normally do. And that can be hard."

Alexis's face lengthened. "And the good news?"

"Two pieces of good news!" Jada continued. "First, anybody can learn to think strategically, which, as you might expect, helps in the strategic process and with strategic management. Second, business strategists over the past few decades have developed tools—we often call them frameworks—that guide executives in this journey and give them strategic insights ... sometimes even answers as to where they should take their company and how. So, while there are no magic answers, there are tools we can use to organize our thinking."

"Ah ha—excellent!" broke in Ian Driscoll, the CEO of Coactum Financial Technologies, a financial software firm. "Frankly, this seemed all very airy-fairy to me when I reflected on it after our separate session with you and Conrad, but it sounds like you two do have some formulas you can give us, like the ones we used in finance, my primary business field before I became the CEO. That's what we need—plug in the data and get the answer."

"Hear, hear," said Suzie Nguyen, the founder of Andromeda eGaming. "I'm a technology manager by background, so I'm used to having tried and trusted methods to answer key business questions as well. I'm not looking for plug and play necessarily," she said with a grin, "but it would be a time saver. Without formulas to analyze the data, how do you stop it from being an endless seminar of opinions?"

Jada looked over at Conrad. She could tell they were not off to the most convincing start.

"Any of you parents?" asked Conrad.

"Um …" replied Ian, looking confused. "Yeah, but why does that matter?"

"Well," said Conrad, "how well did rote formulas work with raising your kids? Did you have some go-to ones that always worked, no matter the situation or the child?"

"Heck no," laughed Ian. "Every kid is different, and all that changes with what kind of mood or state the parent or the child is in." He looked around at the faces in the room. "Now, mind you, it isn't totally free-form in the Driscoll house. We have our rules about the way we behave, our goals, our agreements about the best way to communicate or solve problems, and all that. But the situations are all so different."

Conrad smiled.

"Gosh, I hope strategy is not as hard as raising children!" Derrick Jouet, the CEO of Creativia Playsets, said to laughter.

"No," said Conrad. "But it is more situation-dependent and ambiguous than other business disciplines such as accounting, finance, or operations management. A lot of times, there is no 'right' answer. There is only the answer you come to through strategic thinking and how well you can support it with your analysis."

"Even so," said Suzie, "it would be a more straightforward drill if these things you call frameworks kicked out always accurate answers on strategic questions."

Jada nodded at her. "Yes, that's a totally natural desire for executives. Most executives make their decisions based on a logic that either flows from having certainty about the data and what it means for the business, or some short-term goal that is easily defined. Long-term ambiguity and the ever-shifting sands of competitive forces are uncomfortable for most people."

> *Strategy is more situation-dependent and ambiguous than other business disciplines such as accounting, finance, or operations management. A lot of times, there is no "right" answer. There is only the answer you come to through strategic thinking and how well you can support it with your analysis.*

"Most people?" said Alexis. "I can't think of anyone in my field who would be comfortable with that. Our business is based on precision, good information, and predictability."

Conrad looked at the group. "Well, who is comfortable with ambiguity and no 'right' answers? One answer to that question is only four percent of executives."

"Four percent! Geez," muttered Ian.

Conrad continued, "Let's talk about a study that found only four percent of executives in the general business population naturally use a kind of strategic 'action logic' to understand the world around them and how they reason through and rationalize their decisions. They naturally try to link one move to another over a long period into the future and seek to understand the way to shape things over multiple stages."

"Umm, that's a problem!" said Suzie. "The 'future' hasn't yet happened. That's why we call it 'the future.' These four percent got a crystal ball from Santa?" she finished to laughter.

Jada laughed, too. "No, of course not; it's just that they naturally search for patterns in how things operate and interconnect."

Jada was met with confused looks. She pressed on: "Let me give you a sense of how the strategist's mind works. Let's say the management question in the room is 'Why is this report due Friday?' An executive with an *Achiever* mindset might answer that by saying, 'Because it is due Friday. It says so right here on the project plan. Duh!' On the other hand, someone with an *Expert* mindset might answer the same question by saying, 'If we get the report in by Friday, we will have the data we need to make a decision.' According to this study I'm talking about, *Achievers* and *Experts* make up over two thirds of the executive population."[1]

"And how do these four percent of strategic logic people answer the question?" asked Derrick.

"Well," continued Jada, "they might say something like this: 'If we can get this report done by Friday, that will allow us to use it in our planning next month about how we shape the market next quarter. If we can shape the next quarter, that might give us insights into positioning ourselves better next year. If we successfully position ourselves differently next year, that might allow us to compete at a totally different level in three years.'"

"Whoa," breathed Derrick. "Sounds like that movie I just saw about chess. The character was seeing four or five moves that were connected—in advance of playing the game."

"Yes," said Conrad. "Strategic logic could look like that. Chess is a classic strategy game. But let's take a step back and go back to Jada's first piece of good news. Being able to think strategically is not about being lucky enough to be in the four percent of executives who naturally use a strategic 'action logic' in their decision-making. Rather, it is about being committed enough to learn the behavior—and anybody can learn it. In fact, it is considered a necessary skill—or *executive competency*, as leadership development people call it—for executives to perform at the highest levels."

"So," said Alexis skeptically, "my life—my livelihood—is focused on operational performance. Time, budget, schedule. Boom, boom, boom. You're saying you can help a hyper-operator like me or anyone else be a strategic thinker?"

"Absolutely," said Jada. "You may already be a strategic thinker—you just may not conceive of it that way." Jada swept the room with her eyes, briefly locking in on all the executives. "You are the bosses— the leaders. No matter what your dominant executive skills and strengths are, you ultimately make the call about where to take your enterprise, why, how, who is going to do what along the journey, and what rewards you hope to achieve by doing so. You do that every day already—just by being in charge. You determine the direction of the company, aided by your executive team."

> *Being able to think strategically is not about being lucky enough to be in the magic four percent of executives who naturally use a strategic "action logic" in their decision-making. Rather, it is about being committed enough to learn the behavior, and anybody can learn it. Strategic thinking is considered a necessary skill—or executive competency—for executives to perform at the highest levels.*

"The buck stops with you, yes?" added Conrad.

There was a pause in the room while that sunk in. Suzie broke it. "Hard to wriggle out of that one, friends!" she said to laughter. "I guess we're all going to become strategists."

Conrad smiled. "Yes ma'am, that's right. But you must start somewhere."

What is strategic thinking and how is it different?

"Before we get into the details on thinking strategically and how you know when you thunk it," grinned Jada, "let me start with a story."

"A few years ago," she continued, "I was engaged as an executive coach for a promising young leader in a company—with the goal of helping him prepare for the C-suite. One day, during a board meeting, we were reviewing up-and-coming executives, and a director shared his thoughts about this leader. 'He's a fantastic operator, it seems,' he said to me. 'But I'm worried that he doesn't think strategically. And that's really necessary for a C-suite role and boardroom presence.' 'What does that mean to you? To think strategically?' I replied. 'Well …,' he stammered. 'You know … think strategically.'"

"To cut a long story short," Jada continued, "as you might imagine, the director couldn't really articulate what he was looking for from this leader or any other. He was correct that thinking strategically is considered a core competency for corporate leaders, but he couldn't describe it himself."

"Hmm, I can relate," said Suzie. "I had my leadership team do an executive skills assessment, and that came up as a category we knew we needed, but came up short in. Our firm is full of developers and engineers constantly … well … doing, not thinking—if you know what I mean."

"I get it, Suzie," said Conrad. "Almost every executive rises through the ranks based on their technical and tactical prowess—their ability to get stuff done in their specialty area. But at a certain point in their career, when they are put in charge of somebody or something, their success starts to depend not on their technical and tactical skills, but rather on their strategic and interpersonal skills. Charting a path forward for their company and dealing well with the people on their team."

"Here, let me diagram this to show you what I mean." He jumped up and started drawing on the whiteboard.

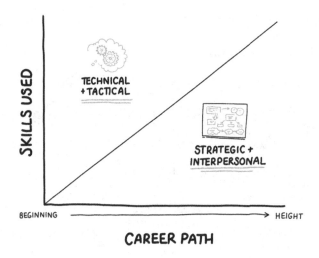

Figure 2.1 Why having a strategic mindset is necessary for executive development

"As you move along this horizontal axis in your careers and accumulate more responsibility as a leader, the skills you use to get your job done—on a day-to-day, week-to-week, and quarter-to-quarter basis—shift to the strategic and interpersonal skills needed to succeed. Your expertise in certain areas of the business are no longer the prerequisite for your success at this stage."

"That makes sense to me," Suzie said. "Even our CTO at the company doesn't really write a line of code. He oversees dozens of software projects and over a hundred engineers and developers."

"Exactly," said Jada. "And this can happen at a relatively early stage in a career—usually when someone is put into any management role. This is well recognized in the executive development realm. Let me draw up a common model of leadership skills that firms want from any budding executive. There are hundreds of these models defined all different kinds of ways, but here is one I like to use—with four categories of executive competencies that are related but different kinds of skills."

She drew on the board:

Figure 2.2 The four categories of executive competencies

"So it's the conceptual realm we are after in strategic thinking then?" asked Ian as Jada finished her drawing.

Jada nodded and turned to him. "Yes, in this particular framework."

Ian paused. "But all of us in here spend a good bit of our time creating a vision for our firms, looking at the market, and setting direction. I would call that part of good management. How does that distinguish itself from strategic thinking?"

"It depends *how* you do it, Ian," chimed in Conrad. "Let's add a couple of key criteria for thinking strategically on the board, and you can see if that is where your headspace is when you are doing those things."

He wrote up on the board:

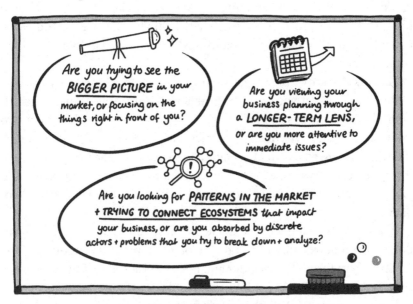

"I see what you mean about strategic thinking being very different from day-to-day management thinking," said Derrick. "But doesn't a working executive need to think about both all the time?"

"Yes, I suppose so," replied Conrad. "You can't always look past the things right in front of your nose. But if I was able to color code your thoughts that you use in running your firm—with blue for thinking that is big-picture, long-term, and connecting events and systems that impact you; and then red for the detailed picture, short-term issues, and analyzing today's crisis—how would the color balance look on your calendar?"

"Oh—very red! Depending on the day," blurted Ian to laughter.

"Points for honesty!" smiled Jada. "You lot are in the mix after all—running lively businesses. There is no right or wrong answer here. But our point is

> Strategists think long-term, big-picture, and seek to connect ecosystems and dynamics shaping their business.

that the times your headspace is in the 'blue,' to stay with Conrad's framework, you are thinking strategically. You are even, quite literally, using a different part of your brain."[2]

"Makes sense—and I certainly understand your points about big-picture and long-term thinking—when we spoke about vision and mission, both of those fit these criteria, I think," said Alexis. "But what about this business of connecting things? What does that look like when someone does it?"

"Let's go back to a blue versus red headspace to address that, Alexis," said Conrad. "Or, if you want to think about it this way, right versus left brain. Your strategic senses allow you to see patterns in a lot of data, to understand the larger context in which data appears, and even to interpret the data by what scientists and engineers call 'separating the signal from the noise.' Everyone has some level of innate ability to do that—and pull the important bits of information they need from a swirling world of data, information, and activity."

"Okay, I'm tracking you," said Alexis. "Last year I had my whole team do the CliftonStrengths test and one of my top five strengths was the ability to 'sort through the clutter and find the best route.'[3] I thought at the time, duh—of course, I'm in logistics and delivery!" she laughed.

Conrad grinned. "Well, that category in CliftonStrengths is the 'Strategic' strength, so you are halfway home. You have one of the key skills of strategic leaders in your top five strengths—the ability to interpret."[4]

"What's the other half?" broke in Derrick.

"Putting that pattern recognition to work," said Jada, "by pulling that interpretation into a greater context and tying things together. Strategic thinkers are what we call 'systems thinkers.' They are always seeking to connect systems that interact with each other and synthesize those patterns to discern what might be important for them."

She paused. "Think about it this way: the analyst mindset attacks complex problems by breaking them down into their smallest bits to understand them. The systems-thinker mindset addresses complexity by searching for the relationship between different events and systems and pulls this information together into a meaningful pattern. So, think of the way you try to make sense of the broader connections underlying the behavior of your customers, the economy, technology, your supply

Strategic thinkers seek to be "systems thinkers." They try to connect systems that interact with each other and synthesize those patterns to discern what might be important for them.

chain, the actions of your rivals, and other forces that press on your business every day. These forces are not entirely discrete—they interact and change each other, along with many more ecosystems impacting your business. The strategic part of your brain pulls all that together, rather than simply trying to break down its separate pieces."

"So," said Ian skeptically, "my business is largely based on quantum mechanics, algorithmic trading, even string theory. We're talking serious mathematics here—'left-brain' activity. Are you saying that even those of us who grew up in an analytical world focused on perfecting these skills can *also* access the strategic thinking part of our brain?"

"For sure!" said Jada. "When you know what it looks like, it's just a matter of activating it and understanding it—just like you would activate a certain muscle in some kind of physical activity."

The group drank this in.

Conrad stood up. "I tell you what, I like to frame this issue in 'How will I know it when I see it?' terms. Let's put some sure signs of a strategic mindset up on the board, what they might call in Vegas a 'tell.' That way when you run into it, even in yourself, you'll know it."

Jada went to the whiteboard and looked at the group. "Hit me with what you heard. If you walk down the hallway and bump into a strategic mindset in action from an executive, what did you see?"

The group started throwing out thoughts and Jada wrote them down:

- They take the long view.

- They look at the big picture.

- They make sense of things by synthesizing and connecting systems rather than just analyzing and dissecting information.

"I like it," said Conrad. "Let me throw on a few more that we can discuss before our next break. I think if we add these to the list you started, you can really see what a strategic mindset looks like in action." He went to the board.

- They ask strategic questions rather than giving immediate answers.

- They observe and reflect, searching for the context of events and issues.
- They challenge conventional wisdom and consider opposing ideas.
- They use analogies and design thinking in their reasoning.

"This is coming into clearer focus for me," said Derrick. "I can see it 'in action,' as you say. It strikes me as a kind of thoughtfulness, removed from the immediacy of the crisis of the day or even the weekly work rhythm. In my experience, thoughtful people ask a lot of questions—they're curious. They ponder the answers and perhaps offer alternatives. I once had an adviser to our business who would constantly say things like, 'Have you considered trying this and why not?' to push us into thinking and perhaps acting differently."

"I like that," said Conrad. "I would only caution you not to think of this thoughtful big-picture view as being a chin-stroking academic exercise in the ivory tower. Ultimately, strategy is meaningless unless it leads to action—so action and results must always be the end goal of a strategy."

> Strategy requires a lot of thinking. But ultimately, strategy is meaningless unless it leads to action—so action and results must always be the end goal of a strategy.

"I buy all that," broke in Suzie. "But what about this last line—analogies and design thinking?"

"Think about it this way: it's another manifestation of thinking differently—using the creative right brain rather than the more analytical left brain," said Jada. "Most business thinking is based on deductive logic—what strategist Roger Martin calls the 'the logic of what must be.' Pretty straightforward thinking—like math. For instance, let's say that one of Ian's customers is unhappy with his experience accessing tech support because it took so long to get help. Ian can assume that if the cause of the pain was dissatisfaction with how long it took, then that customer would be happier with a faster response. Straightforward logic, yes?"

Everyone nodded.

Jada continued, "Other types of reasoning also use a combination of hypotheses, theories, assumptions, and observations. People also use inductive reasoning, trial and error, and similar methods to unpuzzle things.

That's all great. But strategists also use analogic reasoning—drawn from relevant analogies—and try to take lessons from one business setting and apply them to another. Or even a non-business setting. Conrad started off life as a military strategist, and he still likes to use military history to give us lessons for business occasionally."

"This morning, though, Conrad used the analogy of raising children with standard formulas," chimed in Suzie.

> Strategists often think with analogies rather than deduction. Analogic reasoning can help take leaders out of their usual business focus and see if there are lessons to be learned or insights to be gained from other settings.

"Yes—better for the occasion," said Jada, smiling at Conrad. "Analogic reasoning can be very powerful because it lifts strategic thinkers a little out of their business focus to see if there are lessons to be learned or insights to be gained from other settings. Two business school professors named Gavetti and Rivkin once analyzed this and pointed out that Car-Max's strategy was in large part based on Circuit City's, and that Merrill Lynch's founder looked to the analogy of supermarkets in designing his financial services firm."[5] It can be a really powerful tool, but it requires responsible use. To be effective in helping stretch strategic creativity, you must understand the key features of different business problems and see if the patterns apply to your present challenge. A superficial analogy is worse than no analogy."

"What about design thinking?" said Derrick. "We like to think that is the dominant logic at Creativia Playsets."

"Us too," said Suzie. "Our games have won awards for creativity and inventiveness."

"You tell us," said Conrad. "What does design thinking mean to you in this context of strategic thinking?"

"Well, when we design new playsets, instead of starting with an observation of current behavior," said Derrick, "we start with pondering future behavior we'd like to see in customers—trying to open up our minds to what could lead to a whole new play experience."

He paused. "Then we bring the creative ideas to the engineers and manufacturing teams, and we ask them not to shoot down any ideas but to simply ask themselves what it would take to make these playsets before they think of any issues. Underneath the new designs are a set of assumptions, and instead of questioning them right away, we all force ourselves to answer questions like, 'What would it take for this to be true?'"[6]

"Our process is similar," said Suzie. "We think we know at any given time what technology can deliver, but we don't shackle the creative directors to it as a first step. We work backward from an ideal design and make best guesses about how it could come about. Then we see how much of that design we can realistically meet. Usually more than we think."

"There you have it, team," said Conrad. "Design thinking, or for you logic nerds, abductive reasoning. It's not necessary to remember all those terms—or any of them. The takeaway today is that a lot of strategic thinking is characterized by a kind of creativity, future orientation, and an 'art-of-the-possible' attitude."[7]

Strategic thinking is characterized by a kind of creativity, future orientation, and an "art-of-the-possible" attitude.

"I'm not the most out-of-the-box person in the world," said Alexis. "Based on what we've talked about and put on the board, I can see when I am thinking strategically versus when I am not. But it still feels a bit like a dreamy seminar to me rather than an action plan that changes a business by giving it a revised strategy. As that old Wendy's commercial said, 'Where's the beef?'"

Everyone laughed.

"Fair enough, Alexis, and now you've made everyone hungry for lunch," Conrad chuckled. "I tell you what, let's take a quick stretch and we'll have a short introduction to the way that strategists use tools to take this style of thinking out of the clouds and put it into action."

Using frameworks and the strategic process

When the team filed back into the room, Jada stood up and went over to the board. "Alexis pointed out something important before we took a break—strategy ultimately must be a call to action. It is a full game plan to move the enterprise to the place where it is most likely to thrive in the future. Our introduction to strategic thinking this morning simply opened our minds and gave us an idea of the mindset needed to consider and start the strategic process."

Ian broke in, "And even once we've started it, you've also told us that there is no magic formula for getting the right answer for our strategy. Correct?"

"Yes, there are probably a lot of possible paths that could lead to different outcomes—not one set of rules." Conrad paused. "Though don't take this approach with accounting. You'll end up in prison."

Everyone laughed.

"I joke," Conrad continued, "but executives really do struggle with strategy because it has fewer rules and formulas that lead to one definitive answer that is right every time."

> *Strategy ultimately must be a call to action. A full game plan to move the enterprise to the place where it is most likely to thrive in the future.*

"Three of us in here are engineers or operations management professionals," said Alexis, looking a bit exasperated. "Rules and right answers are the currency of our trade."

"Fair enough," said Jada, "nobody is asking you to drop what works for you in software engineering or logistics management. But let me give you one more thought from strategist Roger Martin," she continued. "He said that to be a great strategist, we have to step back from the need to find a right answer and to get accolades for identifying it."[8]

Kurt looked at the faces in the room and thought he would attempt to bridge the gap between what Conrad and Jada were selling, and what his team was buying.

"For my part, I think you guys all have the capacity to think strategically—and not just Derrick because he happens to be in a creative industry. Every one of you has moved your business forward when you didn't know the future perfectly—and even before we invested in your companies you weren't daunted by that. I didn't see anyone frozen and unable to look at choices, weigh risks, take chances—and make a course correction if it was not working out. Isn't that the mindset we're talking about here?"

"Yes, Kurt, thank you!" said Jada. "Exactly. If you look back on your own history as leaders, you can probably find examples where you moved without perfect data or the formulaic answer. You've done this—even if just by instinct. Now we can give you a little more structure—even if we stop short of rote formulas."

Conrad spoke up. "Yes, we are not talking about a shot-in-the-dark free-for-all here with strategy. We have a disciplined way to move down the strategy path. Since we don't want to start with the illusory 'right answer,' we can start with the right questions instead. If we ask the right questions about the business—questions about our external environment, our internal capabilities, our business model, and more—we can then know what tools in the strategist's toolbox to reach for."

"Tools? What does that look like?" said Ian.

Conrad replied, "Our tools are analytical prisms that might force us to think differently—we call them *frameworks*. We look at the data through the analytical framework and see if it gives us any insights that might help shape our strategic choices. Think of these frameworks like a lens—be it reading glasses, binoculars, a microscope, or anything else. When you hold that lens up to your eye, the thing that you are looking at appears different. It appears clearer if you are using the right lens for the job. Strategic frameworks are like that; we use them to see things differently. That new look might give us the insights we need to start framing and analyzing choices—possible courses of action."

"Here is the sequence," said Jada as she wrote on the board:[9]

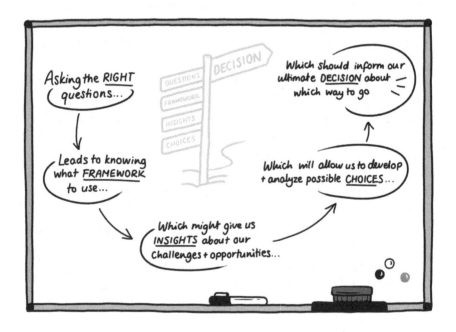

Asking the RIGHT questions...

Leads to knowing what FRAMEWORK to use...

Which might give us INSIGHTS about our challenges + opportunities...

Which will allow us to develop + analyze possible CHOICES...

Which should inform our ultimate DECISION about which way to go

QUESTIONS
FRAMEWORK
INSIGHTS
CHOICES
DECISION

"So, at the end of the day, it's all about making a decision and going for it," offered Alexis.

"For sure," said Conrad. "The essential activity of an executive is decision-making. That is what you are paid to do. For top executives and leaders, it includes weighty decisions about the direction of the enterprise and charting a way into the future. US president Dwight Eisenhower had a two-part equation for leadership. He said that leadership was 'the ability to decide what has to get

> *Strategy frameworks are analytical prisms that can force us to think differently. We look at the data through the analytical framework and see if it gives us any insights that help shape our strategic choices.*

done and get people to want to do it.' Strategic thinking and the strategic process are meant to equip you for that first part of the equation. To decide what has to get done."

"My top team and I have already come up with a lot of good ideas about the future," said Suzie. "Naturally, because we are living it day to day, these ideas have been shaped by our competitive environment, evolving customer behavior, other trends, our own capabilities, and all that. I'm not asking if you think we can skip ahead of this process you refer to, but can we move through it quickly—since we already have an inkling of what would make for a better future?"

"Perhaps," replied Jada. "There are a bunch of tools we can use to stress test your initial thoughts. But it is probably worth emphasizing that being a strategic leader is *not* about coming up with great ideas. Rather, a strategic leader oversees a disciplined way of thinking about the world and the role you want your company to play in it. And then what to do to get to that better place. That process could well lead to brilliant ideas ... or similar ideas to some of your current thoughts ... or just good ones. It's worth going through to double-check your gut instincts, yes?"

"Yeah, I suppose you're right," sighed Suzie. "What if we spent a ton of money and time making a certain move and it turned out we missed something or made a flawed assumption or simply overlooked an opportunity."

"Just so," said Conrad. "All those things can still happen, but a disciplined strategic process—undertaken with your strategic mindset switched on—can prevent common mishaps. The corporate graveyards are full of strategies that were poorly thought through or poorly executed."

Being a strategic leader is not about coming up with great ideas. Rather, a strategic leader oversees a disciplined way of thinking about the world and the role you want your company to play in it.

"I'm starving, so I'm all for lunch at this point," said Ian. "But before we break, give us a thumbnail of where we might go next in this process, now that we have a better handle on what strategy is and how a strategic mind functions."

"I'll leave you with this," said Jada. "We have an expression in our partnership: all strategies are formed outside-in but conducted inside-out."

"What does that mean?" asked Steve.

"It means many things that we will get into over the course of time, Steve," replied Jada. "But for now, it means for us that we tend to start with the external world. Remember that chart we drew up last week? One of the first steps in the strategic process is to analyze and understand the external environment in which your firm exists and competes—deciding where you want to play and what that playing field really looks like, given that there are others on it. Then, in the second step we turn the lens inward—and try to really understand your company at a visceral level: its core competencies, the dominant genes in its DNA, its people, resources, culture, ability to change, its strengths and weaknesses."

"Once we've put those together," Conrad added, "we have a better chance of seeing if there is a preferred new reality we want for the company. Perhaps the firm can move to a new position in its industry where it can gain a better advantage ... and sustain it in the face of changing circumstances."

"So, it's not really until that point that you would start thinking about developing a detailed strategy or strategic plan, then?" asked Derrick.

"We think so," said Conrad. "After all, a strategy will guide you in considering options, making choices, allocating resources, developing processes, and aligning the talents of leaders and followers to get to your goal. Getting to your goal might require changing your product or service mix, perhaps creating a new product or service, doing an acquisition or divestment, changing your business model, going international—who knows?!"

"Big decisions," sighed Suzie. Her colleagues nodded in agreement.

"Big decisions indeed," said Jada. "But less daunting when they are approached—'tamed' even—by a sound strategic process. It can give you the confidence to make those big decisions."

Conrad and Jada's key takeaways

A strategic mindset:
- Is **long-range**, not short-term (most often about the future).
- Is **broad** in scope, not narrow in focus.
- Tries to **connect** many different things, not isolate actions or processes.
- Thinks in the context of a **competitive** environment.
- Thinks about outcomes that will give the company an **advantage** in this environment.
- Uses the process to make hard **choices** and explain purpose and pathways.

Strategic thinkers:
- Ask strategic questions.
- Take the long view and look at the big picture.
- Observe and reflect.
- Start from the context (formulating strategy outside-in).
- Challenge conventional wisdom.
- Consider opposing ideas.
- Make sense of things through synthesis.
- Pull things together instead of breaking them down (analysis).
- Are realistically optimistic.
- Ask "What would it take for this to be true?"
- Use many forms of logic.
- Use analogies and design thinking in their reasoning.

The strategic-thinking process:
- Starts with asking the right questions ... →
- Which leads to knowing what analytical frameworks to use ... →
- Which gives us insights about our challenges and opportunities ... →
- Which will allow us to develop and analyze possible choices ... →
- Which should inform our ultimate decision about which way to go.

Works cited and recommendations for further study

Books

De Kluyver, C. A. (2000). *Strategic Thinking: An Executive Perspective*. Upper Saddle River, NJ: Prentice Hall.

Dixit, A. K., and Nalebuff, B. J. (1993). *Thinking Strategically: The Competitive Edge in Business, Politics, and Everyday Life*. New York, NY: W. W. Norton.

Editors of Harvard Business Review Press (2019). *HBR Guide to Thinking Strategically*. Boston, MA: Harvard Business Review Press.

Martin, R. (2009). *The Design of Business: Why Design Thinking is the Next Competitive Advantage*. Boston, MA: Harvard Business Review Press.

Montgomery, C. A. (2012). *The Strategist: Be the Leader Your Business Needs*. New York, NY: HarperCollins.

Olson, A. K., and Simerson, B. K. (eds.) (2015). *Leading with Strategic Thinking*. Hoboken, NY: Wiley.

Articles

Carucci, R. (2016). Make strategic thinking part of your job. *Harvard Business Review*. https://hbr.org/2016/10/make-strategic-thinking-part-of-your-job, published October 26, 2016, accessed September 16, 2024.

Gavetti, G., and Rivkin, J. (2005). How strategists really think: Tapping the power of analogy. *Harvard Business Review, 83*(4), 54–63.

Martin, R. (2014). Why smart people struggle with strategy. *Harvard Business Review*. https://hbr.org/2014/06/why-smart-people-struggle-with-strategy, published June 12, 2014, accessed September 16, 2024.

Randall, D. (2020). Winning the long game: Developing a strategy mindset. *Real Leaders Magazine*, October 14, 2020.

Rooke, D., and Torbert, W. (2005). Transformations of leadership. *Harvard Business Review, 83*(4), 66–76.

Schoemaker, P., Krupp, S., and Howland, S. (2013). Strategic leadership: The essential skills. *Harvard Business Review, 91*(1–2), 131–34.

Stobierski, T. (2020). 4 ways to develop your strategic thinking skills. *Business Insights*. https://online.hbs.edu/blog/post/how-to-develop-strategic-thinking-skills, published September 10, 2020, accessed September 16, 2024.

Van den Steen, E. (2021). Strategy and strategic thinking. *Harvard Business School Technical Note* 721-431, January 2021 (revised March 2021).

Notes for Chapter 2

1 Rooke, D., and Torbert, W. (2005). Transformations of Leadership. *Harvard Business Review, 83*(4), 66–76.
2 See, for instance, Schmidt, K. (2013). The neuroscience of strategic thinking and executive coaching. *Forbes.* https://www.forbes.com/consent/ketch/?toURL=https://www.forbes.com/councils/forbes-coachescouncil/2023/07/10/the-neuroscience-of-strategic-thinking-and-executive-coaching/ Forbes, published July 10, 2023, accessed October 21, 2024.
3 Rath, T. (2007). *StrengthsFinder 2.0.* Omaha, NE: Gallup Press, p. 163.
4 Ibid.
5 Gavetti, G., and Rivkin, J. (2005). How strategists really think: Tapping the power of analogy. *Harvard Business Review, 83*(4), 54–63.
6 Lafley, A. G., and Martin, R. L. (2013). *Playing to Win: How Strategy Really Works.* Boston, MA: Harvard Business Review Press, p. 186. The authors phrase the question as "What would have to be true?".
7 See especially Martin, R. (2009). *The Business of Design.* Boston, MA: Harvard Business Review Press.
8 Martin, R. (2014). Why smart people struggle with strategy. *Harvard Business Review.* https://hbr.org/2014/06/why-smart-people-struggle-with-strategy, published June 12, 2014, accessed September 16, 2024.
9 Kryscynski, D. (2019). Questions mindset. YouTube video. https://youtu.be/9eTaes-blopQ?si=p0bSkvH49mnriOlf, published November 13, 2019, accessed September 16, 2024.

Chapter 3

The World Around Me: A Dialogue on How to Analyze the Competitive Environment

"The most incomprehensible thing about the world is that it is comprehensible."

—ALBERT EINSTEIN

....

Derrick Jouet, the CEO of Creativia Playsets, meets with Conrad and Jada to discuss his thinking about his competitive environment. Along with Kurt Amery and two other CEOs, Derrick learns that the best starting point for any strategy is conceptualizing the firm's setting relative to other players in the landscape. They learn how to 'map' their industries to better plot a route to a position that gives them a competitive advantage. They also come to understand that the competitive environment is not just their direct competition, but other dynamics that act as forces of competition on their businesses. The executives are given several tools they can use to assess their market environment and the currents shaping it—the strategic positioning map framework, the PESTEL framework, and the Five Forces of Competition model. The group sees ways to understand an ever-changing competitive landscape and starts thinking about positions of future advantage based on those dynamics.

....

Seeing and mapping the market

"Look, Conrad," said an exasperated Derrick Jouet, the CEO of Creativia Playsets. "Nobody sees my competition more than I do every day, but I'm just not following you when you push me to explain where I 'sit' in the market. I mean, I'm small, and they're big. What else is there to explain? You say you want to 'map' my competitive market. I'm not following you."

"Well, surely you can compare yourself to the competition in more ways than big and small, yes?" rejoined Conrad. "What else makes you the same as or different from any of them?"

"Okay, let me throw some things out there," said Derrick. "The big dog in the creative play market is quite obviously Lego. We try to price our playsets in a similar range to theirs—they set the market, really. But they can produce a lot more varied playsets because they're so big. They can also afford hot culture 'tie-ins'—licensing deals with movie franchises and so on."

"So, if you price the same and offer fewer products, why should anybody buy from you?" asked Jada. "Lego is one of the greatest brands of all time!"

"Because we're a better fit for today's kids," said Derrick. "We create products for trending technology tastes, habits, and interests."

"So, you're differentiated from Lego in terms of the type of play experience you offer children?" asked Conrad.

"Oh my gosh, yes," said Derrick. "Look at our line. We orient every playset to children growing up with intuitive technology—and who want to customize their experiences using physical and virtual tools."

Conrad and Jada nodded, waiting for Derrick to continue.

"That is the 'hole in the market,'" Derrick added. "That's what pushed me to start Creativia in the first place!"

Sitting to the side, Kurt Amery wasn't sure Derrick was getting the benefit of this analysis, but at this point he took it on faith that Conrad and Jada were on the right track. They had said that the next step in creating a strategy for any of his businesses was to conduct an "external analysis." Kurt had recruited Derrick to go head-to-head with Conrad and Jada to demonstrate to all of his executives that this analysis was a fundamental step in thinking strategically. That's just what was needed to school his whole team in understanding the outside forces buffeting their companies.

"Derrick, what about non-Lego offerings like the other building-block toys?" said Kurt. "Not the Mega Bloks ones for toddlers, but the more advanced ones like K'Nex, Vatos robot building sets, all the marble run sets, chemistry kits, and stuff like that?"

"We're different from all of those," said Derrick. "First, we set ourselves apart from purely physical playsets with our virtual element. Second, we are different from the purely virtual playsets because of our physical element. Those offerings and others are all over the map regarding price, appeal to different market segments, and in other ways."

"Right you are!" said Conrad, smiling. "Did you just say *map*?"

Derrick raised his eyebrows.

"You're speaking our language," said Jada. "Map is the key word. Any company can 'map' its competitive market and its position versus competitors."

"And if you analyze that map," said Conrad, "you can see if there is a future place in the market you may want to move into—because you see more future customers there or less competition or some other advantage."

A strategic position in the context of the market

Liz Fiscella, who was sitting in on Derrick's external analysis along with Alexis Chapman and Kurt Amery, chimed in. "Derrick said the initial business opportunity for Creativia was his perception of a 'hole in the market.' Could a map show that hole, so to speak?"

Conrad smiled and nodded. "A map of where everybody is—or isn't—can show you many things."

> A company can "map" its competitive market and its position versus competitors. That map can show the company a future place in the market it may want to move into to gain some advantage—more customers, less competition, or some other benefits.

"Hmm," said Derrick. "I get the concept, but what does that look like?"

"How about this—let's map something," said Conrad. "Everyone get out a sheet of paper. Draw me a map of Paris in two minutes."[1]

"Paris?" said Liz. "Paris, France?"

"Can't do," said Alexis. "I've never been."

"You have some idea of Paris, yes, Alexis?" asked Jada. "Give it a shot. Map whatever is in your head."

A few minutes later, Conrad posted four maps on the board. Derrick's detailed the Seine River, the Eiffel Tower, the Louvre museum, major boulevards, and even a grid dividing the city into sections. Liz drew a half-dozen stick figures in notable places—a bookish man balancing a cigarette on the Left Bank, a woman with a feathery hat on the Right Bank. Kurt drew a dozen straight lines, circling and labeling key locales such as "Opera" and "Madeleine." Alexis drew a river adorned with a beret, a baguette, an arch, a tower, and a tricolor flag.

"Four useful depictions of Paris," Jada said. "Tasty looking baguette, Alexis!"

Alexis took some good-natured ribbing.

"Derrick's even has the districts on there," said Jada.

"Yes, the *arrondissements*," Derrick said, smiling with self-satisfaction.

"Liz," asked Jada, "what gives with those stick figures?"

"When I think of Paris, I think of caricatures. The intellectual at a book stall, the wealthy madame on the Champs-Elysées."

"Part of the *human* geography of Paris," said Conrad, "and definitely tourist highlights."

"Kurt," said Jada, "it looks like the last time you were in Paris, you didn't get much sunlight? Your drawing reminds me of a map of the Paris subway."

"It stuck in my head," said Kurt. "That's what happens when you don't want to get the family lost."

"And Alexis," smiled Jada. "You've never been to Paris, but your map is altogether different from what you might draw for, say, Berlin or London or Rome, yes?"

Alexis nodded and smiled. "Thanks for cutting me some slack. But what's the moral of this mapping story?"

"That all of you have an innate mapping ability," said Conrad. "You can contextualize things, sense patterns, and show actors or objects in relation to one another."

"Well," said Derrick, "I love Paris. But that was hardly enough time to show all the context and patterns I had in mind."

"We gave you only two minutes for a reason," said Conrad. "A lot of strategic thinking is intuitive, not analytical. You get a lot of fresh insight if you let your intuitive right brain do the talking. It sees things in relation to each other and their environment."

> *A lot of strategic thinking is intuitive, not analytical. You can gain fresh insight if you think with your intuitive "right brain." It sees things in relation to each other and their environment.*

"So, how does this relate to helping Derrick see his competitive environment in a way that will help him formulate his new strategy?" Kurt asked.

"Remember a few weeks ago when we talked about how a company positions itself in its market—in many ways, the fundamental point of strategy. That competitive position has to be related to the environment in which you compete.[2] Being able to map an environment is the first step."

Conrad explained that on a physical map of a place, you can't change certain reference points—such as the Seine River in Paris or the cardinal directions (north, south, east, west). On a strategic positioning map, however, you can change your parameters at will. Different parameters yield different perspectives.

"Here's a map Jada and I did last week," he said, putting up a map showing automobile brands. The map had labels for its parameters on a 2x2 matrix. The horizontal axis represented a range from utility and reliability at one end to exotic and high performance at the other end. Conrad called it "from plain to fancy." On the vertical axis was a scale from upmarket and expensive at one end to economical at the other end—from "pricey to cheap" in Conrad's words.

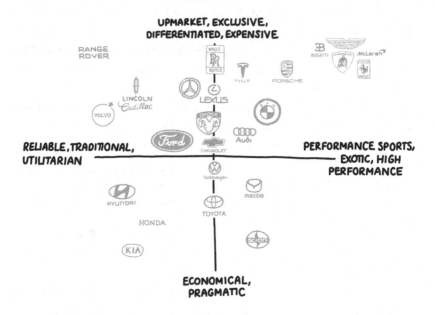

Figure 3.1 Example of a strategic positioning map

"You all know car brands," said Jada. "You can intuit why these brands and companies are generally where they are on the map. The purpose here is not to argue about the exact accuracy of the positioning of each brand on the map—rather we want to represent two things strategically: first, this concept of the context of the market, and second, the relative position of the players in it."

Kurt leaned forward. "Pretty accurate to me," he said. "And probably not an accident I would think. It strikes me that these brands and companies position themselves exactly where they want to be—in a particular place in the market."

Conrad and Jada nodded in agreement.

Jada drew a matrix opposite Conrad's. "So, Derrick, you already mentioned several characteristics of offerings in your market that could serve as competitive parameters. One was the physical aspects of the playsets—blocks and pieces. The other was virtual aspects—is that something like app-assisted play?"

"To simplify, yes," said Derrick. "We do something pretty cool. Our blocks and their configuration—whatever it is—can be read by our app. So the physical creation can be changed and used in our virtual world too based on what the player builds and how they want to use it. I suppose you could have a scale ranging from conventional to innovative, at least in a technical sense."

"You also mentioned price," said Kurt. "Wouldn't a classic scale from low- to luxury-priced be useful?"

"For sure," said Conrad, drawing it up. Derrick then described which company should be where on the emerging map.

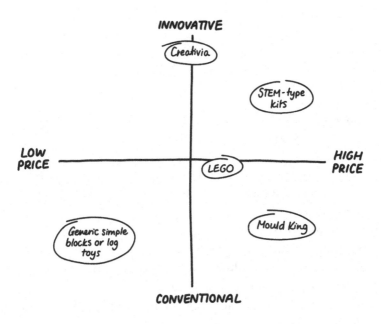

Figure 3.2 A competitive landscape map for playsets

"You know, Derrick," said Kurt, "I remember your investment pitch. You said you set out to build a company that did not exist, but the market was there for it. A company that would make affordable playsets with a virtual element that could allow for a choose-your-own-ending story."

"That's right," said Derrick. "You can see on the map the hole in the market I sought to fill."

"But this map's only about price point and technology," said Kurt.

"A map with two dimensions has limitations," said Conrad. "You could add a Z axis for a third dimension—perhaps a scale of how customizable a play experience might be."

"Or a fourth dimension or more," said Jada. "Each map dimension characterizes key features of the market and then shows which neighborhood in the city your company lives in and why."

"You also want to ask another question in the process," said Conrad. "Are you there on purpose, as Kurt pointed out, with the car brands ... or by accident? Or is your neighborhood still a good one? Might you want to move to a different neighborhood for some reason?"

Alexis pointed at the whiteboard. She had another question. "This map shows how Derrick differentiated Creativia from other imagination-based playset-type providers, but I don't see how it helps direct him to a better future."

"Hold that thought," said Conrad. "This map, like any strategy tool or framework, gives us just a starting point. It shows how a firm sits relative to others in its market. It highlights conditions or parameters that might define market differences. It can give you insights about who is where and doing what in your market. Now, if you had additional analysis saying, for instance, that there was an unfilled need in the market—say on our automobile map this blank area in the lower right corner for cheap high-performance sports cars," he pointed to the diagram. "In theory, some company could move a brand over or down to that spot. Or create one from scratch—like Toyota did with Scion."

"I would think a lot of people would want a cheap high-performance sports car," Kurt offered.

"Indeed," said Conrad. "But making them at a profit has yet to be figured out. So, demand does not make a market!"

"One last thing to remember," Jada added. "A map like this offers a snapshot in time, but the competitive landscape changes as if in a video. Real insight comes from knowing what forces are moving the marketplace 'video' in what direction."

Analyzing the forces of the competitive environment

"How's the video of your marketplace look, Derrick?" asked Jada.

"Hugely dynamic!" replied Derrick. "Running at double time—the way kids behave and spend their playtime, the preferences of parents, the attempts by competitors to add value propositions to their basic playset model. I mean, Lego has leveraged its brand into clothing, watches, board games, books, home decorations. The demise of dedicated toy stores has shifted the whole manner of where and how people buy toys. And don't get me started on how fast technology is changing."

Liz broke in, "Don't tell me we have to add three more axes on the map to capture these things? I'm losing track of all the parameters."

"No worries there, Liz," said Jada. "Let's not overburden our strategic positioning map. Instead, let's introduce some different frameworks to capture more insights."

She wrote "P-E-S-T-E-L" on the board.

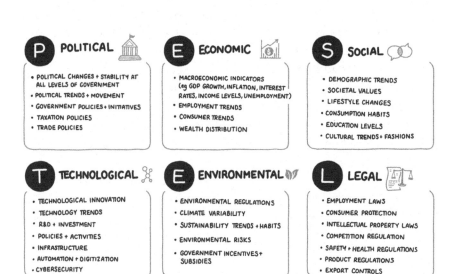

Figure 3.3 The PESTEL framework

"Is that the creature Harry Potter was flying around on?" laughed Liz.

"No," smiled Derrick. "That was a Thestral. But what does PESTEL stand for?"

Jada explained that the "P" stands for political trends or dynamics shaping the marketplace, "E" for economic ones, "S" for social changes, "T" for technological trends and movements, "E" for environmental elements, and "L" for legal ones.

"Imagine if you spent a few hours using PESTEL with your top team of market watchers," said Jada. "Itemize all the things in these categories that are changing right now, and then chart the way they will shape your market."

"Wow, yes, very worthwhile," said Derrick. "My team has an instinct for this stuff. We will pounce on opportunities, but we've never thought out our moves so deliberately. I can't remember the last time we took a deliberate and organized look at the undercurrents shaping our market-place. Let me give you an example: working-from-home trends ended up being a boon for our industry. Building toys and playsets sales went up and have stayed strong since then. I'm not sure anybody was prepared for that or if they thought through what it means for the future."

"Seems like a combined political, economic, social, and environmental phenomenon," said Kurt.

Jada nodded. "It's a great exercise—even if it only flexes your strategic-thinking muscles periodically."

"A caveat, though," said Conrad. "Like all strategic frameworks, it organizes your thinking. It may even suggest options and alternatives. But it does not spit out a magic answer."

Strategic frameworks, like PESTEL, are tools to organize thinking. Looking at data and facts through the lens of the framework allows the strategist to gain different insights.

"But it gets you through the starting gate," offered Kurt.

"Yes," Jada agreed. "It forces you to question basic assumptions you and your team have about the world in which you compete."

"But it's not the destination," reiterated Conrad. "Just the starting point. Early in the strategy process you have to make an appraisal of the world in which you exist, who else exists in it, and what forces are shaping all that existence."

"We know the 'who else exists' bit—that would be Derrick's competition," said Liz.

"Know your enemy and know yourself, and in a hundred battles, you will never be in peril," offered Jada. "Wisdom from Sun Tzu—one of the great strategic minds of all time."

"Sun Tzu was right," said Conrad. "But the 'enemy' isn't always the big dog that's in your face—or even the little dog snapping at your heels. The enemy might be forces in the market that are not your rivals."

Conrad looked at the blank stares in the room.

"Forces?" said Alexis. "Like the Force in Star Wars?"

Jada stepped in. "Sort of. Let me walk you through what Conrad is talking about."

While Conrad was drawing on the board, Jada explained that certain dynamics in the marketplace can feel to a firm like business rivals by exerting competitive pressure on a company, even though the forces are not direct competitors. The forces can compete with you without actually being on the list of industry competitors.

"Sounds like the ghosts that you didn't see in the night," said Liz. "Ghosts from behind a door you wish you never opened."

"Hah!" Jada said. "Not far off the mark. A good analogy. I may have to steal it!"

Conrad put down his marker. "Think about it this way: what an executive should worry about from a direct rival is not simply that they exist, but the competitive effect their existence has. For instance, if a direct competitor cuts prices to start a price war, its force and impact—on your margins in this case if you follow them—are the effect that needs to be a factor in your strategy."

"Concern yourself with the effect, not just the cause?" asked Kurt.

"Absolutely," said Jada. "There are a lot of competitive forces other than direct rivals. It's the ghosts that come back to bite you in the dark if you don't take them into account. They are in the shadows and are as important as 'knowing your enemy.'"

Conrad turned to what he had drawn on the board. "Here is another concept from Michael Porter: the Five Forces of Competition model."

"Smart dude, this Porter guy," muttered Liz under her breath.

"No doubt," said Conrad as he finished drawing. "In some ways, this model of his to creatively analyze competitive forces in an industry started what many people call the strategy revolution. Let's look at what he offered us."[3]

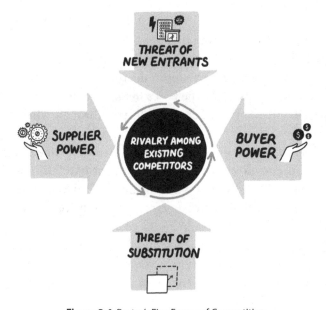

Figure 3.4 Porter's Five Forces of Competition

(Source: Figure 1.1 from Porter, M. (2008). *On Competition*. Boston, MA: Harvard Business School Press, p. 4. Reprinted with kind permission by Harvard Business Publishing)

Jada let the drawing sink in as they studied it. "Derrick, you are our focus today. Let's start in the center, with the most conventional force of competition—your direct rivals. We've focused a bit on this already with our mapping exercise, but the most important decision you need to make there is to decide who is truly a competitive firm—in other words, who is providing similar toys or experiences for customers. So, Derrick, would you, for instance, compete with companies that produce fixed-model playsets or advanced chemistry sets or robotic kits?"

Derrick considered this for a moment. "I suppose we wouldn't. They might nibble at the edges of our business, but I think of them more as competing in a market adjacent to imagination-based playsets and kits, even the most advanced ones."

"So you place them outside that 'circle,'" said Jada. "In other words, those firms are *related* to your industry. They can impact it with their business models. But they are not direct rivals."

"You don't try to fight the whole world competitively," said Conrad. "The circles in the rest of this model will bring in enough for you to worry about."

"Oh … joy," said Derrick.

"Hey," rejoined Jada, also laughing. "We say that if you don't enjoy thinking competitively about everything, don't go into the strategy business. There's a reason the founder of Intel called his strategy book *Only the Paranoid Survive*."

Certain dynamics in the marketplace can feel to a firm like a business rival by exerting competitive pressure on a company, even though these forces of competition are not direct competitors.

Insights from the Five Forces model

Conrad directed their attention back to the diagram. "We mentioned that something like a PESTEL framework can help you see the bigger picture of trends affecting your firm. And we've talked about direct competition—that is generally easier to see. The insights from the rest of the forces in Porter's model can help you analyze the industry in which you compete—especially the forces of competition that can shape price, profit, and demand. These non-direct 'forces of competition' don't get the attention they deserve. Let's look at them for Derrick's industry."

"When you say 'buyers' in the model, do you mean customers?" asked Derrick.

"Could be," answered Conrad. "Who buys your playsets?"

"Parents for their kids, of course," said Derrick. "Or a relative. The adults make the buying decision. We've done a lot of market and customer surveys to confirm that. The kids certainly put the pressure on, though."

"How much pricing power do these buyers have over you?" asked Conrad.

"Not much, really. We price reasonably—mid-market. And with our virtual features, we won't lose kids to cut-rate imitators. Our differentiation is our best protection there."

"Okay, that's good news about your end users," said Conrad.

Derrick's eyebrows went up at the mention of "end users."

"Let me ask you—how many Creativia playsets do you sell directly? Through your website?"

"Tiny share, perhaps ten percent," answered Derrick. "Walmart's the biggest toy seller, followed by Amazon and then the other big-box retailers. It's been that way since Toys"R"Us initially went out of business a few years ago."

"Could you also consider the retailers as your buyers?"

"I suppose. We definitely have to negotiate with the buyers at Walmart, Costco, Target, and the rest."

"Do they have pricing power over you?"

"They pressure us. Walmart's or Costco's goal is to move products—move them as soon as possible. If a toy doesn't fly off the shelf, they give the shelf to something else, not necessarily a toy."

"So price matters," said Jada. "A slow-selling playset sits on the shelf, and the big-box retailers then return it to you?"

"I see where we are going," said Derrick. "Yes, these intermediate buyers sell probably seventy-five percent of our sets. So, they do have pricing power—probably more than our end users."

"You might want to think of the big-box toy buyers as your customers," said Kurt. "It's not just end users who pit you against your rivals."

"A powerful insight," said Conrad. "That could shape your decisions about where and how you grow your business."

"Next up, suppliers," said Jada. "How's the balance of power work there? Are they able to exert control over you by charging higher prices? Or can you pit them against alternative suppliers to neutralize their power?"

"You know," started Derrick, "I didn't think about duplication and resiliency in our supply chain until that global supply chain slowdown a few years ago. That caused us to want to have some redundant options in the supply chain. But I can see your point," said Derrick. "If I only have a single source of supply, that supplier could squeeze me."

"For sure," said Jada. "And yet times change. If you look at buyers and suppliers together, you see how they can exert forces that affect your prices and profitability—factors you usually attribute to direct rivals."

"So now, let's move on and look at the bottom of the diagram," said Conrad.

"Substitutes, wow!" said Liz, jumping in. "Everything a kid might do with their time is a possible substitute for Derrick's products—from soccer practice to homework."

"True enough," said Conrad. "But that is an expansive view. Let's look at the question of substitutes more narrowly. What do you see adjacent to playsets or even virtual toys that could lure customers away from your offering and other similar toys?"

> *Considered together, buyers and suppliers can exert competitive forces that affect a company's prices and profitability—factors the company might usually attribute to direct rivals.*

"Oh, phones, phones, phones, and more phones," Derrick said. "It's all about mobile games these days."

"Do they substitute for just about every indoor play activity these days?"

"Oh yes, largely. That's why we can only win with the virtual element in our playsets, so as not to be completely pushed out by a game on the phone."

"That's a good defense against an available substitute," said Jada. "Offering richer value and more accessibility to the play experience is better than going only physical or only virtual."

"I never really thought of it that way—it's a powerful concept," said Kurt. "If you ignore or allow substitutes, your addressable market of buyers can shrink."

Conrad moved over to the last category on his diagram—new entrants—and Liz spoke up. "Going back to our maps," she said, "how can you put a new, unheard-of company on the map if you can't see it in the market? It won't be on your competitive radar."

"Then you need a better radar," said Jada. "The graveyard of once-great companies is full of those that failed to take new entrants seriously. They missed how someone they didn't see was doing something innovative. Think of once mighty Sears and upstart Walmart back in the day, for instance. A new entrant to the industry who is doing smart new things can pressure existing companies to spend to keep up—and that whittles away profitability."

"Well, other than acquiring a government-sanctioned monopoly or building an illegal cartel, how can you defend against a new entrant?" asked Alexis. "It's a free market, after all."

"By using a few basic strategic moves," said Jada. "Make it hard for them by elevating the fixed costs of competing—either with new points of differentiation, or by protecting intellectual property, increasing spending on research and innovation, or locking up suppliers with exclusivity."

"Playing hardball—I like it," said Liz. "But wouldn't spending on defensive moves have the same effect, reducing your profitability?"

"It absolutely could," said Jada. "That's why we consider it a competitive force, the same as a rival in a price war."

> *Once a company understands what gives it leverage (or doesn't) with competitive forces, it can adopt strategies that limit its exposure to the leverage that rivals, buyers, suppliers, substitutes, or new entrants might have over it. A strategically shrewd company might position itself where the competitive forces are the weakest.*

Conrad looked around at the faces in the room. "Look, I know this involves looking at the totality of competitive forces more comprehensively than you might have in the past, but it's not that bad. You simply need to recognize a few things. First, the situation is always in flux in all five of these areas, so analyze these things not as a snapshot but as changing dynamics. Second, they are all relationships of a sort—and at any given time, one party has leverage over the other party in the relationship. Once you understand what gives you leverage or doesn't, you can adopt strategies that limit your exposure to the leverage that rivals, buyers, suppliers, substitutes, or new entrants might have over you."

Everyone in the room nodded. "But!" he said, rising to his feet. "That is not your chief takeaway from the Five Forces model. The benefit you get from this exercise is not just tactical responses. Rather, it is to see if you can position your company where the competitive forces are weakest and you have the most leverage to exploit changes in the forces. That would be how you use this tool strategically."

"And then you can decide what to do—where to position yourself on the market map, yes?" asked Derrick, hoping for an easy answer.

"Well," said Jada. "Not quite yet."

Jada explained that, before everyone started to think about having practical goals that might form the basis of a strategic plan, they had more to consider. Using a few tools for external market analysis was the start that would help everyone remove the risk of forming objectives in isolation, a mistake many firms make. The external analysis reveals market opportunities and threats. But the next question is, what is feasible for a firm? That requires turning the analytical lens inward. What internal capabilities and constraints may or may not allow the company to make the move wanted in the market?

Conrad and Jada's key takeaways

- Strategy is formulated **"outside-in."** Start by understanding the world in which the company exists and the dynamics shaping it.

- **"Mapping" a company's competitive position** relative to market characteristics and other competitors is a tool for helping envision a company's current competitive position. This can help to determine whether a strategic move can be made to give a company a unique or differentiated strategic position within an industry.

- A **PESTEL framework** can help a company discover the impact of the bigger trends shaping the industry and affecting the company.

- Don't just think of direct rivals as exerting competitive pressure on the company. **Porter's Five Forces model** adds four more "forces of competition": understanding the changes in supplier power, the changes in buyer power, the threat of new entrants, and the threat of substitutes. This can help a company understand the dynamics of a particular industry— and forces of competition that can shape price, profit, and demand.

  » Rivals and the threat of new entrants can affect profitability.

  » Buyer and supplier power can affect price and profitability.

  » Substitutes can affect the total number of buyers.

Works cited and recommendations for further study

Books

Greenwald, B., and Kahn, J. (2005). *Competition Demystified: A Radically Simplified Approach to Business Strategy*. New York, NY: Portfolio Books.

Porter, M. E. (1980). *Competitive Strategy: Techniques for Analyzing Industries and Competitors*. Republished with a new introduction 1998. New York, NY: Free Press.

Urbany, J. E., and Davis, J. H. (2010). *Grow by Focusing on What Matters: Competitive Strategy in 3-Circles*. Sterling Forest: Business Expert Press.

Articles

Barrows, E., and Frigo, M. (2008). Using the strategy map for competitor analysis. *Harvard Business Publishing Note* Nr. B0807E-PDF-ENG.

D'Aveni, R. (2007). Mapping your competitive position. *Harvard Business Review*, 83(11), 110–120.

Day, G. S., and Schoemaker, P. J. H. (2005). Scanning the periphery. *Harvard Business Review*, 83(11), 135–48.

Editors of Harvard Business School Press (2005). SWOT analysis I: Looking outside for threats and opportunities. Boston, MA: Harvard Business School Press.

MacMillan, I. C., and McGrath, R. G. (1997). Discovering new points of differentiation. *Harvard Business Review*, 75(4), 133–145.

Porter, M. E. (1979). How competitive forces shape strategy. *Harvard Business Review*, 57(2), 137–145.

Urbany, J., and Davis, J. (2007). Strategic insight in three circles. *Harvard Business Review*, 85(11), 28–30.

Watkins, M. D., and Bazerman, M. H. (2003). Predictable surprises: The disasters you should have seen coming. *Harvard Business Review*, 81(3), 72–80.

Notes for Chapter 3

1 Inspired by an exercise used for other purposes by Dr. Mark Nevins. www.nevinsconsulting.com
2 Porter, M. E. (1980). *Competitive Strategy: Techniques for Analyzing Industries and Competitors*. Republished with a new introduction 1998. New York, NY: Free Press, Chapter 1.
3 Porter, M. E. (1979). How competitive forces shape strategy. *Harvard Business Review*, 57(2), 137–145.

Chapter 4

Understanding Ourselves: A Dialogue on Internal Character and Competencies

"Gnōthi sauton. Know thyself."

—*Inscribed above the entrance to the temple of Apollo at Delphi, site of the sacred oracle*

....

Liz Fiscella, the Founder of Healthy Family Foodstuffs (HFF), is in the hyper-competitive grocery industry. She is meeting with Conrad and Jada to mull over the foundation on which she might be able to expand the number of HFF stores. She is joined by Kurt Amery, who will judge whether Argo Ventures should invest in her expansion plans, and two other executives. Liz discovers that to expand her stores into an even more competitive space, she needs a profound understanding of HFF's sustainable source of competitive advantage. She learns that this must be a competency of HFF that is valuable, unique, rare, difficult, or costly to imitate, and hard to substitute. If she can put her finger on this, then she has a stronger position from which to expand. The executives learn from Conrad and Jada several frameworks they can use to understand that foundation of their core competencies—sources of durable competitive strength. Liz also learns how to take the well-known SWOT framework and turn it on its side into a TOWS matrix—allowing her to take her insights on the shape of the market (threats and opportunities) and match them with the strengths and weaknesses of HFF that she has been discussing. This helps point her to certain basic strategic choices she should analyze before launching any plans.

....

Sources of competitive advantage

Liz Fiscella leaned back into her chair and puffed out a big breath of air. "Okay, Jada, I get why you are pushing me on this, but I am telling you that Healthy Family Foodstuffs' competitive advantage *is* our positioning in the market. For our customers, we uniquely represent some of the things they like about other grocers—but all together in one place. First, we are fairly priced like Trader Joe's; second, we have a healthy organic orientation like Whole Foods; and third, we have a Costco-style family bulk approach. We fill that gap in the market for growing health-conscious families."

"Fair enough," responded Jada. "And the strategic positioning map you did for your external analysis showed that. We loved the way you used three axes of price, health-consciousness, and packaging size/convenience. It was clear where you fit in the market." Her voice trailed off.

"Umm … but?" asked Steve Adlar of Secure Home Suite, sitting in on Liz's session with Suzie Nguyen of Andromeda eGaming and Kurt Amery.

"But you are here in the room today, Liz, because you want to scale your business outside of a few niche stores in supportive environments," explained Jada. "Your vision of filling this market gap and picking those spots got you this far—a fantastic achievement. But going to the next level will require some real soul-searching about what is *truly* your *sustainable* source of competitive advantage, and making *that* the engine of your strategic move."

Jada paused. "Think about it this way. There is something—some activity, some competency—that HFF does particularly well. Unusually well! Something your competitors might find difficult or costly to imitate. We would call this attribute of HFF a core competency, and whatever it is, it will underpin to your customers the competitive advantage of having an HFF store."

Liz looked skeptical. "I mean, outside of our value proposition to growing families, which a cynical customer could say is marketing as much as anything else, it's hard to think of things that fit your description—especially the ability of others to copy our model. We all know that the grocery business is a bit of a commodity industry, yes?"

Kurt leaned forward. "Yeah," he said. "I'm where Liz is on this right now. In marketing HFF to a certain kind of customer, her company has a really unique selling proposition—or value proposition—however you want to say it. In the grocery industry, it's hard to distinguish yourself, except for the convenience of a store location for certain shoppers. Our investment decision in Healthy Family Foodstuffs revolved around this fantastic and unique value proposition of it being the shop that could appeal to a growing segment of budget-conscious, health-oriented family buyers."

"I understand," said Conrad, jumping into the conversation. "Nobody is doubting the utility of a distinctive selling proposition in the market. It's the basic building block of strategically positioning yourself in the market, as the maps we did last week showed. But Jada is talking about digging a little deeper to understand what underpins that uniqueness—and it is more than marketing campaigns."

"Let's try this," said Jada. "Let's push this excellent conversation into some frameworks so we can look for internal sources of competitive advantage. This drill may prompt us to recognize some finer points of differentiation that HFF has, on which Liz can base her company's growth. My guess is, Liz, there is

> A core competency is something a firm does particularly well and can be the source of a sustainable competitive advantage.

something you do particularly well at HFF that can sustain what advantage you can gain over competitors or competitive forces."

While Jada was talking, Conrad stood up and went to the board. "Here is a way we can start looking at this puzzle in a competitive context," he said when Jada finished. He was drawing a Venn diagram with three interlocking circles.[1]

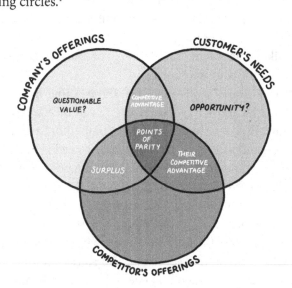

Figure 4.1 Competitive strategy circles

(Source: Urbany, J. E., & Davis, J. H. (2007). Strategic insight in three circles. *Harvard Business Review, 85*(11), 28–30, p. 29. Reprinted with kind permission by Harvard Business Publishing)

Conrad finished drawing and turned around to look at the group. "Now, I drew these somewhat symmetrically for ease of understanding, but of course, in real life, they don't have exactly this perfect shape. For instance, my guess is, Liz, that you don't carry a whole lot of products that have little or no appeal to your customers?"

"No," laughed Liz. "Those would be on the 'going out of business soon' shelf and we want that shelf to be realllllly small."

"Naturally," said Conrad. "So let's focus only on two bits of this diagram as a way to start seeing sustainable competitive advantage in our mind's eye. The middle segment, usually the magic place in a Venn diagram, here is uninspiring—and cannot power a business forward. It is a necessary place you have to be, but your competitors are there too. In a commodity industry, it's hard to create a compelling case for why someone would pick your bag of apples over theirs, so to speak."

Jada looked at Liz. "Liz, how many of your products or what percentage of your sales do you reckon fall into that category of parity with your competitors?"

"Maybe forty percent?" answered Liz. "I mean, these are the things I have to have in the store so that the busy family shopper doesn't have to make two other stops to pick up necessary items while juggling a baby and half the local youth sports team."

"It sounds like table stakes," said Suzie. "You must have these to be in the game, but it's not your winning hand."

"Great analogy, Suzie," said Jada. "Yes, the winning hand is this area in Conrad's diagram above the middle, where you meet a customer need with something only you can do, and your competitors are absent. Here, you are unique—and valuable—if that customer need is acute."

"Which probably means you have some pricing power?" asked Kurt.

"Perhaps," answered Conrad. "It depends on the elasticity of demand and the availability of substitutes. If a customer is unwilling to pay more or can find an acceptable substitute for their need, then your pricing power dissipates even if you are the only one in the market fulfilling that need."

"I'm following," said Steve. "But to build on Kurt's question, what is the best way for a business to spend its energy in that little magic segment of the diagram? Play with increasing pricing and margins if you can? Or grow that area and achieve better results through scale?"

"Depending on circumstances, it could be either," said Conrad. "More importantly, Steve, you've opened us up to the strategic insight we can gain from this framework. The operational thought is to play with pricing where you have a customer captive, so to speak. The strategic thought is to expand the part of the market where you have a competitive advantage—and sustain it."

"What's the formula for that, then?" asked Suzie. "Although I should know better at this point than to ask Jada and Conrad for formulas."

Jada smiled. "We charge nothing for formulas … but double for frameworks!" she said to laughter. "Seriously, no formula, but let's look at a framework for determining the building blocks of expanding and sustaining that area of competitive advantage."

Finding core competencies

Jada started drawing a big tree on the whiteboard as the small group settled back into the conference room after a break. She started speaking even as she filled out some details—limbs, branches, leaves, and roots.

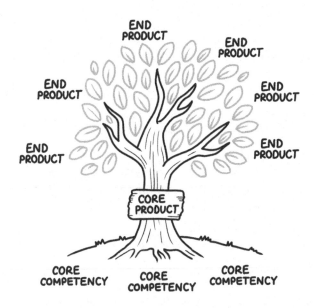

Figure 4.2 Core competencies are the roots of a firm's activities and advantage

"So," she said to the group, "let's start with the concept of what C.K. Prahalad and Gary Hamel, two great business thinkers, called a core competency. In defining this concept, these thinkers used the analogy of a tree for the company. The branches, leaves, fruit and such are the business units and the products or services. But the roots of the tree are its core competencies—resources, processes, activities, capabilities, or attributes that ultimately are the foundation of the firm's competitive advantage."[2]

"Do you mean like intellectual property?" asked Steve. "We've filed for several patents in our company to protect some competitive advantage we think we might have from an inventive new technology, but it takes forever to get approved."

"IP could be a core competency for an innovative firm that depends on unique inventions protected by IP laws to give it a competitive edge in its products and services," answered Conrad. "But the concept is more expansive than that—it could include many things ranging from assets to processes to even values and culture. Whatever it is, it has to meet a certain set of criteria to be a core competency on which a firm can base its competitive advantage. These are the things that ultimately underpin the moves you might make to grow that precious segment of our Venn diagram."

"Okay," said Kurt, "I'll bite. What are those criteria?"

Jada went up to the board and wrote:

- The competency provides access to markets. So, it is valuable.
- It might be rare or expensive to have.
- It is difficult or costly for others to imitate.
- It is hard to substitute for.
- It is absolutely necessary for our product or service.
- It underpins the benefit of the product/service as perceived by the customer. It captures why a customer picks us over a competitor.
- It can be sustained and we know how to make it durable.

She turned back around to the group. "This is a more drawn-out list. For shorthand, some people like to remember the acronym VRIN: Valuable, Rare, Inimitable, and Non-substitutable. "The key thing to remember is that these competencies are in the roots of your firm—not necessarily its products."

"I'm not sure I'm following," said Suzie. "Can you give us an example?"

"Sure," said Jada. "Let's stick with our subject for today—Liz's company and industry. Liz, in a general sense, why do people shop at Whole Foods?"

"Well, certainly not for the bargain prices," scoffed Kurt. "Nine dollars for a little bag of organic kale?"

"Seems crazy, right," laughed Liz. "But the customers in Whole Foods have accepted that price. Some are there for the vibe—healthy and hip. Friday nights at Whole Foods are one of the better singles scenes in town for single shoppers with healthy tastes and lots of disposable income."

She continued, "But Kurt may have put his finger on it with his poke at Whole Foods. The Whole Foods shoppers I know, me included, go for really fresh organic or all-natural products—especially produce, meats, and dairy. And lots of variety too. We'll pay up for that quality and wide selection."

"Okay, let's follow that thought," said Jada. "You're describing the end product you see in the store that is drawing you in." She pointed to the leaves on her tree diagram. "But conceivably, anybody who wanted to could put thirty different kinds of English cheeses out in the cabinet daily. And fresh lobsters, organic dragon fruit, and so on. They might lose a bunch of money doing so, but they could do it. So, what underlies Whole Foods' ability to make money with that variety of expensive fresh products?"

Liz didn't hesitate. "Oh, I would say their supply chain for sure. That's their secret weapon. They have an amazing supply chain for fresh produce that meets all kinds of sustainability, organic, and environmental standards. They know how to get a wide variety of fresh products to their stores. They even had a fleet of fishing boats working exclusively for them that use sustainable fishing practices. They do use some third-party distributors, but they also have their own distribution network that specializes in what people want from them—a wide and high-quality variety of fresh produce and other perishables."

"That sounds super expensive," Kurt chimed in. "If a refrigerated truck full of produce or fish breaks down, that's a bad day for Whole Foods."

"Yes, but they really focus on that part of the supply chain, recognizing it as key to their business model—and they price in its extra expense," replied Liz. "Last time I checked those fresh produce categories drove the majority of their revenue and probably more than two thirds of their profits. Sure, there is a ton of great product in their stores, and it's marketed really well to the customers they know want to be there, but I think their secret sauce really is their fresh produce supply chain and the care they take with that."

"Ah ha!" cried Conrad triumphantly. "*Secret sauce*—great term. Could that be another way of saying core competency? In other words, their core competency is not the organic gold beets or free-range eggs but rather the process of getting them to the store. It seems difficult and costly to imitate, hard to substitute for, certainly valuable to their business, and it definitely is at the root of what their customer wants from them. Companies like Whole Foods link certain business activities—in this case their unique fresh produce supply chain—to the value they provide to their customers. Whole Foods invests in this supply chain and it becomes a competitive edge for the company."[3]

> A core competency is often valuable, rare, difficult, or costly for competitors to imitate, and hard to substitute for.

"I see it," said Steve. "But I don't spend much time in Whole Foods— I'm a Trader Joe's guy, really. What do you think is *their* secret sauce, Liz?"

"Well," she answered, "on the surface, they also have that natural vibe— with a funky twist of a smaller store footprint, though. But their business model is very different. The vast majority of their products are frozen or dry packaged goods—so no need for an expensive fresh produce supply chain. And over eighty percent of those goods are private-label products with a third-party manufacturer. So, like Costco they can lock in good private-label deals with their supply chain."

"Sounds like the opposite of the Whole Foods' profit formula," said Suzie. "Now I understand why the Trader Joe's produce section is so small—that's not where they make their money. But what about the Hawaiian shirts, diagonal aisles, tiny parking lots, and the way they make many popular products only available periodically? Can't figure that out."

"Part of the vibe and appeal—they are going for a certain kind of buyer after all," said Liz. "They're not trying to appeal to shoppers who want big generic grocery stores. Their founder once said that Trader Joe's was for overeducated and underpaid people—classical musicians, museum curators, college professors, journalists, and so on."[4]

"Great observations!" said Conrad, who had been drawing yet another diagram up on the board while they were talking.

"Keeping exactly these points in mind," he said, "let's look at how all this fits into this framework of how you might find or derive your core competencies."

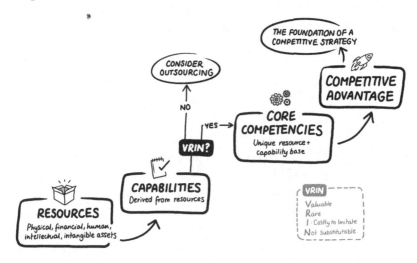

Figure 4.3 The Core Competencies framework

"As you can see," Conrad continued, "every enterprise has the resources and capabilities to do whatever it is that they do. And for many firms, wrestling with these resources is the alpha and omega of their internal analysis—what do they need to get their strategy done? It's a necessary question but not sufficient in our view."

"Let me guess," said Liz. "I need to keep moving up that chain to explore core competencies that meet those criteria for sustainable advantages?"

"You've got it," said Jada. "And when you look at what those things are—be they activities or capabilities or resources or something else—you protect them and reinforce them. They are likely the foundation on which you make your next strategic move."

"What does the 'consider outsourcing' bubble imply?" asked Kurt.

"Well, if you've done a value chain analysis of all the activities that go into making your firm tick, and identified the secret sauce in that value chain that you want to protect and build on, then other activities in the value chain could be candidates for outsourcing. For instance, if Trader Joe's has only a few fresh products since they aren't central to their business model, they could consider outsourcing that supply chain. Whereas they would probably never want to outsource those key private-label deals they strike with suppliers for their so-called white-label products—the Trader Joe's brands. A good firm never outsources core competencies, but they might outsource other activities that aren't important to them or are relatively generic pieces of their value chain."

Liz was looking carefully at the diagram. "I think that's helpful," she said. "We have to look hard at that if we're going to launch an expansion strategy. But I'm even thinking that if we can get to grips with our core competencies, then we will also know where to allocate our resources and put our best people. I guess those could be our investment areas."

"They very well could be," answered Conrad. "The question you want to ask yourself as you drill down on identifying a core competency is how long you might be able to succeed in your market if you *didn't* control that competency? That answer can steer you to where you need to invest time, energy, money, and talent. On other things that are not core competencies, you might be able to get away with being just good enough."

> *A good firm never outsources core competencies—but might outsource other activities that are not important to it or are relatively generic pieces of its value chain.*

"I know we're running up against the lunch break," said Liz. "But how is this core competency concept different from a unique selling proposition or a unique value proposition? We did an exercise at HFF in which we looked at all the different attributes that customers value in the niche grocery market, and then we ranked ourselves in all those areas against our competitors. So, for instance, we beat Whole Foods on price in most categories, we beat Trader Joe's on family-style packaging, we beat Costco on ease of the shopping experience, and we beat everyone on the family environment—we provide a play area, like some IKEAs. That exercise allowed us to see our differentiation in the market."

"Great exercise," said Jada. "Essential in many ways, but think of it this way. Those things—your unique value proposition or points of differentiation from your competitors—are like the part of the iceberg you can see above the water. A core competency is the secret weapon underpinning your ability to have those points of differentiation—it is oftentimes below the waterline. Understanding this—and what it is—can make your new strategy much more foundational because you want to build on that unique competency."

SWOT versus TOWS

Liz was looking pensive when everyone settled back in after lunch.

"How are you feeling about all this, Liz?" asked Jada.

"I'm still circling around this concept of drilling down to the part of the iceberg under the water and seeing what truly underlies our competitive advantage—then sustaining it with the expansion plan I aim to put in front of Kurt and the board."

"Yeah, it may take some serious discussion with your team and perhaps some objective market experts who know HFF, but also know the market," said Conrad. "But it will be time well spent. In the meantime, would you like another framework to approach the issue from another direction?"

"I don't know," said Liz. "I'm not a finance or operations management person by background, but even I'm yearning for a formula with a ready answer rather than frameworks that *might* provide some insights which *might* point me to some choices which *might* give me a direction to go. That's a lotta *mights*!" she said with a laugh.

Conrad smiled. "Well, I could stop here and sing 'I Never Promised You a Rose Garden,' but instead, let me give you a respected framework to look at your core competencies for more insights. Everybody here has heard of SWOT, yes? Strengths, Weaknesses, Opportunities, and Threats?"

"Ah …," said Suzie, "even buried in our world of coding and software development we know about SWOT—and we use it too!"

"Excellent," said Jada. "What do you use it for?"

"I guess you could say we use it for something like an annual physical," responded Suzie. "We update our strengths and our weaknesses, which might have evolved. And we look at the opportunities and threats in the market—the external pieces—which definitely will have evolved. And then we might make a course correction to our business plan based on all that."

"Hmm, good," said Conrad. "Everyone else use it the same way?" Heads nodded around the room.

"It's useful, no doubt," he continued. "And as you can easily imagine, your self-examination of strengths and weaknesses can certainly give you great insight on what might or might not be a core competency, so it is a useful tool. But …"

"I expected that," jumped in Steve. "There is always a 'but' with you two!" he said to laughter.

Conrad smiled. "But …" He paused for effect. "Just running a SWOT analysis often leaves firms with simply a list of observations. These are pretty useful observations in theory; perhaps some get acted on in some fashion. But in and of itself, your standard SWOT analysis does not naturally point you in a more determined way toward what might be your strategy."

Jada drew a simple SWOT matrix on the board.

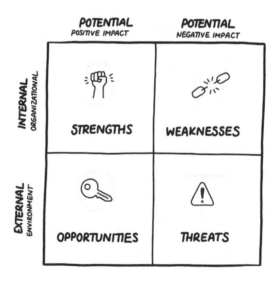

Figure 4.4 The SWOT analysis

"What Conrad is getting at," she said as she drew, "is that to get more than a list of observations from this matrix, you want a SWOT-type framework that drives toward some strategic insight that can lead you to strategic action. Consider the questions Liz is asking herself at this point in our process for Healthy Family Foodstuffs."

Jada wrote on the board:

- *How does the company rank relative to its key competitors?*
- *Does the company enjoy a distinct sustainable competitive advantage?*
- *Given all that ... will the company's competitive position be strengthened or weakened if the present strategy is continued?*
- *How well can the company defend its current position?[5]*

Kurt asked, "This first question we looked at when we did our strategic positioning maps—the 'Map of Paris' exercise, yes?"

"Correct," answered Conrad. "And the second question is what we are exploring here with Liz today."

"And ... they lead us on to the third and fourth questions—the 'so what?' questions," said Jada. "Understanding our competitive position and understanding ourselves is really useful. But 'what to do about it?' is the game we are in. What do we need to do to improve our competitive position? Where do we want to 'live' in the market we are in? Our current neighborhood? A different one? What are our options and alternatives for moving neighborhoods? That journey from one place to the other is going to be your strategy. And to really get a better launch into this from SWOT, we like to turn it on its side and use the TOWS framework instead."

> *Understanding a competitive position is necessary, and understanding core competencies is critical. But the strategic question that follows is: based on that, what does a firm need to do to improve its competitive position?*

Conrad drew a new matrix on the board next to the SWOT matrix.

"Oh, I see," said Steve. "Because you like to start the strategic process with the external market analysis, you moved Threats and Opportunities to the beginning of the framework, since those are really about the outside world."

"True enough," said Jada. "But to see how TOWS can be more useful than simply reordering the process, let me write in the boxes."

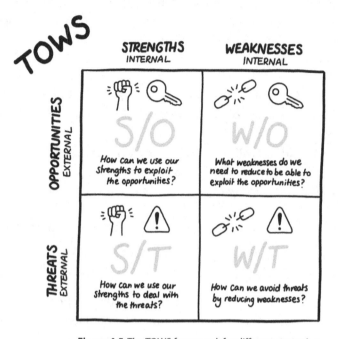

Figure 4.5 The TOWS framework for different strategies

"I don't believe in magic," Jada said as she finished. "But as a figure of speech, this is the magic of the TOWS approach. While a classic SWOT may help push you toward a good analysis of the environment and yourself as a firm, a TOWS framework will move you toward identifying strategic alternatives because you are *combining* the insights in a way that suggests possible alternatives for the basis of your strategy."

Jada continued, "You can see here in the boxes, four different strategic approaches could emerge in this simple matrix. An SO strategy for Liz would use HFF's strengths to maximize opportunities in the market. This could be a good guide for her planned expansion. Or, she could adopt a more defensive strategy: an ST strategy would use HFF's strengths to minimize threats—for instance if she saw Trader Joe's or Costco or Wegmans coming after her market segment."

"That makes sense to me," said Liz. "And I guess if I were to put my money on the WO box, I would have a strategy to minimize weaknesses by taking advantage of opportunities. For instance, we are pretty weak in our ability to scale—we carry only two thousand products. That is half of Trader Joe's and like thirty times less than a Wegmans store. But I see opportunities in small markets that Trader Joe's and Wegmans would not consider and thus could be right for our expansion."

"Exactly," said Conrad. "And a WT strategy would be a defensive variant of that."

"Wow," said Steve. "So much to consider here. If you had asked me at the start of this morning about my point of competitive advantage, I could have given you an answer in three seconds flat. But now I think I need to understand what my answer is at a deeper level, *and* I need to know what that means in terms of building our next move on it. My head is swimming."

Using the power of frameworks

"I hear you, Steve," sympathized Conrad. "But, great strategists always seek to simplify, so let's end that way today. We're talking today about Liz and everyone else building on some competitive advantage that delivers higher profit, growth, or more market share—whatever she and Kurt decide measures success, yes?

"To make that point about simplification, Michael Porter would tell you not to worry about juggling lots of answers, because he maintained there are really only two general categories of competitive advantage. Every firm is either a cost leader—in other words, low cost—or a differentiator who provides a special product or service."[6]

He turned to Jada, who was drawing another diagram on the board. She continued the explanation. "He then went on to say that the second major decision a firm makes is where it will compete. It either goes after a niche market and, therefore, has a relatively narrow market scope, or it goes after a large and general set of consumers and, therefore, has a broad market focus. Which looks something like this:"

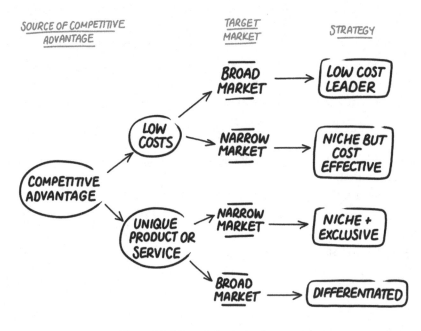

Figure 4.6 A Generic Strategies framework

Liz broke in. "Simple enough—but I don't think I'm in just one box. On the one hand, we go after a niche market—growing families seeking organic and healthy foods. So, that is a focus strategy. But our Trader Joe's- or Costco-like appeal to those same families is that they are on a budget and can't afford Whole Foods for a family of five or six. So, that would make us a low-cost player. But, at the same time—I really do think that we are differentiated. How does that work?"

"Well, no map shows everything and no matrix solves everything," said Jada. "They seek to simplify and even provoke. So, the insight you just laid on the table is that you may not be in one box or the other, but rather driving down the middle of the diagram. So, the task in front of you is which of your competencies do you lean on, going forward—the competencies that led you to be a cost leader ... or that led you to be differentiated?"

"Or both," sighed Liz.

"Or both," agreed Jada.

"Pretty simple framework," said Kurt. "Perhaps oversimplified?"

"Perhaps in some circumstances," said Conrad. "But firms that use this along with other tools pour a lot of complex analysis and energy into it—and it can tell you a lot. It's as good a tool as how you use it. But don't discount it as too simple. Remember what former Supreme Court Justice Oliver Wendell Holmes said: 'I would not give a fig for the simplicity that lies on this side of complexity, but for the simplicity that lies on the other side of complexity, I would give my life.'"

"Fair enough," said Kurt. "And a great quote—but even so, this generic strategies concept can't be the alpha and omega of sorting out strategic alternatives that could stem from core competencies and the market environment, correct?"

"Correct," said Conrad. "All the frameworks we are using help give us the 'first word,' not the 'last word,' in our process to flesh out a strategy."

"So," said Jada, "in that spirit, let's leave you with one more tool that can help you connect our topic today of 'who are you and what *really* makes you special?' with where that might lead you strategically."

She went back to the board one last time. "A few years ago, a book called *The Discipline of Market Leaders* came out. Its core argument was that the best firms really understand what authors Michael Treacy and Fred Wiersema call a 'value discipline'—what I like to call the dominant gene in their DNA.[7] It's the trait or characteristic that really makes them tick, the thing they are particularly excellent at, the thing that underpins their identity—their personality—their success."

"Sounds like more secret sauce," laughed Liz.

"Yes," agreed Jada. "This value discipline is a company's core competency in some ways—but more broadly thought of than some single thing. When a company really commits to the value discipline that drives its uniqueness or success, it then orients almost all its energy and investment around that discipline—sometimes almost at the expense of simply being okay in other areas. This understanding and relentless focus on who they *really* are allows them to succeed—it is their enduring source of competitive advantage."

"Makes sense to me," said Kurt. "Play to your strengths."

"Right," said Jada, as Conrad was drawing on the board. "These authors further posited that there are generally three types of dominant genes in a firm's DNA."[7]

Conrad had written:

- **Excellence in Process companies:** *these firms focus on operational efficiency above all else. Think FedEx, Walmart, Amazon.*

- **Excellence in Product companies:** *these firms focus on delivering a superior and distinctive product. Think Apple, Tesla, LVMH.*

- **Excellence in Customer Service companies:** *these firms focus on customized service and tailored solutions for the customer. Think Ritz-Carlton, Neiman Marcus, Abercrombie & Kent.*

"So every company in the world is only good at one of three things?" said Suzie skeptically.

"No," said Conrad. "That's not really their only point. In fact, in our work we expand their three disciplines—a kind of core competency—to five." He quickly sketched on the board:

Figure 4.7 The dominant gene in an enterprise's DNA

"In addition to their three disciplines—let's call them innovation, operational performance, and customer affinity—we also see firms whose outstanding discipline is marketing, such as beer or soda companies, and also just proximity—where getting the right real estate or territory is the most important thing a certain kind of business could do for itself."

Jada jumped into the conversation. "What Conrad is getting at, and what we take away from this framework, is that there are ways other than just cost leadership or differentiation to characterize basic strategic choices. This 'disciplines' framework shows us that many market leaders focus on an area—a discipline—where they are unusually good. That becomes the basis of an alternative source of competitive advantage as opposed to cheaper or different."

> Core competencies underpin a firm's point of distinction. Generically, a firm is differentiated by being either low cost or having a unique offering. But firms can also differentiate themselves through "value disciplines"—a value at which the firm passionately excels, which drives its competitive advantage, and around which revolves its fundamental value proposition.

"Let me see if I get this," volunteered Kurt. "If I think about some of our portfolio companies this way, I could see that Celar Logistics, which focuses on operational excellence and process, probably uses that to force their competition to keep up with their efficiency—so that would be their source of competitive advantage?"

"That makes sense to me," answered Conrad. "And what about Secure Home Suite, Steve?"

"Well," said Steve, "I don't have a ready answer. In my heart, I think we are an innovation company whose unique products force competitors to keep up with our inventiveness. But I also think that because we chose a niche market we know very well, and that the big guys don't care about too much, we are a customer affinity player—we've won the loyalty of our customers for years with outstanding service. I think that combo of disciplines is our competitive advantage."

Jada and Conrad nodded. "Companies can have a real talent or passion for a discipline or two," said Jada. "But more than two and I usually start to wonder if they are thinking hard enough about who they truly are and what truly drives them or makes them special."

"Hmm," said Liz. "For Healthy Family Foodstuffs, this may be another model where I may be a bit in between the points on your frameworks, so to speak. We have an amazingly loyal customer base who loves feeling like they are shopping at a place that cares about them and their kids. We will even sculpt our supply chain around their expressed wishes for what they want from HFF. Yet, in an industry with a single-digit margin, we have to be efficient to succeed financially. I cannot keep prices low unless we kill it with excellent operational performance and good business processes."

"Makes sense to me," said Jada. "Sounds like you two are straddling two value disciplines—maybe three since you already mentioned marketing success."

Conrad sat back down at the table. "Look, none of these frameworks are meant to label or pigeonhole anyone—so don't obsess over that. Rather, they are meant to prompt exactly the discussion we are having today—having right now!—about how to look within and see a platform from which to grow."

"Is there a good test to see if you're being honest about your organization?" asked Suzie.

"Sure," said Jada. "Here is one I like: if you think you lie between categories, ask a customer why they chose you. You might discover that their answer points you to the dominant gene in your company's DNA."

"Or," added Conrad, "I sometimes use an internal question when looking for the value discipline that drives an enterprise. Who is the key type of employee in the firm? If the most valuable employee is the ruthless process engineer or supply chain manager, I get one kind of answer. If it's the coveted account manager, or the brilliant design team, then I have different answers."

"Whew," breathed Liz. "I definitely have enough to work with here. I need to huddle with my team for a few days, drill down on what we do, where we are uniquely good, and come up with answers to some of these questions that the frameworks raise."

"Excellent," said Conrad. "When we next assemble, we'll take that work you've done examining your market and determining your enduring source of advantage and work that into various strategies that might move you forward."

Conrad and Jada's key takeaways

A **core competency** is not what the company does, but what it is uniquely good at—*better* than others—*and* what customers value.

- It is a unique strength (or strengths) embedded in a firm.
- It allows a firm to differentiate its products or services.
- It can find its expression in structures, processes, routines, people, actions in the value chain, or ways of doing things.
- It can provide a sustainable competitive advantage if it can endure.
- It can underpin most strategic decisions—trade-offs, resource allocation, direction setting, strategic alliances, outsourcing, etc.

The best core competencies:
- Are valuable
- Are rare
- Are hard to copy
- Are hard to substitute
- Are durable
- Can't be appropriated by others to capture value
- Are sustainable
- Confer competitive superiority on the company

Questions to probe for a core competency:
- How long could we dominate with our business if we didn't control this competency?
- What future opportunities would we lose without it?
- Does it provide access to multiple markets?
- Do customer benefits revolve around it?

Turn internal analysis of strengths and weaknesses into possible future action plans by using the TOWS framework instead of SWOT.

A core competency or a value discipline can be an internal foundation on which to build a solid strategy.

Works cited and recommendations for further study

Books

De Kluyver, C. A., and Pierce, J. A. (2013). *Strategic Management: An Executive Perspective*. New York, NY: Business Expert Press, chapter 5.

Editors of Harvard Business School Press (2006). *SWOT Analysis II: Looking Inside for Strengths and Weaknesses*. Boston, MA: Harvard Business School Press.

Porter, M. (1985). *Competitive Advantage: Creating and Sustaining Superior Performance*. New York, NY: Free Press.

Prahalad, C. K., and Hamel, G. (1993). *The Core Competence of the Corporation*. Boston, MA: Harvard Business School Publishing Corporation.

Treacy, M., and Wiersema, F. (2007). *The Discipline of Market Leaders: Choose Your Customers, Narrow Your Focus, Dominate Your Market*. London, England: Basic Books.

Urbany, J. E., and Davis, J. H. (2010). *Grow by Focusing on What Matters: Competitive Strategy in 3 Circles*. New York: Business Expert Press.

Articles

Duncan, W. J., Ginter, P. M., and Swayne, L. E. (1998). Competitive advantage and internal organizational assessment. *The Academy of Management Executive, 12*(3), 6–16.

Ghemawat, P., and Rivkin, J. (1998). Creating competitive advantage. *Harvard Business School Background Note* 798-062. Boston, MA: Harvard Business Publishing.

Hamel, G., and Prahalad, C. K. (1989). Strategic intent. *Harvard Business Review, 67*(3), 63–76.

Ly, B. S., and Vroom, G. (2012). Sustaining competitive advantage. *IESE Industry and Background Note*. Boston, MA: Harvard Business Publishing.

Minsky, L., and Aron, D. (2021). Are you doing the SWOT analysis backwards? *Harvard Business Review*. https://hbr.org/2021/02/are-you-doing-the-swot-analysis-backwards, published February 23, 2021, accessed September 16, 2024.

Prahalad, C. K. (1993). The role of core competencies in the corporation. *Research Technology Management, 36*(6), 40–47.

Prahalad, C. K., and Hamel, G. (1990). The core competence of the corporation. *Harvard Business Review, 68*(3), 79–91.

Treacy, M., and Wiersema, F. (1993). Customer intimacy and other value disciplines. *Harvard Business Review, 71*(1), 84–93.

Urbany, J., and Davis, J. (2007). Strategic insight in three circles. *Harvard Business Review, 85*(11), 28–30.

Valentin, E. K. (2001). Swot analysis from a resource-based view. *Journal of Marketing Theory and Practice, 9*(2), 54–69.

Van Den Steen, E. (2017). Creating and sustaining competitive advantage. *HBS Industry and Background Note* 717-479. Boston, MA: Harvard Business Publishing.

Notes for Chapter 4

1   Urbany, J., and Davis, J. (2007). Strategic insight in three circles. *Harvard Business Review, 85*(11), 28-30; Urbany, J., and Davis, J. (2010). *Grow by Focusing on What Matters: Competitive Strategy in 3 Circles.* New York, NY: Business Expert Press.
2   Prahalad, C. K., and Hamel, G. (1990). The core competence of the corporation. *Harvard Business Review, 68*(3), 79–91.
3   For more on this type of approach, see Porter, M. E. (2001). The value chain and competitive advantage. In Barnes, D., *Understanding Business Processes.* London: Routledge/The Open University, pp. 50-66.
4   Colin D. (2020). Joe Coulombe, founder and namesake of Trader Joe's, dies at 89. https://www.npr.org/2020/02/29/810693474/joe-coulombe-founder-and-namesake-of-trader-joes-dies-at-89, published February 29, 2020, accessed September 16, 2024.
5   DeKluyver, C. A., and Pearce, J. A (2012). *Strategy: A View From the Top.* 4th ed. Harlow, England: Pearson.
6   Porter, M. (1985). *Competitive Advantage: Creating and Sustaining Superior Performance.* New York, NY: Free Press, New York.
7   "Dominant gene in a firm's DNA" is an evocative phrase and concept I learned from Ron Jones, my chief strategy officer at Sotera.

Chapter 5

Charting a New Path Forward: A Dialogue on Basic and Advanced Business Strategies

"Change is the law of life. And those who look only to the past or present are certain to miss the future."

—JOHN F. KENNEDY

....

Steve Adlar, the CEO of Secure Home Suite, has experienced a good run of success in launching his office suite software company in a niche market—small home-based and mobile businesses. He wants to expand into new markets or create new products and services to grow in his current market. He meets with Jada and Conrad, along with Kurt and Ian Driscoll of Coactum Financial Technologies, to discuss how he and his team should consider their options. Steve discovers how to weigh choices between expanding into into new markets or creating more products and services in his current market. He learns about more creative strategies such as being a category creator or defining a new kind of customer and offering in a "blue ocean." Finally, they discuss the promise of disruptive innovation to penetrate a mature market and the innovator's dilemma that may result from it.

....

The basis of any business strategy

Steve Adlar, CEO of Secure Home Suite, took a long look at the whiteboards he had filled with the help of Conrad and Jada. Like his fellow company bosses, he was much more of a strategic thinker now, thanks to Conrad and Jada's regimen of introspection. The mental testing and frameworks had grounded his whole team, affirming their basic strategic position.

"We're now so much surer of ourselves," he said, joining Conrad, Jada, and others for a new session. "We walk taller, talk strategy with more authority."

He explained that the strategic positioning mapping exercise helped update the team's view of the company's position compared to market competitors. The Five Forces of Competition model gave them a more sophisticated perspective on what competition meant for Secure Home Suite. The SWOT framework and the TOWS analysis clarified what mattered in the external environment. They showed how much better the company could compete as it focused on its strengths and weaknesses.

"So, you know where you are—good," said Conrad. "Leadership scholar Warren Bennis once said that the first duty of a leader is to define reality for followers. You've done that. What about where you're going in the future?"

"I'm having trouble with that one," said Steve with a wry smile. "I'm still waiting for the magic answer."

Jada gave him an exaggerated evil eye.

"No magic answers!" exclaimed Conrad. "Just insights!"

Steve had gained many insights from Liz's session. He had learned from the Generic Strategies framework that his target market was narrow—his company was not going to go after every kind of customer who uses an office suite of IT applications. He had also learned that his company's competitive advantage depended on differentiation—it was not going to focus on winning customers based on price.

For Steve, the core competency analysis highlighted one thing above all: his company did best by offering quickly developed products, simplicity, and security with its productivity apps custom-made for certain kinds of businesses that would be overwhelmed by the big office suite systems for huge corporations. That's how Secure Home Suite made huge inroads into the mobile and small home-based business markets—markets where customers don't want or need an expensive suite of tools and applications from big providers.

But he wasn't sure he had the pathway outlined for the future. "Okay—insights. But when is the other shoe going to drop?" he asked. "All this analysis doesn't reveal the best strategy for scaling my business."

"But your realizations so far may be a platform to launch your next big move," said Conrad. "You've got your team centered on those most fundamental of business questions. You know who you are, what you are best at, where you compete, and where you really add value for your customers."

"The basic questions of strategy, as you've said," said Steve. "Sure. But that still doesn't seem to me a compass pointing to a clear direction for the future."

"Well, think about what the Generic Strategies framework did for Liz," chimed in Kurt. "At the end of her analysis, she realized that her growth strategy needed to be a bit more like an Aldi's than a Trader Joe's—only carrying things her niche customers want and on which she can get excellent bulk deals from suppliers. That basic positioning insight made her realize that Healthy Family Foodstuffs probably needs to put new stores with fewer products in the same shopping centers as regular grocery stores, so HFF won't need to carry generic items that her shoppers can get next door. That's not a common thought in that business—to be in the same shopping center as another grocery store."

"On top of that," said Kurt, who as usual was sitting in on the session, "I thought her position right in between being a company with a cost advantage versus one with a differentiated offering advantage gave her some extra insight. Liz realized that while Healthy Family Foodstuffs is a niche grocery with a very differentiated offering, it still needed some cost advantage since it targets families on a budget, even if her customers are health-conscious families who will pay a little bit more for organic or non-processed food."

"Yes," nodded Jada. "Liz's business did not fit neatly into one box or another in the Generic Strategies framework."

"That framework helped us too," said Steve. "Frankly, going through the drill with my team using that framework allowed us to narrow our strategic options by putting the kibosh on some ideas we had about competing on price or marketing toward more generic customers—both of which seem to represent an opportunity in the market for someone, but probably not for us given our positioning and core competencies."

"Ah ha," laughed Jada. "Please tell me you invoked our First Commandment—that strategy is not an 'anybody-have-a-good-idea?' game; it is a thought process?"

"Well," smiled Steve, "I didn't say it exactly that way, but I remembered the point—you said that a market opportunity for someone does not necessarily make it a market opportunity for us."

"You were paying attention!" said Jada. "Music to my ears! But you have to make hard choices. What if it looked as if the *only* space in the market to expand was with the big corporate customers? And perhaps to create a low-cost offering to nudge in there against the major league competitors?"

"We would have to consider it," said Steve. "But we see plenty of market share to gain in our mobile and home-based businesses niche, especially with how people are shifting their work routines these days."

"Let me ask you this," said Conrad. "When you looked at the Discipline of Market Leaders framework and asked yourself which of the five dominant genes in a company's DNA was most present—innovation, operational performance, customer affinity, proximity, or marketing—which one was it?"

> *Strategy is not a contest to judge good ideas about market opportunities. It is a disciplined thought process to work toward ideas that fit. A market opportunity for someone in the industry does not necessarily make it a market opportunity for a particular firm.*

"Definitely product leadership through innovation," answered Steve. "Our entire jam is inventing—and coming up with a better way for our customers to do things than the clunky tools the major IT companies offer mobile and home-based users. We can excel at that and be good enough to stay competitive at the other things."

"So that's a useful insight," said Kurt. "It is the foundation of your next move, I suppose?"

"No doubt," said Steve. "We won't outrun who we are. But, while we grasp what our core competency is, we don't know exactly what new opportunities we should direct that energy toward."

"Well," said Jada, "in the strategy process, you've landed us where we want to be—which is starting to formulate business strategy options that might lead us to a better future. We just spent a few weeks on all the frameworks—from PESTEL to the competitive strategy circles and all the rest. Those frameworks gave us insights about where we are, where we might want to be, and what we have to work with. Next, we generate options to consider. Alternative strategies—or 'moves' as you called them."

Basic strategic alternatives

Conrad restarted the session. "Steve, in the TOWS analysis with your team, what was the principal opportunity you saw in the market for growth?"

Steve drummed his fingers, hesitating. "Well, the team was split to tell you the truth. Half wanted to add more apps to our current product suite—to gain more market share with current customers in our current market niche. The other half wanted to move upstream with what we have into the bigger market with more customers—where big competitors might be vulnerable in spots."

"A choice between economies of scope," said Conrad, "and economies of scale."

Steve hesitated again.

"The first half of your team," said Conrad, "proposed offering more products or services for the same people, yes? You'd grow and profit from the additional value-added activities for current customers or perhaps a few similar, new customers."

"Yes—we see people doing that," said Steve. "Some formerly niche competitors, such as Slack and Whoop, are moving from where they started—making one killer app for the office—and are now presenting a whole set of tools and apps for collaboration. So, they are making more stuff for the same customers."

"Yep—economies of scope," said Conrad. "Could that work for you? What's your gut reaction?"

"Depends," said Steve. "We'd have to model what the profit uplift might be. Doing more things for current accounts would run up development and support costs. We'd probably get some new customers too, though."

"Mostly scope, then, but perhaps a little additional scale as well," said Jada. "Now, let's say you looked at this strategic direction. You would build a new product or service to make it happen, wouldn't you?"

"For sure," said Steve. "But that's fun for us. There's no shortage of ideas from my techies and customer account leads when it comes to whizbang features. We always survey our current customers about what they might need."

"And these new features or products or services," asked Conrad, "would they flow from what you believe to be your core competencies—speed and inventiveness?"

"For sure. And we *really* know our customers, so we don't waste a lot of development or rollout time with unneeded or confusing features."

"So you grow in your market with an expanded offering," said Jada. "Good option. But what about a pure economy-of-scale play? Attacking the much larger generic market with your current offerings?"

"We'd face a learning curve," said Steve. "How do we sell our suite to that market? Large-scale customers might view our offering as too simple—or feel we're bush leaguers who lack the infrastructure and support of huge IT companies."

> Basic growth strategies often involve gaining economies of scale by adding more customers for the same offerings, or gaining economies of scope by offering more value (i.e. adding products or services for the existing customer base).

"You'd have to probe that and make a call," said Conrad. "But let's leave it on the table as a strategic option. Let's say you accomplished this—you'd achieve growth with the economies-of-scale effect, because you'd spread your fixed and sunk costs over more paying customers."

Kurt spoke up. "I love growth—especially profit—so I see why you'd do this. But when I hear 'learning curve,' I hear investment costs."

Steve nodded. "Going after the big market—a broader market in our Generic Strategies framework—would require more than just a marketing campaign. A different kind of customer requires that we learn a different way of selling."

Jada leaned in. "Why, then, would some of your team call that the next great opportunity for Secure Home Suite? Surely those customers already get gold-plated service from some of the world's best technology providers?"

"Simple," said Steve, "When the FBI asked notorious bank robber Willie Sutton why he targeted banks, he replied, 'Because that is where the money is.' And when you ask my team why we should target the larger market, they say, 'That's where the customers are. Far more than in our current niche market of mobile and small home-based business users.'"

"Hmm, now we are getting to the 'why' of that strategic option—

moving in our Generic Strategies diagram toward the bottom box—a broader market." Conrad pointed back to the whiteboard. "Would that move also require a new product or service from Secure Home Suite?"

"Not necessarily," said Steve. "Our simplified ecosystem and our speed in bringing out new features and fixes could peel off the ultra-frustrated big-company customers. We'd need more support infrastructure, though. But I'm not sure we'd have to add new and expensive gadgets, bells, and whistles."

"I see more dollar signs flashing," said Kurt.

"But what about those frustrated users?" asked Conrad.

"They're not the ones who sign the purchase orders," said Steve.

"They're not at the point of sale?"

"No, not at the bigger companies. The real customers there are the IT procurement managers. They inflict their choices on the users."

"So, you might need to develop an enhanced offering based on their enterprise needs?" asked Kurt. "Not just bells and whistles but tools for, say, cross-company collaboration?"

"Maybe, yes," said Steve. "And there's the rub. What we come up with would probably differ from what we might develop for folks in our current core niche market."

"Alas, the devil is always in the details," said Conrad.

Silence filled the room.

"Look, take heart," said Jada. "So far, we have discussed only two options. There are many categories of basic strategic moves—some of which fuel the two we have discussed."

She went to the board and started making a list. She finished with nine items, a green star after the first two:

1. Economies of scope in the current market ⭐
2. Economies of scale in a new market ⭐
3. Develop and deploy a new product
4. Add a new service
5. Gain a new kind of customer
6. Approach a new market
7. Enter a new geographic area

8. Add a new role or place in the value chain
9. Make a change to the business model

"Those don't seem like either/or choices to me," volunteered Ian. "In some scenarios, Steve might need to develop a new product *in order to* gain a new kind of customer for an economy-of-scale strategy, yes?"

"Correct, they are not exclusive," Conrad answered. "These basic moves can be used in various combinations or alone. Usually, combinations. Remember that a strategy is a series of interconnected moves—not just one shift in tactics."

Steve nodded. "Yeah—I can see that. There are scenarios where I might have to do number four—add a new service with current customers simply as a defensive measure without gaining economies of scope. One of those ST strategies we saw from the TOWS framework—deploying our strength against a threat. But, in general, in terms of whether I expand in my current market with more stuff or do the same stuff for different customers, it looks like some of these other moves would be necessary to enable either of the first two strategies."

"Yep," said Jada as she put down her marker. "Moves three to nine on this list can fuel the first two strategies or generate their own strategic paths. What they have in common is that they are all centered on doing something new."

"And I would add that I think they are all in reach," said Conrad. "All of these options require Steve to do what his company does best—rapidly invent simple problem-solving tools. Each play to his core competencies, in other words."

"So I probably need to take this back to my team and see how these options mix and match with each other," said Steve. "Just in this initial conversation I can see that undertaking strategy number one requires number three and perhaps number four—maybe even number eight!"

> Almost all strategic moves that would improve a company's competitive position require doing something new.

"And these options are just a start," said Conrad. "Your analysis might consider other moves too before finally yielding a clear strategic path."

Considering a new business-level strategy

Steve looked at the whiteboard. "It seems deceptively simple—these basic options we should consider to grow. What am I missing?"

"At the business level, most strategies should be focused and simple," answered Conrad. "At a corporate level, it can be much more complicated. Here is a quick test: at Secure Home Suite, do you consider each of your different applications to be distinct lines of business, with different resources and costs and so on?"

Steve looked thoughtful but was silent.

Jada turned to the whiteboard again. "Here is a good way to think about whether you need a more straightforward business strategy or a more complex corporate strategy. Think about Conrad's question in the context of these questions,"[1] she said, writing down:

- Where do we compete?
- What unique value do we offer to customers?
- How do we deliver that value?
- How do we sustain our ability to deliver that value?

Steve thought for a minute. "We really are one business, not several. We compete at the office solutions level—not the individual app level. We certainly only sell the full package to customers. We share engineering and development resources, even if different apps have different project levels and teams at certain points—depending on whether they're fixing bugs or adding new features. We're too small to think of ourselves as a bunch of different app businesses. In fact, the magic of what we do comes in tying them seamlessly together into a simple suite. We are in the mini-ERP business, not in eight separate productivity-app businesses."

"Okay, good," continued Conrad. "As Jada alluded to, at the level of a corporation that has several lines of business, it can get much more complicated. We may get to that later. But at this stage in developing basic strategic options, the 'Why?' of considering a new business strategy is more important than the 'What.' You need to look into all the details of the 'Why.'"

Ian leaned forward. "I'm starting to appreciate now all the pre-work, so to speak, we did before getting to where all of us action-oriented managers want to be: doing something!"

"Right," said Jada. "It seems almost reckless to make a move—whether any of these basic ones or many others not on the board—when you have not considered the whole picture. You don't simply want to run after the first decent-sounding idea. Good strategists probe the rationale and ramifications of several ideas."

She then summed up what had been going into their thinking so far: the analysis of the competitive environment; the strengths, weaknesses, and strategies of key competitors; the anticipated moves of key actors, influencers, and stakeholders; the shifting sands of market forces; and each firm's own nature as an enterprise. Each of these analyses, she said, had to be done with careful thinking to bring out the most devilish details. Only then could you move to generating strategic options and analyzing and choosing alternatives.

"That's the beauty of frameworks!" she said. "Engage the whole brain. Unearth all the details!"

"My whole brain is zeroing in on what looks like two basic choices," said Steve, "with variations of each of those we must analyze. But either one could take us to the next level of growth and profitability."

Good strategists use questions and frameworks to probe the rationale and ramifications of many ideas.

Conrad and Jada looked at each other. Steve could see by their looks that they were interested in mining more details.

"Yes ... and no," Jada said with a smile.

Innovation and more creative strategies

"Before you do some drill-down analysis on what you think are your strategic choices so far," said Jada, "we might want to come at the job of generating choices in yet another way: what is called a blue-ocean analysis."

"It's good for us to broaden our thinking," said Conrad. "One of the choices you are considering is to try and make headway in a mature market dominated by the likes of SAP, Microsoft, Oracle, and Google—and you'd be doing it by competing with the same core competencies they claim to have: innovation and invention."

"We know David can't kill all the Goliaths," interrupted Kurt. "We invested in Steve's company because he saw parts of the market that those behemoths weren't serving, or serving poorly. Secure Home Suite planted its flag on the shores of neglected turf and has since moved inland with an attractive new offering."

"And we're flying our flag farther and farther inland each year," said Steve, "and everyone can see that."

"And what allowed you to plant your flag in the first place?" said Conrad.

"Probably our ability to innovate to solve an unmet or poorly met need. And that could well allow further expansion," replied Steve.

"Steve," Jada asked, "when you started making headway in your business, were you creating a new product or service category or offering something better?"

"We just went after the underserved customer," said Steve. "Take a guy with a tree service business. He wants to run his business right on the spot, next to his chainsaw and truck. In other words," he continued, "many small businesses want to handle the whole value chain—from sales to proposals to delivery to invoicing and collection—from their phones or tablets, with all their applications seamlessly integrated. In the past, all the workplace office suites forced the business owners to shuttle to and from the worksite to the home office to get everything done. Secure Home Suite pioneered and offered them an easy phone- or tablet-based solution that spanned the business lifecycle."

"The small mobile or home-based business folks," Kurt added, "were crying out for a way to run themselves with a virtual office."

"So you're creating a bit of a category?" said Jada.

"Well, we didn't invent anything new," said Steve. "We just chased a market that was too small for the big guys, really. And designed around what the little guys really needed."

"Don't sell yourself short," replied Jada. "Keurig didn't invent hot coffee either. But they invented a new and convenient way to deliver an old value, which appealed to a certain kind of customer. That is why we call Keurig a category creator."[2]

Steve liked that thought. "That accounted for our fast growth in the beginning," he said. "But if we created a category, it was in a small market. I'd have to think hard if our next stage of growth could come from creating a new category of product or service for more mainstream, larger businesses."

By innovating in a customer's value chain, a category creator can fashion a new or unconventional way to deliver a traditional value.

"You'd have to look at whether you can eliminate or improve activities in a customer's value chain—like you did with the mobile businesses," said Jada. "Or perhaps explore offerings adjacent to the core office suite functions where your ability to innovate could make a difference."

Conrad nodded as Steve took notes. "Or you could go where the enemy ain't."

Steve looked up, not speaking. Kurt looked confused.

"Go where the ocean is blue and fresh, not red and bloody," said Conrad.

More confused looks greeted him.

"Okay, here's how the reasoning works," said Conrad, "Am I right that all your competitors can see where your current customers are just as well as you can?"

"For sure," agreed Steve. "Not many secrets in this market."

"Okay," Conrad said as he stood and went to the whiteboard. "Then let's talk about going where customers are *not*. This is called a blue-ocean strategy, so labeled by two business thinkers named Kim and Mauborgne.[3]

For a blue-ocean opportunity, go where the enemy ain't!

It might seem a bit counterintuitive, but perhaps it is something to consider. To start with, think about focusing your strategy on noncustomers."

Steve and Kurt looked at each other. "Um … are you okay, Conrad? Low blood sugar, perhaps?"

Jada laughed. "Well, we got your attention, eh?"

Conrad kept drawing on the whiteboard, undeterred. He finished drawing and pointed to the board, circling the right-hand column in his diagram.

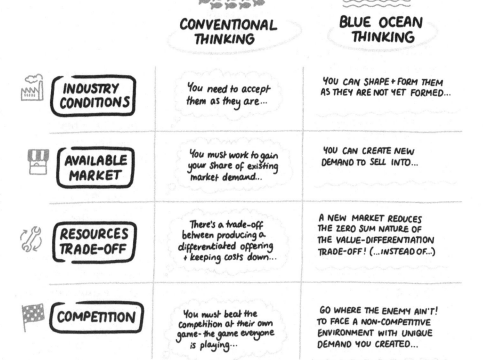

Figure 5.1 The Blue Ocean framework

"Noncustomers sounds nonsensical," said Conrad. "But the concept makes sense when you examine a strategy that would create new customers in a place of *noncompetition*. This place—at first a place that is all your own—can allow you to grow when you use your innovative tendencies to spur new demand there."

Conrad explained that the term 'blue ocean' was coined by its creators because the place of noncompetition is not a red ocean colored by blood in the water from sharks fighting over the same customers. It is clean, fresh, open. So the idea is to go where customers might be present, but competition is not—and *create* demand.

"Who knew we needed cool home computers, minivans, made-to-order laptops," said Conrad. "We embraced them only after they came out from Apple, Chrysler, and Dell."

"But everybody can eventually access the blue ocean," said Steve. "Just look at the first minivan. Everybody ended up copying it."

"True enough," said Jada. "Competition happens—if the blue is good, it might turn red over time."

"And all the big guys have more resources than we do," said Steve. "Even if we get to a future spot in the market ahead of everybody else, the big guys will soon invest and compete with us in a feeding frenzy."

> A blue-ocean strategy allows companies to invent and capture new demand in a market not defined by intense competition.

"Perhaps," answered Jada. "If demand is robust, yes, competitors will cast their nets for customers in the same place you do. But you gain an advantage in being there first."

The early gains, she explained, can endure for a while. That's the beauty of going into an uncontested market space where competition is irrelevant. By inventing and capturing new demand, and—by doing so—offering customers a leap in value, a company can enjoy an ocean of its own for years. She cited Cirque du Soleil's way of reinventing the circus. It revolutionized a well-known business model by combining different art forms. The new show had some traditional circus features but also elements of opera, dance, and design. In its ocean, it created a whole new kind of customer: people willing to pay high prices for a new type of show.

"Moreover, it wasn't a huge risk to test this new market," said Jada, "Cirque didn't have the most expensive pieces of a traditional circus—such as animals and superstar performers."[4]

Conrad nodded. "New demand—that's the key to a blue-ocean strategy. Think of Yellow Tail wine from Australia. When they came on the scene in 2001, they didn't want to deal with cutthroat competition for the current market of wine drinkers. Instead, they focused on non-wine drinkers—their blue ocean—and converting them to the wine experience via Yellow Tail wines."

"It's a really cool concept," said Steve. "But I'm having a hard time imagining where we'd sail to find a piece of ocean without blood in the water."

"Me too," agreed Jada. "But, like good strategists, let's use a framework instead of dismissing the idea out of hand. Building a strategy canvas like this is one way to get to a possible blue-ocean strategy."[5]

Jada drew on the whiteboard. "By charting the performance value of an offering on the vertical axis and then different product features or criteria that customers want or might want, sometimes you can see a path to a blue-ocean value proposition."

She drew up a simple diagram:

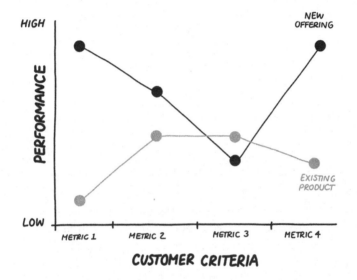

Figure 5.2 A generic Strategy Canvas framework

"You know, we did that at Coactum Technologies," exclaimed Ian excitedly. "We didn't know it was called a strategy canvas, but we did take a look at what we were providing versus our competition—the traditional stock exchanges and brokerages."

Ian went to the board and started drawing. On the horizontal axis he labeled a few criteria that customers trading financial securities wanted from the platform on which their trades are executed: speed, transparency, price, ease of use, and the level of service provided. He described the vertical axis as representing the relative importance to a customer—from low to high.

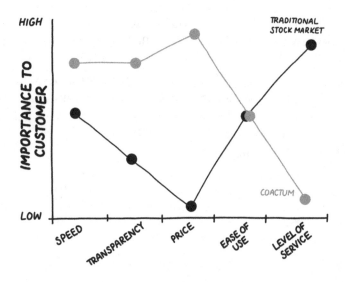

Figure 5.3 The Coactum Technologies Strategy Canvas framework

"What you can see here is how we stack up in these features against traditional stock markets or brokers," he said, pointing out the various advantages of Coactum or its competitors in the various areas.

"Okay," nodded Steve. "I see your point; you are better at some things than they are, but they are better at other things than you are. Where does the blue ocean come in?"

"Here!" said Ian, drawing a big circle around the upper left of his diagram. "When we created these advantages in these categories, few customers wanted those things. They had been frozen in time by custom, regulation, and the lack of technology into slow, nontransparent, and expensive trading through third parties. When technology and the regulatory environment changed, we jumped in with software offering these criteria at a totally different level, and that ended up creating a whole new kind of customer—the high-speed, high-volume, price-sensitive trader."

"Wow—a new customer where one didn't exist before," said Kurt. "Day traders, quant traders, automated trading desks—all your current customers."

"Yep," said Ian, putting down his marker. "As the movie said, 'if you build it, they will come.' We created a capability in a blue ocean—and new customers showed up for it. But it's starting to get pretty red now—we have to think about our next move."

"Very cool. I like how you break out the criteria a customer will value," said Steve. "I can see the value of singling them out. I need to sit with my team, especially my account leaders, and get a handle on what customers are looking for in their office suite tools."

"Yes, indeed," nodded Jada. "Even then, if you can see a path to creating viable new demand and a product or service that might create and satisfy that demand, you will need to think hard about the price point that works for these new future buyers and whether you can build it at an acceptable cost."

"Yes, and leaving the math aside," said Steve, "I'm guessing there would be other big challenges to not-yet-customers adopting a not-yet-offering."

"It's not for the faint of heart," said Conrad. "But even if you don't pursue a blue-ocean strategy, going through the thinking with your team will make you so much more attuned to three things we've been stressing all along: the market, the future, and yourselves."

"A reminder to bear down and get the homework done right," said Steve. "A nice thought to finish the day with." He started pulling his various notes together into a pile.

Jada held up a finger. "But before calling it a day, Steve, let's explore one more innovation-based strategy idea. This one may fit Secure Home Suite best."

Steve sat back in his chair. "Wow, a lot to consider here."

Even if a firm doesn't pursue a blue-ocean strategy, going through the thinking process and creating a strategy canvas will make leaders much more attuned to three things that are key for maintaining a strategic focus: the market, the future, and the company.

"But here it comes, Steve," crowed Kurt. "The moment you've been waiting for. Your secret sauce for the next phase of success!"

"Ha ha, guys," said Jada. "So sorry to disappoint you, but the sauce—and its cooking—that's up to you."

"Like everything we've discussed in the past," she continued, "what we are about to discuss is intended to help you and your team with how to think strategically, not what to think or ultimately do—that is up to you."

"Rats!" laughed Steve. "Well, we tried for the easy answer to my strategy challenge. Okay, I'm ready for another framework to think through."

The power of innovation at the low end of the market

"We know at this point," Jada said, "that you need to strongly consider moving upstream, if you will, toward the huge market of conventional office suite customers—or at least some part of that segment."

"Agreed," said Steve. "Carving off even a few percentage points of the mainstream market would ensure our future. Even if our next move is to expand some services for our current niche market, I don't see how we can avoid going after parts of the larger market."

"So, you'll need to find some way to penetrate that market, or parts of it. The conventional head-on approach is to make a better product than, say, Microsoft and convince customers of that fact."

"That's not a strategic sauce that appeals to me," sighed Steve. "Let's keep cooking."

"Right," said Jada. "There is a third way to come up with that sauce—besides going for a new category or blue ocean. You can use a disruptive innovation in the mainstream market to peel off customers from the major providers."

"You mean beating them at their own game?" asked Steve. "We ruled that out as too costly and risky for a small company like ours."

"Ah, but you cook up a strategy that uses different rules," said Conrad. "Use guerilla warfare, not a conventional assault."

A firm can penetrate a mature competitive market with an innovation at the low end of that market's needs, avoiding competition. With that foothold it can then work upstream to compete for the more profitable parts of the market.

"Or if you leave the military out of it," said Jada, nodding toward Conrad, "you work smarter, not stronger."

Jada explained that in this strategy, Steve would not play in a major arena where big companies flex their strengths. Instead, he would use an innovation to meet minor customer requirements or needs at the low end of the market, a long-haul strategy to disrupt the mainstream market over time. This "low end of the market" might be a place where Microsoft Office or Google Workspace solutions don't yield much profit.

"So you pursue the part of the market the big guys don't go after or don't serve well," said Jada.

"I read you," said Steve. "Go after the nonprofitable, pain-in-the-butt customers and requirements."

"I'm sure there are some of those," said Jada.

"But even if we could figure them out, why would I want to go in and bottom-feed for the least profit?"

Conrad drew another diagram on the whiteboard in the only space left. "Because it is your entry point into the market. You don't take the front door. You go in the side."

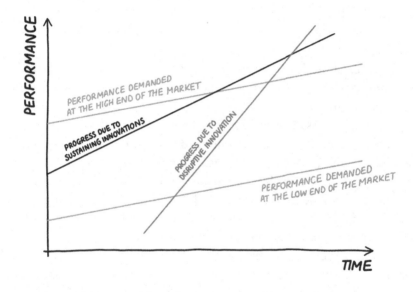

Figure 5.4 The Disruptive Innovation framework by Clayton Christensen

(Source: Figure I.1 from Christensen, C. C. (1997). *The Innovator's Dilemma: When New Technologies Cause Great Firms to Fail*. Boston, MA: Harvard Business Review Press, p. xvi. Reprinted with kind permission by Harvard Business Publishing)

He explained that if a company could provide an innovation at the low end of the market, it would force the big competitors into what famous business school professor Clayton Christensen called "the innovator's dilemma."[6] The big companies have to decide to come down-market to compete for customers and needs they'd rather not focus on, or to simply abandon part of the market to small companies and their innovations.

Ian was thinking about how this might affect his company. "Why wouldn't they just stamp out this incursion into the market?" he asked. "Why give a new entrant a foothold?"

"Because business isn't really warfare," answered Conrad, nodding back at Jada. "It turns out successful companies rarely want to mess with the small fry. Why distract yourself with the little fish when you're pulling in the big ones? What harm can ignoring them do?"

When big companies are at the top of their game, he explained, they want to spend their time doing all the "right" things: listening to their best customers, and investing in and even innovating their best and most profitable products and services to make them better. They carefully study market trends and allocate investment to the projects with the highest return on investment.

"Sensible stuff, don't you think?" said Conrad. "The small pains-in-the-butts don't buy enough to pay the bills, let alone give a decent return on investment."

"I'm with you," said Kurt. "Let's keep the focus on returns."

"And in doing so," Conrad continued, "they often make the equally sensible decision to not compete against new entrants at the lower end of the market, where profits are slim and customer needs are pedestrian."

Conrad explained that the history books are full of company executives who followed that approach. Why chase the down-market for little return, their thinking usually goes, when you can you milk the best part of the market for maximum profit? That was the decision made by the leaders of the big American car companies in the 1970s, when unexciting but cheap Japanese subcompact vehicles came onto the American market. GM, Ford, and Chrysler—the "big three"—found it much more sensible to continue with their high-profit cars and, over time, SUVs, rather than chase the low end. Like most successful big firms, they found it easiest to sustain or slightly improve their cars for the same kinds of customers.

"I think that probably made sense for them at the time," offered Kurt. "I can't imagine a finance meeting where someone suggests de-emphasizing a sustainable business that has great margins to chase emerging, insignificant, or low-profit markets."

"Exactly!" said Conrad, putting down his marker. "We rarely see successful mainstream firms respond to the disruptive innovation at the low end of their market. And that provides an opening for firms like yours. The leaders of the big firms aren't stupid, of course, and they are often haunted later by their decision, as this diagram shows."

Steve eyed the whiteboard. "If I'm interpreting this correctly, I can establish a foothold at the low end of the mainstream market and then move to the high end?"

"Yes, and that's not only the theory. That is the experience of many low-end disrupters over many different industries," answered Conrad.

Continuing with his car example, Conrad noted how quickly the low-end Japanese entrants moved up the American market to make competitive, high-profit luxury vehicles and SUVs. A few decades later, the cycle repeated with Korean car companies entering via the lower end of the market. In fact, the cycle has repeated itself many times in many industries.

"Mainstream competitors very rarely respond in a way that defends their turf until it is too late," said Conrad.

"Guerilla warfare!" said Steve with a smile. "Love it!"

Jada leaned forward. "Before you put on your war paint, think hard about whether Secure Home Suite's skill at innovation can produce something disruptive as a market entry tactic. Then, if you can also climb the curve of performance—and profit. Otherwise, you'll be condemned to low-profit bottom-feeding."

"Hmm," said Steve. "Yes, not a tasty prospect. Even so, while the Generic Strategies drill helped me see the movement I might need in the market to grow, these other innovation-based strategies might be my best way to penetrate bigger markets. That will help focus our analysis as we wrestle with the idea of new products and services for our next growth phase."

"We hope so," said Jada.

"Question," said Ian. "How should I think about this for Coactum Technologies? As I mentioned, we have lived the disruptive innovation curve and had a temporary blue ocean to get us going. But, as Kurt reminds me, we are barely breaking even due to the investment it took to build that disruptive technology. It will take a long time to dig out of our investment hole and climb the profit curve through scale in our industry."

"That's a big parting question," said Conrad. "I'll tell you what, when we resume, you and Coactum will be the focus of our conversation. It might be your business model you need to play with, not your strategy."

Conrad and Jada's key takeaways

Differentiation and positioning, based on generic strategies, choice of market, or other differentiators, are at the heart of a strategy.

Most basic business strategies are relatively simple, but the **repositioning requires something new or different**, such as:

- A new product or service
- New customers
- New markets
- New geographies
- New value proposition
- New place or role in the value chain
- New activities for current customers (economies of scope)
- Same activities for more customers (economies of scale)

Good questions to help you with "Why this strategic move?":
- Does it help create a *profitable* competitive position for you in a specific industry or market segment?
- Is that segment attractive? Why? Is it growing?
- Can you successfully compete there? What is your relative position?
- What is your relative advantage? Can you sustain it?

Blue oceans are uncontested market spaces where competition is irrelevant. You invent and capture new demand and offer customers a leap in value.

The innovator's dilemma:

- The downfall of many industry-leading firms starts to occur when they are at the top of their game, doing all the "right" things with their best customers and allocating investments to the highest return on investment.
- They avoid competing against disruptive innovations at the low end of the market that may create their competition of the future.
- This offers a market-penetration strategy for low-end disrupters who can move upstream.

Works cited and recommendations for further study

Books

Christensen, C. M. (1997). *The Innovator's Dilemma: When New Technologies Cause Great Firms to Fail*. Boston, MA: Harvard Business School Press.

Editors of Harvard Business Review (2005). *Harvard Business Essentials: Strategy*. Boston, MA: Harvard Business School Press.

Kim, C. W., and Mauborgne, R. A. (2005). *Blue Ocean Strategy*. Boston, MA: Harvard Business Review Press.

Kourdi, J. (2015). *Business Strategy: A Guide to Effective Decision-Making*. 3rd ed. London: The Economist/Profile Books.

Porter, M. E. (1985). *The Competitive Advantage: Creating and Sustaining Superior Performance*. Republished with a new introduction 1998. New York, NY: Free Press.

Porter, M. E. (2008). *On Competition*. Updated and expanded edition. Boston, MA: Harvard Business School Publishing.

Rumelt, R. P. (2011). *Good Strategy, Bad Strategy: The Difference and Why It Matters*. New York, NY: Crown Business.

Articles

Christensen, C. M. (2003). Beyond the innovator's dilemma. *Strategy & Innovation, 1*(1) (March/April 2003).

Christensen, C. M., and Overdorf, M. (2000). Meeting the challenge of disruptive change. *Harvard Business Review, 78*(2), 66–76.

Christensen, C. M., Raynor, M., and McDonald, R. (2015). What is disruptive innovation? *Harvard Business Review, 93*(12), 44–53.

De Jong, M., Marston, N., and Roth, E. (2015). The eight essentials of innovation. *McKinsey Quarterly, 2*, 36–47.

Kim, C., W., and Mauborgne, R. A. (2002). Charting your company's future. *Harvard Business Review, 80*(6), 76–83.

Kim, C., W., and Mauborgne, R. A. (2005). Blue ocean strategy. *Harvard Business Review, 82*(10), 76–84.

Yoon, E., and Deeken, L. (2013). Why it pays to be a category creator. *Harvard Business Review, 91*(3), 21–23.

Notes for Chapter 5

1   See Professor David Kryscynski's video on corporate vs. business strategy, https://youtu.be/X50pX-orhtjY?si=LLxBBzL-n6lKnnaY, published January 31, 2020, accessed September 19, 2024.
2   See Yoon, E., and Deeken, L. (2013). Why it pays to be a category creator. *Harvard Business Review, 91*(3), 21–23.
3   Kim W. C., and Mauborgne, R. A. (2005). *Blue Ocean Strategy*. Boston, MA: Harvard Business Review Press.
4   Kim, W. C., and Mauborgne, R. A. (2005). Blue ocean strategy. *Harvard Business Review, 82*(10), 76–84.
5   blueoceanstrategy.com (n.d.). Strategy canvas. https://www.blueoceanstrategy.com/tools/strategy-canvas/, accessed September 19, 2024.
6   Christensen, C. M. (1997). *The Innovator's Dilemma: When New Technologies Cause Great Firms to Fail*. Boston, MA: Harvard Business School Press.

Chapter 6

Choices Within Our Strategy:
A Dialogue on Business Models

"The real voyage of discovery consists not in seeking new landscapes
but in having new eyes."

—MARCEL PROUST

....

Ian Driscoll, CEO of Coactum Financial Technologies, sits down with Conrad and
Jada to examine the business model within his strategy. Ian's strategy is a sound
one and it delivered what a strategy should: Coactum has positioned itself in a
competitively advantageous place in the market. Operating in a blue ocean, Coactum's
value proposition has even created a new kind of customer for the securities trading
business. But Ian's business model seems not to be capturing the full value of
Coactum's strategic success. Ian and two other executives learn that if a strategy
describes what a business is trying to achieve and where and against whom the
company competes, its business model describes how the company works. A business
model is the design for delivering value to customers and making profits—the internal
engine working inside of the strategy. As Ian will discover, there are many business
models to choose between within any given strategy, and choosing poorly can deflate
outcomes from even the best strategy.

....

What is a business model?

Ian Driscoll, the CEO of Coactum Technologies, no longer needed convincing that Conrad and Jada offered answers to strategic questions he
had long been wrestling with—but he still felt a bit in the dark. One the
one hand, he prided himself on the way Coactum had cracked into the
stodgy securities trading industry on the back of disruptive technology—
finding a blue-ocean market along the way. But not a day ended—not one
night did he fall asleep—without Ian knocking himself on the side of the
head as if to shake loose an answer to his most vexing question: *how is
Coactum going to convert this strategic success into decent profits?*

To Conrad and Jada, he now said, "We're barely breaking even, and that's driving me nuts. We're sitting on a technology goldmine, and we've cracked open the market—I'm convinced of it—but we're not extracting the money we deserve from the gold ore."

Everyone in the room could see the frustration on his face, a frustration he shared with Kurt. *We've got the technology and a winning strategy,* both were thinking. *But what are we missing?*

As if to reassure himself and seek validation, Ian tossed a half-dozen copies of a news story from *The Trader Times* on the table: "Coactum Promises a Revolution to Democratize the Markets."

"You want to talk about innovative disruption?" he said, pointing to the story. "There you have it. In spades. In the securities industry's leading journal. Front-page proof of our differentiated strategy. People in the know say we have top-gun technology and are changing the market."

Everyone in the room was impressed, but didn't, at first, take in Ian's focus on the technology and strategy. What popped out at them instead was Ian's caricature. He was portrayed in a cape and tricorn hat as George Washington crossing the Delaware, gleaming technology sword held aloft.

Everyone chortled.

"I envy you!" Jada said, suppressing her giggle. "How many people see their cartoon in a mainstream industry magazine? You're a star!"

Ian wasn't to be humored. He was frowning, and so was Kurt. Amid the friendly ribbing, they had a tough time softening up.

"Okay, okay, any publicity is great publicity," Ian said, finally rolling his eyes. "My kids got a kick out of it, too. The black boots and the cape. Kind of dashing, don't you think? I didn't expect the attention, but I'll take it."

"I think it—and your general situation—captures some good news and some bad news here," said Conrad. "And I think it applies not just to Ian but to everyone here."

Conrad gestured to the others in the room. Along with Kurt, Derrick Jouet of Creativia Playsets and Suzie Nguyen of Andromeda eGaming were on hand. They, too, enjoyed taking part in the teasing, but they realized they had to face the same concern as Ian. *Does my strategy capture the full value of the business I have created?*

"Good news first," said Conrad. "All of you have come a long way as strategic thinkers." He went to the board. "Let's look at three questions strategic thinking has to answer."[1]

- *How will our business differentiate itself from competitors?*
- *How will it create value for customers?*
- *How will it make a profit for us and our investors?*

"All of you now have sound strategies and thus good answers for two of these three key questions—that's the good news. You are well positioned in your markets for sustainable competitive advantage," he continued. "The bad news is that your financial results probably don't reflect your market success or value creation—at least not as much as you would like."

"Well, that's for sure," said Kurt. "I can't wait to see more dollars dropping to the bottom line."

"And that's what we're here today to talk about," said Conrad. "Question number three is the question of the hour. Today we need to work on how our George Washington," he winked at Ian, "unlocks some potential for better results."

"And we're going to do that," said Jada, "by talking about the business model that sits within your strategy. We do that by pulling your strategies and business models apart."

"Hmm. Maybe it's just the circles I run in," offered Derrick, "but I hear these terms used interchangeably—like they mean the same thing."

Jada heaved an exaggerated sigh. "A common error that leads to sloppy thinking, I'm afraid."

"'Strategy' and 'business model,'" she explained, "are words that get tossed around too casually. Strategic thinkers should look at their strategy and business model separately—even though they are connected and codependent. The better thinkers recognize that a strategy, focused on being competitive and well positioned in the market, is generally oriented externally. A business model, focused on how the business runs and delivers its value proposition, is oriented internally."

"When you disentangle the two," she said, "you see how the external logic of the strategy connects to the internal logic of how your business runs. You can then evaluate the strategy and your business model on their own merits while never losing sight of their connection."

Ian nodded. "I am feeling good about the strategy piece—my team and I put together a short statement with those elements you talked about a few weeks ago. In putting it together, we started by looking outwards from the company—at our competition, our customers, and all the other forces in the market. We tried to articulate why Coactum exists, what we are hoping to achieve in that market, what kind of work we do and what kind we don't, where we do it, against whom we compete, and whom we service."

"Good on you!" offered Suzie. "That's a lot to get into a strategy statement—did you get it down to thirty-five words though?"

"You count," said Ian, who cleared his throat before reading from his notebook.

"Coactum Technologies," he read, "distinguishes itself by bringing fast, efficient, and low-cost execution to financial transactions in the capital markets that no longer need a fee-based middleman. By doing so, we make the capital markets more efficient and accessible to the investing public. Over the next three years, Coactum hopes to gain thirty-five percent market share of trades in the most liquid securities. We do that not in the traditional fashion—hosting a floor of professional traders or an electronic network connecting them—but by using sophisticated software to create a virtual marketplace that automatically matches buyers and sellers at the most efficient market price. Buyers and sellers in the market will choose us over competitors because of our speed, efficiency, and low cost—all of which distinguish us from the status quo."

> A strategy leads with an external logic—it describes _what_ a business is trying to achieve and _where_ and against _whom_ the firm competes. The business model has an internal logic—it tells _how_ the firm delivers value.

"Nicely done," said Conrad. "Hard to resist going over thirty-five words, isn't it?"

"Well, it was a lot to pack in," said Ian, apologetically. "Mission, vision, values, objectives, market position, competitive advantage—like stuffing a suitcase for vacation."

"But that gives you a neat, portable package for you and your people to rely on to guide the business," said Conrad.

"That's great that you have an excellent basic strategy—and solid positioning in the market," said Jada.

"For sure," said Ian. "We know exactly how we want to shape the market and where we position ourselves. As I described at Steve's session, we're a kind of a category creator and disruptive innovator."

"But it isn't enough to make it a successful business?" asked Jada.

Ian looked abashed.

"A great business," offered Kurt. "But we are still short of translating Coactum's success into sustainable profits. It makes us all crazy. Ian's people have created the most amazing nonprofit in the portfolio—our favorite charity!" he said, chuckling.

"Funny," said Ian, wincing. "No matter how good we are at wielding our core competency to disrupt stock markets, we're still coming up financially short as a going concern."

Conrad stroked his chin. "Okay, let's take a crack at solving this profit mystery. As you discovered, a good competitive position in and of itself does not guarantee financial success. Let's put aside the strategy for now and examine the business model working underneath your strategy."

"*Underneath?*" said Ian quizzically. "I'm not sure—"

"Underneath as in the motor under a car hood," said Jada. "Or the engine in the belly of a ship. The business model is the engine that propels the car or ship. The strategy prescribes the direction and purpose—the path of the car or ship in relation to everything else around it."

"I get that analogy," said Ian. "Our strategy explains our competitive position and direction, but our business model explains … what?"

"How you make your money," Jada answered. "At least, that is how business writer Michael Lewis described it."

"Was he right?" asked Kurt.

"In a way," answered Conrad. "He's great with phrases, and it's a good shorthand for looking at how a firm's revenue model, cost model, profit model, delivery model, and many other features of the business combine into its business model—how it delivers its value proposition."

On the board, Jada drew the distinction in two columns:

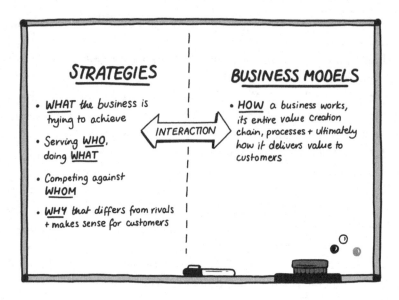

"Okay," said Kurt, "that helps a lot. With strategies, it appears we mostly look out from the business. With business models, we look into the business. But how much play could Ian possibly have in his business model? Coactum has been succeeding for a few years now; the cake is kinda baked in the way it does its thing at this point, yes?"

"Depends," said Conrad. "Let me ask you what you could change: what prevents you from simply raising prices on your customers if you have a blue-ocean advantage?"

"Well," said Ian, "it's blue because these new kinds of customers came for the low price to execute trades, among other things we do that others don't. That's why they swam over here. It would be hard to convince these high-volume, high-speed, low-cost customers we've created with our technology to pay large licensing fees to access our trading software. They would swim away."

"And on the cost side of the equation—the profit model," volunteered Kurt, "Ian and I have scrubbed every part of his cost basis. We cannot find much more profit by focusing on cost control."

Conrad and Jada eyed each other. In their mutually telepathic way, they were thinking the same thing: *here's the nub of the profitability problem for Ian. Here's where we need to delve deeper to unlock his potential profit machine.*

Jada was the first to speak. "Ian, you basically charge for your value by selling software licenses. Yes?"

Kurt and Ian looked at each other. "Umm," said Ian. "Is this a trick question?"

"No tricks!" said Jada.

"Yes, then," said Ian. "We're a software company after all. That's what we build, that's what the customer wants, that's how we deliver it to them, that's how we charge. Our unique advantage is our killer trading software. We started off as a single software program—and we grew a company around that. We're a piece of software disguised as a company in some ways."

"Okay—I get that," said Conrad. "But hang on a minute. When you did your strategy canvas in our blue-ocean discussion, I thought you said you competed against traditional stock markets, not other types of software."

"In a way, yes," Ian responded. "Our software allows users to use our platform as a virtual stock market—that is the effect of Coactum, if you will. The software creates a virtual stock market. But at the end of the day, *the* transaction with our customers is that they buy software from a software company that allows them to trade securities off the traditional market floor."

"Is it possible to price for the effect and not the means that cause the effect?" asked Jada. "It strikes me that the value your customers get from Coactum is the experience of low-cost trading not done through traditional, slower, and pricier marketplaces, correct?"

"Absolutely. For certain kinds of trades in liquid securities and for customers who want speed and price transparency, Coactum crushes the old way of trading."

"Okay, I rest my case then."

"What case?" said an exasperated Ian.

"That the *value* you are selling your customers is not a software package. The value you are selling them is the business outcome they get using your software."

Jada paused. Ian just stared at her, brow creased in puzzlement. Then she said, "So, why don't you consider charging them for the business outcome they get rather than the enabling software? Charge them for the outcome, not the tool that allows them to have that outcome."

The room went quiet. Ian's mind was turning. "I understand your point, Jada—your provocation really. But I run a software company—full of software engineers, software sales people, software account managers, and finance people and systems that understand software sales. You might think you have a revelation, but to my ears, it sounds like it might be a revolution!"

Conrad said encouragingly, "Yes, well—it's all connected. Changing one part of the engine might require changing parts of the car, too."

The gears were whirring in everyone's minds now, not just Ian's. Suzie was wide-eyed. She couldn't help but see the parallels in her business. Gaming companies like hers had toyed with ways to make money besides selling game licenses. She was now having the same double-take as Ian. *Is Andromeda eGaming using the right pricing model?* she thought. *Am I leaving money on the table, too?*

"Okay, I see the implications, but I don't have the right answer," said Ian. "Let me take some time to think about it."

Designing your business model?

When the group returned from a break, Ian checked the whiteboard. It was mostly blank. He'd been talking with Kurt, and he sighed. Why was it blank? On the other hand, Kurt was grinning and flashing Ian a thumbs-up.

Ian turned to Jada: "I just lost a bet with Kurt. I was sure you would have a 'how to design your business model' framework on the board."

"Don't pay out just yet!" said Jada. "You know how I love tools. More coming! Just remember that with each framework, you are not going to get an easy answer, but—"

"Yes, yes, but I will get insights that might lead to answers. No worries. Your strategic tools and frameworks philosophy has sunk in."

"You've won some disciples, Jada!" joked Conrad. "You no longer have to soften them up with croissants."

Ian had liked those croissants. "So what comes next?" he asked, at this point more hungry for answers than anything else.

"Let's put the philosophy into practice," said Jada. "You've got an innovative company that has an excellent competitive position in the market but whose software licensing business model may be underserving its true value proposition. Fair?"

"Fair," agreed Ian. "But what are my realistic alternatives?"

Conrad went to the board. "Before we run through another framework, let's list a bunch of common business models as a way to take stock of their variety. Let's take turns. I'll write down the kind of business model, and each of you tell me what kind of company you buy from that makes money that way."

After ten minutes of listing and kibitzing, Conrad and the group had built a rich list of models and business examples.

- Advertising fee-based, e.g. **Facebook**
- Advertising plus subscription, e.g. **Hulu**
- Advertising plus data sales, e.g. **Google**
- Brokerage fee for matching, e.g. **realtors**
- Freemium: the basic product is free, upgrades cost, e.g. **LinkedIn**
- Cell phone—levels of use/use time, e.g. **cell carriers**
- Subscription, e.g. **magazines**
- Pay as you go, e.g. **utilities**
- Tiered pricing, e.g. **cloud services**
- Value to customer, **e.g. pharmaceuticals**
- Costs plus margin, **e.g. automobiles**
- Razor and blades (low-margin product, high-margin refills), e.g. **printers/ink**
- Reverse razor and blades, e.g. **Kindle**
- Bundling, e.g. **value meals, cable plus internet**
- User communities, e.g. **Angi**
- Product to service, e.g. **Zipcar**

Conrad put down his marker. "Whew, my hand is getting cramped." Without much thought, he reeled off more models while he worked the cramp out of his writing hand. He mentioned disintermediation, which removes intermediaries and connects producers directly with consumers; standardization, which offers uniform products or services to achieve economies of scale; fractionalization, which sells partial ownership or access to high-value assets; and leasing, auctions, reverse auctions, and more.

"So, for every strategy," concluded Ian, "there's a business model?"

"Or several that could work," said Jada. "But the main thing to remember is that your business model is both connected to your strategy *and* distinct from it. You can have different strategies and the same basic business model. Subway, Anytime Fitness, Chem-Dry Carpet Cleaning, and Hampton Inn have very different strategies, but their business models are basically the same. They are franchises, a model not even on our whiteboard."

"Can the opposite be true?" asked Kurt.

"Sure," said Conrad. "Mix and match. You can have the same basic strategy and different business models. Look at the airlines. They all perform the same business function, and some have similar strategies, but they make money differently."

"I can't wait to run this back to my team," said Ian. "I will tell them we're going to open up frequent trading accounts and issue co-branded credit cards. We're copying the airlines!"

"Well, it's no joking matter for the airlines," rejoined Jada. "Today, those programs you are making fun of provide forty percent or more of the revenue that major airlines generate, and it is their most profitable revenue!"

Ian looked at Jada. He went slack-jawed. *What is she suggesting?*

Jada persisted: "In that business where you can't control most of your cost base—fuel and organized labor—the airline credit cards have turned out to be a genius tweak to some of their business models."

She let that sink it.

"But, that is them, and this is you," she added, to Ian's relief. "You're playing different games on different ball fields. The point is that now you've shaken the foundation of status-quo thinking, you want to sort out if there are better business models to fit Coactum."

She drew a diagram on the whiteboard:

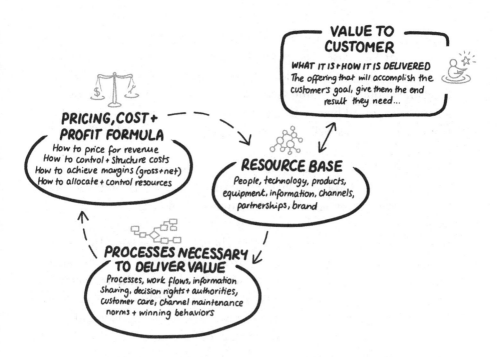

VALUE TO CUSTOMER

WHAT IT IS + HOW IT IS DELIVERED
The offering that will accomplish the
customer's goal, give them the end
result they need...

**PRICING, COST +
PROFIT FORMULA**
How to price for revenue
How to control + structure costs
How to achieve margins (gross+net)
How to allocate + control resources

RESOURCE BASE
People, technology, products,
equipment, information, channels,
partnerships, brand

**PROCESSES NECESSARY
TO DELIVER VALUE**
Processes, work flows, information
sharing, decision rights + authorities,
customer care, channel maintenance
norms + winning behaviors

Figure 6.1 Designing Your Business Model framework

She turned back to the group. She could see Ian was feeling run over by this juggernaut of fresh thinking.

"Think about what goes into a business model per this diagram. We've been talking about the customer value proposition—and it sounds to me like your customers value what your software lets them do, not the software per se. But what else is involved in a business model? Powering any business model are resources, processes, and profit formulas that support the way that company will make money from its value proposition. This model gives us an organized way to consider all the pieces of a possible different business model."

Ian looked thoughtfully at the diagram.

Conrad leaned in. "Ian, you said that Coactum offers an alternative to the old stock-exchange model for trading securities. What does their business model look like—the pieces of it, like their profit formula and their key resources?"

Ian explained that the mainstream stock exchange is a venerable system that has existed for a few hundred years. The exchange's basic value proposition is to provide a location where buyers and sellers can meet and conduct a binding securities trade at a price they agree on. The location, approved by regulatory authorities, was once only physical but is now electronic as well. Accredited experts and financial professionals staff the exchange.

"How do they make their money?" asked Conrad.

Ian moved to the board. He drew a triangle showing a traditional stock market's three revenue streams. The first stream comes from charging listing fees to the companies that list on their market, allowing them to make their securities available for buying and selling. The second stream comes from selling the data from their marketplace to financial information services. The third comes from charging the traders a fee to work there—to be on the exchange floor, like the New York Stock Exchange; to be on an electronic network, such as Nasdaq; and to be licensed to negotiate and conduct the trades for their clients. The traders, he said, make money by charging their clients in a way that covers their cost of being "on the floor."

Figure 6.2 Stock-exchange revenue streams

"Wow," said Suzie. "Sounds like they make money coming and going."

"Exactly," said Ian. "But the system was pricey ... and closed. If you were not on the old exchange's floor, you were literally shut out from what was happening. They've faced some regulatory issues around putting themselves ahead of their customers over the years. So, that was our opening."

As technology and connectivity improved *and* the regulations changed to allow for alternative trading systems, Ian said, his company saw a chance to create a virtual market for liquid securities that basically trade themselves. He gave an example. On any given day at any given moment, a certain number of people want to buy Microsoft shares at a certain price and a certain number of people want to sell at that same price. The parties don't necessarily have a place to see and meet each other in real time— except through intermediaries on the approved exchanges. For people trading a liquid stock like Microsoft, however, there is no need for intermediaries to look for a match. There just needs to be a way for the people on either side of the potential trade to find each other easily.

"Our software," said Ian, "creates that virtual exchange where these liquid transactions can easily happen—get consummated—*without* help."

"It's very cool," said Kurt, clearly pleased to be an investor. "Coactum has upended the middleman-dominated marketplace. They have disintermediated unnecessary players. This is a game changer."

Conrad and Jada looked at each other again. You could tell they were ready to open a new line of questioning.

"And what do you do with your market data, Ian?" asked Jada.

"We show everything live in real time to anybody with an internet connection," he said. "We want to make the markets more transparent, more democratized, and less expensive."

"Okay, so you can't charge listing fees, you don't sell your data, and you don't have middlemen to do the work that will pay you to do the trading?" queried Conrad.

"Exactly," said Ian, suddenly sensing he was walking into another of Conrad and Jada's strategic-thinking traps.

"Hmm," smiled Jada. "Maybe Coactum should have been a nonprofit. Register it as a charity and take the tax deduction, Kurt."

Ian winced. "What do you mean? *Not funny*."

"Just teasing!" said Jada. "To think this through, let's return to the value proposition box at the top of our Designing Your Business Model framework. Your software is the means by which you give high-volume traders a way to get to the exchange. The customer wants to be on a regulatorily approved and reliable system to conduct transactions. You've been selling them technology on an old pricing model. But they don't necessarily want to buy your technology; they want to buy the use of the virtual stock exchange your technology creates, correct?"

"I'm with you now," said Ian. "Yes, I do think that is our ultimate value proposition to them. Entrance to the low-cost, high-speed, no-intermediary exchange."

"Alright, let me take you a step further with an example—an analogy. You remember we said that strategists often think in analogies?"

"Okay," said Ian, "hit me with it."

"What do you know about commercial power tools?"

"I've done a lap or two around Home Depot."

"Okay, then you'll like this one." Jada then described how most commercial power tools are sold to companies that do construction and repair jobs. The tool manufacturer sells the tool for cost plus margin. The point of sale is often at the project-manager level, requiring a large hustling sales force to go from jobsite to jobsite. It's a high-turnover, competitive, relatively low-margin business. She pointed to the profit formula box on the diagram as she made the last point.

She went on to say that in mulling this conventional business model over, leaders of a Swiss tool company called Hilti realized that what their customers really wanted to buy was not the tool itself but rather its *use*. "That use was the value proposition to the construction and repair firms. They needed the use of the tool, not the tool itself, to get their work done and make their money."

"Okay," said Ian. "I get the analogy. My customers value the use of the Coactum trading platform, not the software that gets them there. But how does that point to a pricing strategy or profit model that is different?"

"Consider what Hilti did with the insight," said Jada. "They went from a model of selling tools to leasing them. They concluded comprehensive tool-leasing deals with the major construction firms, allowing Hilti to make much higher margins by charging for what the customer really wanted—the use of the tool."

"Victory, right?" said Conrad. "But, there were big implications for the firm as a whole when they changed their pricing methodology."

He pointed to the other boxes on the business-model diagram. The strategic takeaway, he explained, is that Hilti's move impacted the company's entire business model, especially the way the sales team worked. Leasing-based pricing moved the point of sale from the construction project manager, who was getting a few tools at a time, to long-range, years-long deals done almost at the top executive level with CFOs and chief procurement officers. Hilti, in turn, maintained, repaired, and replaced the tools—and charged for that in the leasing arrangements.[2]

Conrad pointed to the resources and processes boxes on the diagram. "As you can imagine, this was not just a change in pricing policy that created far better margins. It changed everything else about the company—from the kinds of skills they needed from executives to the type of workforce and facilities they maintained and even to their management information systems. That is why you must look at all these things in designing a business model—it's not just about tweaking sales terms to change the revenue model."

"Whew," said Ian. "If we decide to have a different pricing model than software-license sales, we will likely need to change much else."

"You can bet on it," said Conrad. "Think about how Netflix had to change over time. The basic business model was simple to start with. They bought movies from studios and shipped them on DVDs to homes from warehouses. Then, as technology allowed, they added a new delivery system—streaming—to the same basic business model

A change to any part of the business model, be it pricing or the form of value delivery, should prompt possible change in all other aspects of company activity. From the skills of key executives to the type of workforce, to the structure, processes, and systems by which the firm manages its operations.

and value proposition. That changed them from a warehouse-based distributor into a tech company. But now they make their own movies and shows as well, so they are a full-fledged entertainment company."

"And they started just as we did," said Ian. "As one simple business doing one thing, in their case a mail-order delivery company, and they built from there."

"They evolved," said Conrad. "And over time their business comprised basically three different kinds of companies—a logistics company, a creative arts company, and a technology company. All with different resources, processes, and people. So, they have re-evaluated their business model as the world around them changed—and they still are."

"Yes, I can see how all the pieces in a company's operations need to fit together to support how it makes money," said Ian. "It's not just about how you charge your customers."

"Even so," said Kurt, "this business-model question does seem to start with pricing your value proposition. And for Coactum that may mean going back to capturing its value proposition in a different way—the way its customers do rather than the way it thinks of itself as a software company."

"Good thought," said Conrad. "Can you see some possible business models you would consider?"

"Software as a service, for one," said Ian, "probably with volume-based pricing. In our industry, people are used to paying transaction fees with volume discounts."

"That might be one alternative," said Conrad. "Your team could make financial models and test them to find out at what volumes of customer use this could deliver decent profit, which requires modeling the cost of different resources and processes to support that model. I think the key to playing with alternatives is to think about Jada's point: what do your customers really value?"

"Oh, trading operations are not shy; they tell us daily," said Ian. "They love Coactum for certain ultra-liquid securities, but we know they would love us more if we had more participants and securities on our site. More liquidity spurs market popularity in the same way as a bigger crowd at a hip party: the more people show up, the more other people want to be involved."

"Perhaps there is also a transaction-based fee model in there," said Jada. "You could also have discounts or rebates for customers who add orders to your site—making it more liquid and attractive to participants.

Then, you could charge a larger fee for people who remove that order from the pool of orders at the Coactum market."

"We could play with that or variations to see if it works." Ian was now musing about the possibilities. "It's just math, after all. That demands a different back office, sales team, processes, all that … for sure."

"Work on that with your team," suggested Conrad. "Our goal today is not to land on the the answer, but rather to give you ways to work through some frameworks with intelligent, open-minded people, look for insight from analogies in other industries, and model different approaches. Like Hilti, you could be a high-profit firm hiding in a low-profit business model."

"From your lips to my ears," said Kurt.

Testing a business model

Ian sighed and pushed back from the table a bit. "Well, a lot to consider and think through. And here I was thinking that with a cool strategy and a disruptive technology, I had it made in the shade."

"And strategically, you do, Ian," encouraged Jada. "But you're probably leaving money on the table. You might even be stymieing your next moves in the market by using a conventional software licensing business model when, in reality, you are a financial services innovator."

"I don't mind saying this is mind-bending," said Kurt. He looked to Derrick and Suzie, who seconded his assessment. This line of analysis had far more ramifications than they had thought—and prompted more questions.

"Question for you," said Suzie. "Is it possible that a different business model can not only deliver more profitability on the current book of business but also help the company's future strategic position?"

> A different business model can not only deliver more profitability on the current book of business but also help the company's future strategic position.

"Possibly, yes. Remember our diagram of the interaction between strategies and business models," said Conrad. "Sometimes your business model itself can propel your strategic position."

Some strategic experts, said Conrad, would point to Dell on this account. Dell developed a disintermediation and mass customization business model by selling computers directly to end customers and with the ability to create bespoke configurations. The business model and its attractive economics were so disruptive to the conventional computer industry of the time that this created a competitive advantage and enviable position in and of itself.[3]

"It feels to me like that could happen for you as well, Ian," said Conrad. "If this business-model thinking you are going to do leads you to think of Coactum more and more as a platform for new ways of delivering financial services, my guess is that will be the basis of a durable strategic position rather than your initial entry into one part of the market via a disruptive software program."

"I hear you," said Ian. "We thought of ourselves in the early days as the best trading software program in the market. Now we think of ourselves and that tool as a better alternative to an ancient way of doing business."

"So, can you see your way to taking your value proposition and modeling different ways to make money on it?" asked Jada.

"I dunno; my head is swimming," said Ian. "A subscription model, a pay-as-you-go model, a brokerage-fee model, a kind of reverse auction with incentives as you suggested, razor and blades ..."

"Don't make it too complicated to start with. Don't overburden yourself," said Conrad. "You already have a business model built on dis-intermediation and brokering. Now, play with some options. Remember a few principles, developed by business-model expert Joan Magretta."[4]

Conrad wrote on the board:

A sound business model must pass two tests:

1. **The narrative test**—connects customers, offers what they value, shows how you will make money delivering that value.

2. **The numbers test**—the profit and loss formula works.

Conrad looked around the room. "That's straightforward, so let me add a few more 'stress tests' to bring rigor to your business-model thinking." He wrote:

3. Is the new business model aligned with company goals?

4. Does it "feed" the strategy?

5. Is it self-reinforcing—i.e., do all the activities support each other?

6. Is it robust? It should resist easy imitation, manipulation by others, substitution, and complacency.[5]

"You end up making a lot of choices when you change a business model," said Conrad. "Policy choices, resource choices, governance choices, and much more. As you do so, ask yourself: does the model still hold up?"

"That's a good checklist to keep us from going too crazy with considering every possible sort of business model," said Ian, taking notes.

Conrad and Jada's key takeaways

- **Business models** tend to be more concerned with *how* a business works. In contrast, strategies tend to answer questions about *what* the business is trying to achieve, serving *whom*, competing against *whom*, and *why* that makes sense.

- A **strategy** explains how you will beat competitors by being different. A business model explains who your customers are and how you plan to make money by providing them with value and delivering the product, service, or outcome.

- Business models are more internally oriented, while strategies are more externally oriented, but they overlap.

- A sound business model must pass two tests:

  » The **narrative test**—connects customers, what they value, and how you will make money delivering that value.

  » The **numbers test**—the profit and loss formula has to work.

- **Common business models include:** affinity club, brokerage, bundling, fractionalization, leasing, razor and blades, reverse razor and blades, pay as you go, subscription, freemium, auction/reverse auction, franchising, user community, etc.

- You can have different strategies and the same basic business model. (Subway, Anytime Fitness, Chem-Dry Carpet Cleaning, and Hampton Inn have different strategies but are all franchises.)

- You can have the same basic strategy and different business models. (Airlines are one example.)

Works cited and recommendations for further study

Books

Casadesus-Masanell, R., and Ricart, J. E. (2012). Competing through business models. In: Dagnino G. B., *Handbook of Research on Competitive Strategy*, chapter 22 (pp. 460–491). Cheltenham, England: Edward Elgar.

Foss, N. J. and Saebi, T. (2015). *Business Model Innovation: The Organizational Dimension*. Oxford: Oxford University Press.

Editors of Harvard Business Review (2004). *Entrepreneur's Toolkit: Tools and Techniques to Launch and Grow Your New Business*. Boston, MA: Harvard Business Review Press.

Editors of Harvard Business Review (2019). *HBR's 10 Must Reads: On Business Model Innovation*. Boston, MA: Harvard Business Review Press.

Johnson, M. W. (2010). *Seizing the White Space: Business Model Innovation for Growth and Renewal*. Boston, MA: Harvard Business Press.

Osterwalder, A., and Pigneur, Y. (2010). *Business Model Generation*. Chichester, England: John Wiley & Sons.

Articles

Casadesus-Masanell, R., and Ricart, J. E. (2010). From strategy to business models and onto tactics. *Long Range Planning, 43*(2), 195–215.

Casadesus-Masanell, R., and Ricart, J. E. (2011). How to design a winning business model. *Harvard Business Review, 89*(1–2), 100-107.

Casadesus-Masanell, R., and Tarzijan, J. (2012). When one business model isn't enough. *Harvard Business Review, 90*(1/2), 132-137.

Casadesus-Masanell, R., and Zhu, F. (2013). Business model innovation and competitive imitation: The case of sponsor-based business models. *Strategic Management Journal, 34*(4), 464–482.

Christensen, C. M., Bartman, T., and Van Bever, D. (2016). The hard truth about business model innovation. *MIT Sloan Management Review, 58* (Fall issue), 31-40.

Cliffe, S. (2011). When your business model is in trouble. *Harvard Business Review, 89*(1–2), 96-98.

Girotra, K., and Netessine, S. (2014). Four paths to business model innovation. *Harvard Business Review, 92*(7–8), 96-103.

Johnson, M. W., Christensen, C. M., and Kagermann, H. (2008). Reinventing your business model. *Harvard Business Review, 86*(12), 50-59.

Magretta, J. (2002). Why business models matter. *Harvard Business Review, 80*(5), 86-92.

Ovans, A. (2015). What is a business model? *Harvard Business Review.* https://hbr.org/2015/01/what-is-a-business-model, published January 23, 2015, accessed September 17, 2024.

Notes for Chapter 6

1 See the chapter "Building a business model & strategy: How they work together" in Editors of Harvard Business Review (2004). *Entrepreneur's Toolkit: Tools and Techniques to Launch and Grow Your New Business.* Boston, MA: Harvard Business Review Press.
2 Johnson, M. W., Christensen, C. M., and Kagermann, H. (2008). Reinventing your business model. *Harvard Business Review, 86*(12), 50-59.
3 Magretta, J. (2002). Why business models matter. *Harvard Business Review, 80*(5), 86-92.
4 Ibid.
5 Casadesus-Masanell, R., and Ricart, J. E. (2011). How to design a winning business model. *Harvard Business Review, 89*(1–2), 100-07.

Chapter 7

So, You Want to Do a Deal?
A Dialogue on Corporate Strategy
and Mergers and Acquisitions

> "Each player must accept the cards life deals him or her: but once they are in hand, he or she alone must decide how to play the cards in order to win the game."
>
> —Voltaire

Suzie Nguyen, founder of Andromeda eGaming, has multiple business units in her company and faces a range of strategic dilemmas—and opportunities—that challenge her beyond her basic thinking about business-unit strategy or innovation. In some parts of her business that can do more than just produce new games, she sees opportunities for doing different activities in the industry but doesn't quite know how to think through the way that connects to her core business. Elsewhere in the company, she sees the possibility to produce more games under the Andromeda brand. She learns how to use several new frameworks to organize her thinking around her portfolio of different businesses and to considering how these choices come together at the corporate-strategy level rather than focusing solely on individual business-unit decisions. She also learns how to decide between building, borrowing, and buying a new capability for Andromeda—or even merging with another industry player.

Forming a corporate strategy

Suzie Nguyen stared down Conrad across the conference room table. "Look, Conrad," she said. "I'm not telling you that your strategic-thinking progression was useless. It just didn't lead us to a specific answer."

Suzie, the founder of Andromeda eGaming, had worked overtime with her team to re-evaluate Andromeda's competitive market and the changing customer habits in electronic gaming—revealing some market opportunities. Her team had also looked in the mirror and done a deep dive on what made Andromeda unique and what core competencies they could use as a foundation for new growth.

"We were roaring along," she said. Then she hesitated, and her voice trailed off.

"Okay," said Conrad quizzically. "You were roaring along, but—"

"Roaring along but getting nowhere definite."

"You roared until you ran out of gas?"

"Roared until we ran aground. We didn't even get to the finish line."

"Okay, so what stalled you out?"

"After we looked at the frameworks for adopting different business strategies or evaluating business models, my business-unit leaders each gave me a different option for our new best strategy. Totally different answers. Each strategy by itself was an excellent idea. People were pumped. They loved them. The problem was, we got to the point where we had a wish list of options from the business units and no *right* option for the whole company."

She added, "It was such a disappointment. And here I was telling everyone how we would race over the horizon—following your frameworks—and converge on a strategic destination everyone agreed to."

Jada slid her hands onto the table. *I need to defuse Suzie's frustration,* she thought. "Rest assured, we'll get to that destination," she said. "Suzie, we're going to come at strategic thinking from a different angle today."

"A new angle?"

"Bear with me," said Jada. "How many businesses are you in at Andromeda?"

Suzie stared back at Jada, frustrated. "Duh, one. Electronic gaming."

"No, that is your industry," Jada shot back. "How many different *businesses* do you have?"

"My industry? Are we splitting hairs here? What is your definition of different businesses?"

"Ask yourself this: do different units in your company have different kinds of customers, different kinds of resources, different people, different processes not shared across the firm?"

Suzie shrugged. "Some of our units are pretty independent in what they produce and to whom they sell—and how they sell."

"So they're independent in their business models?"

"In their business models, yes." And then Suzie grinned and said, "Yes, I remember Ian's session."

"Okay," said Jada, "so there is some separation between the business units. But they share some resources across Andromeda, yes?"

"For sure."

"And not just your back-office functions?"

"Not just back office. The CTO oversees the sharing of technology resources, some of which are centralized at the 'corporate' level, some of which belong to the business units owing to specialization."

Conrad went to the board. "So, basically, you have a family of businesses, a portfolio if you will, distinct from each other in some ways, cooperating and sharing in others."

"We are all part of the Andromeda team. We deliver on the same value proposition—advanced gaming with cutting-edge AI integration for always-unique playing experiences."

"Let's get those business units up on the board," said Conrad. "We can then talk about common portfolio-management frameworks to see how much of your strategy is shared across the entire business."

"This is the new angle we're talking about today," said Jada. "This is about corporate strategy, distinct from individual business-unit strategy. Your overall Andromeda corporate strategy 'sits above' your business-unit strategies. It allows you to prioritize and coordinate all your strategic moves."

Jada and Conrad knew that this idea would be new to everyone. It applied to many of Kurt Amery's businesses, several of them on the cusp of growing out of their bootstrap phase. For that reason, Kurt had asked for Alexis Chapman, CEO of Celar Logistics, to also join the conversation.

Kurt himself was keen on attending because Suzie was in the midst of a time-sensitive strategic challenge that demanded this very kind of thinking. How should she and her

An enterprise may in fact have several different kinds of businesses within the firm—business units that differ from each other in customers, re-sources, processes, business models, and the skills of the people. The firm needs an overall corporate strategy, not just the sum of the different business-unit strategies.

leaders, who ran a company ready to grow to the next level, take their next strategic step? Kurt was sitting with his elbows on the table, attentive as ever.

Andromeda's portfolio of businesses

At Conrad's request, Suzie explained how she thought about her different business units. First she described the biggest and oldest division—the game studio—which creates Andromeda's core product: AI-enhanced video games. Andromeda sold these games in the traditional way, to video-game publishers like Activision Blizzard and Electronic Arts, and even to console makers like Sony and Nintendo. The Andromeda game studio cut deals with publishers upfront and then produced the creative product.

"It's just like the process a book author goes through," Suzie said. "We create the content, and the publisher handles the marketing, licensing, distribution, and all that."

Conrad wrote on the board:

Biz 1: game development studio

Suzie then explained that because Andromeda's studio invented original technology tools to integrate AI into its games, she and her team had split off certain developers from the studio and made them into a separate division. That division created Andromeda's gaming engine—the baseline software architecture for AI-enhanced gaming. Any game studio other than Andromeda could then license that engine to optimize and simplify the development of video games across platforms.

"We license the engine only to a few other studios making non-competitive games," she said.

"Pretty cool," said Jada. "Sounds like Andromeda is a tech solution leader in the space and not just a development studio."

"It sort of evolved that way," agreed Suzie.

Conrad wrote:

Biz 2: gaming engine

Suzie then explained that both businesses fed the high end of the gaming user base—the serious gamers willing to invest in consoles, sophisticated equipment, and a high-tech experience. Even though

Andromeda's unique AI enhancement is its signature technology—and its differentiator—those kinds of players want immersive experiences. That customer demand led Suzie and her team to create a hardware division that makes a virtual reality headset and other immersive gaming accessories.

"This business has a different customer base, business model, and supply chain from the first two businesses," said Suzie, "so we made it a separate unit."

Conrad wrote:

Biz 3: hardware/VR accessories

"And ... we've gone one step farther," said Suzie, "with our first foray away from the high-end gaming community."

"Games on smartphones!" guessed Alexis, jumping in. "That must be it. If I had a dime for every Candy Crush player I see on my flights, I could retire."

"Absolutely. That's where the mass market is," said Suzie. "Everyone is gaming on their phones. So, we started a mobile gaming division—different kinds of development and technology, different kinds of sales and distribution processes, and a different business model. In fact, we use the 'freemium' model, where the basic game is free, but the player ultimately pays for it with in-app purchases. Anyway, a business with huge potential."

Conrad wrote:

Biz 4: mobile gaming

"Got your hands full," said Kurt approvingly.

"Overfull," she said. "We have so many opportunities—all of which ultimately flow from our AI-enhancement advantage."

"So you're no longer roaring along with our strategic-thinking process," said Jada, "because you and your team don't know how to prioritize strategies for advancing each business unit in its part of the market."

"I guess that's where we are," said Suzie. "All those excellent strategies, but they seem to drag us in different directions."

Jada went to the whiteboard. "If you're torn between businesses, you're not the first. That's the challenge of corporate strategy. It's more complex than a single business-unit strategy."

Jada drew a quick diagram. "Here is a way to think about what we are fleshing out in this conversation—the separation between business-unit strategies and an overall corporate strategy or strategic direction."

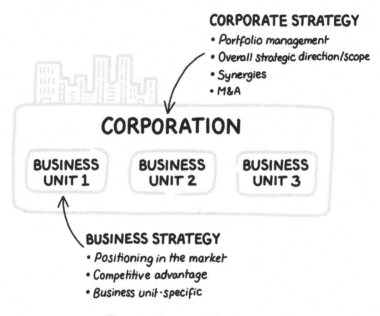

Figure 7.1 Corporate vs. business strategy

Suzie sighed. "Sheesh, do I even have a corporate strategy? I'm consumed by the work of supporting all these excellent strategic ideas in the business units. And there's not enough corporate support or financing to go around."

"We hear you," said Jada. "It would be a lot easier if your job as a strategic thinker was limited to shaping business-unit strategy, which often just involves a new product, expanding a service, or penetrating a new geography."

"These frameworks might help you, Suzie, as well as everyone else." She gave a nod to Kurt and Alexis. "They help diversified firms look at the relative value of many opportunities—to help set priorities. The first," which she started to draw, "is a well-known framework from the Boston Consulting Group—the BCG matrix."

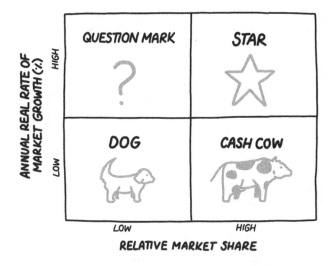

Figure 7.2 The BCG matrix and portfolio management
(Source: Henderson, B. (1970). The product portfolio. https://www.bcg.com/publications/1970/strategy-the-product-portfolio. Copyright © 1970 by Boston Consulting Group (BCG). Reprinted with permission from BCG.)

Along the horizontal axis, Jada explained, a company can assess its competitive position by market share. On the vertical axis, it can assess the growth potential of the market it is operating in. The framework asks strategic leaders to place their businesses based on strength and potential.

"What are the funny icons all about?" asked Alexis.

"Four memorable ways to characterize businesses," said Jada. "You may have heard of them."

Jada explained that a dog is a low-growth business with a weak competitive position. A cash cow is also a low-growth business, but the company's position in the market is strong, and it can milk profits from its position. A star is a strong business with high market potential. A question mark, the most challenging category, is often a business with significant market potential, but the company is not competitive enough to exploit that potential.

Suzie was drawing a 2x2 grid of her own on her tablet.

Conrad looked over her shoulder. "Some early thoughts?"

"Early brainstorming, yes. I don't have one business in each box, but I can see where they roughly fit."

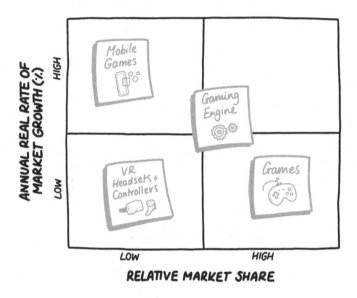

Figure 7.3 Andromeda's BCG matrix

She then displayed her tablet for everyone to see, pointing at different aspects with her pen. "Our bread-and-butter business, where we started, is the game studio. We produce a new blockbuster game for a publisher every year. It's a big business. For instance, *Call of Duty: Modern Warfare* made $600 million in sales in three days when it was released a couple of years ago. We don't ring the bell with that kind of success all the time, but we're good at releasing a profitable annual game. I would call that our cash cow."

Jada wrote it up on the whiteboard. Conrad asked, "Why not a star? I thought the video-game industry was really growing."

"As a whole," said Suzie. "But mostly in areas other than traditional console or PC games. I mentioned mobile gaming, but the new action is from the streaming games market, e-sports, other gaming competitions, virtual reality, and many other things that will drive new growth."

Conrad nodded. "What about your gaming-engine business?"

"I put that one in the middle—edging toward the star category," Suzie said. "We have something really unique there in a market that doesn't offer many gaming-engine choices. More and more game studios need it or want it, and they cannot afford to build it themselves. But I am unsure of how much growth it has if we tie it, as it is today, to the traditional high-end gamer and games market."

"You seemed super interested in mobile games," said Jada. "What about that?"

"Definitely a question mark. We're barely getting our feet wet there, and building for mobile platforms is so different. I'm not sure we've really figured out how to leverage our AI enhancement in mobile games. But much of the future is there for the industry, no doubt—I just don't know if it is there for us."

"And your virtual reality equipment and accessories team?" asked Conrad.

"Like mobile, it's a good business in and of itself," said Suzie. "But I don't know if it is good for us. Keeping up with the Joneses, so to speak, is an expensive proposition—chasing market share from Meta, Sony, Nvidia, HTC, and all the big boys. I love what we have done there, but it feels like it doesn't belong at the end of the day. What phrase did you two use when we were exploring core competencies—does it play on the dominant gene in our DNA? Well, our dominant gene is software development, not tinkering in the garage with lots of hardware."

"So, that's in the dog category?" asked Jada.

"Hmm, I guess," said Suzie. "Seems unfair to call it that, though—it's a good market and my team has done cool work. But you bring me back to my dilemma. So what if I 'grade' these units as a dog, cow, star, or question mark in their relative value to the company? I still need to know what to do about it, not just what animal to call it."

"Exactly," said Conrad. "We want to avoid a bias toward analysis and instead focus on action—that is what every strategic leader should do."

Jada went to the board and started to draw a new matrix. While she was doing that Conrad explained, "There are several frameworks to translate this bit of analysis into possible action plans. One was designed by McKinsey & Company and used by General Electric, among others, and it is meant to prompt thinking about action."

He took a different colored marker and wrote in the boxes on Andromeda's BCG matrix. "Here is what that method might suggest—grossly simplified."

Figure 7.4 Andromeda's BCG matrix and possible strategies

Suzie studied it. "Pretty clear direction. Milk the cash cow—our game development business. I should invest in the gaming-engine unit to grow it. I should continue to improve my moves into mobile ... perhaps. And I should dump the VR accessories stuff?"

"That would be an accurate read if this were a decision matrix," said Conrad. "But this, like all frameworks, serves only to stimulate and organize your thinking—not to spit out a limited set of canned answers. As you can see, these are generalized ways of looking at specific, complex situations. They do help to highlight where you might best spend your energy and analytical effort, but they are not a blueprint."

Jada was now standing beside Conrad. She had drawn a box on top of the BCG matrix with five parts. "Here is one I like to use that seems to allow for a bit more complexity—especially given that no business always fits perfectly into one box or the other. And as you pointed out, you have a business or two in the middle—but stretching toward one of the other boxes."

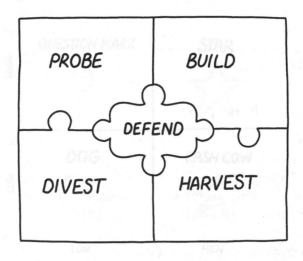

Figure 7.5 Strategic options for a portfolio analysis
(Source: based on an idea by Ronald C. Jones)

"I like it," said Suzie. "I don't feel so boxed in by this framework. I'm not so much a prisoner of other people's categories."

"Yes, here you are freer to exercise your strategic-thinking skills," agreed Conrad. "The major takeaway from all of this is *not* to pigeonhole your analysis of relative value *or* your action plan. Rather, it gives you a foundation to weigh priorities and courses of action."

"And I like this last idea of probing as an interim business strategy," she said. "That is how we started—by experimenting with a new way of video gaming, and then reinforcing what was working, and dropping what wasn't."

"And you'll find other matrices of your own to give you yet other ideas," said Conrad.

Alexis jumped into the conversation. "So, does having priorities among the business units and putting them on different development and investment paths give Suzie a corporate strategy?"

"The beginnings of one, yes," answered Jada. "A good corporate strategy will guide you in how the business units within Andromeda may or may not work together and may or may not share resources. In other words, how they relate to each other, and the whole—the Andromeda strategy and value proposition."[1]

Build it? Borrow it? Or buy it?

"So that all is helpful to me from the standpoint of prioritization and weighing different business opportunities that surface for each business," said Suzie. "But I still don't feel like I have a corporate strategy that is distinct from four different business-unit strategies, no matter how I rank and stack their relative importance to Andromeda."

"At Andromeda," said Jada, "what do you think makes something so-called 'corporate,' versus a business unit?"

"I guess when, as the founder, I spend my energy and attention on something, that would make it corporate. And the same could be said for the other executives on my team."

"What about investment capital, Suzie?" asked Kurt. "You and I and the other board members control that as a corporate resource."

"And we control other things like IP, legal resources, finance," said Suzie. "I mean, the head of the gaming studio can't just run out and borrow money, get a lawyer, and buy another game studio without my team pulling corporate levers."

> Corporate strategy entails more complicated strategic moves than a single business unit developing a new product or going after a new customer. It often requires a long-term and sophisticated look into the market, new investment, outside expertise, and intense corporate leadership energy.

"Perfect example," said Jada. "They point to our answer. Corporate strategy entails more complicated strategic moves than a business unit developing a new product, going after a new customer, and so on. Corporate strategy often calls on you to look a bit wider and deeper into the market because it normally requires investment, outside expertise, and intense corporate leadership energy."

"We went over basic business-unit strategies with Steve a few weeks ago. What are some corporate-strategy moves?" asked Kurt.

"Let's write some down," said Conrad, still at the board. He wrote:

1. Vertical integration (backward)

Suzie joked, "Look, ma, a new gymnastics move! I'm vertically integrating—going backward!"

"Whatever that means!" said Kurt.

"A wonky term," admitted Jada. "But it refers to a simple concept." She explained that Suzie's value chain of activities started with a game idea and ended with the completed game being played. There were links—steps and activities—in the value chain in between. All these links made up the vertical value chain.

"You launched the business with just one big activity in that chain, developing the game, correct?" asked Jada.

"Yes," agreed Suzie. "And like all new studios at the time, we built our first games on a generic game-engine software architecture licensed from a game-engine company. That was in an era before AI had matured enough to integrate into our product."

"But you don't use that game engine now for your development platform, do you?"

"We use our own proprietary game engine, and even—as I was saying—license it to others, thus making it a separate business unit from our studio."

"So," continued Jada, "if we define going 'backward' in the value chain as going toward the point of origination, and 'forward' as toward the customer, you own a business today that you've grown by going backward."

"Right! Yes!" said Suzie. "I guess we did stumble on some vertical integration—going back up the value chain. You need to have the development engine before you can write the code for the game."

Conrad had drawn eight boxes in a vertical row with "Idea of a game" at the top end and "End user plays game" at the bottom. He colored in two boxes in the middle next to each other:

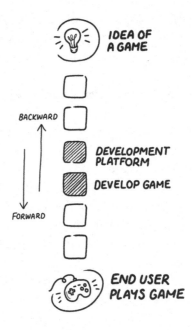

Figure 7.6 The value chain in the gaming industry

"This is just approximate," he said. "Don't worry about the exact number of steps in the game development value chain—but we know that there are many, and not all of them are done by Andromeda. So, if Andromeda thinks it can grow by owning or performing more steps in this value chain, it might want to do it as a strategy of vertical integration."

"Right," agreed Suzie. "I get it. We are doing it now in part. But why does that make this corporate strategy?"

"Because to carry out a move to do more of the process, you would need to either build the new capability for the value chain yourself, borrow it from someone who specializes in that part of the value chain— enter into a partnership or something like that—or buy another company already doing that function so you can own and control it. These are often the possible actions in a corporate strategy: the three Bs." He wrote on the board:

Build it

Borrow it

Buy it

"Keep those Bs in mind as choices in vertical integration. When entering the game-engine business, you chose the first B," said Conrad. "What makes this a strategic move, based on corporate strategy, is that you chose to own more steps in the value chain and you invested in that. Now, at least for that piece of the puzzle, you control the costs and quality of that step when you did not in the past."

"Control over the process, yes," said Suzie. "And creating our own engine has saved us money."

"And that's a big reason for a vertical integration strategy—cost and control. Now, if you were to do more vertical integration forward toward the customer, what would be your next step after game development?"

"Publication, marketing, and distribution of the game," answered Suzie. "We rely on the big game publishers to do that."

Jada added a label in the next box on the value chain diagram below 'Develop game':

> *Corporate strategy often entails a decision to gain more or new capabilities—and a further decision to either build it oneself, borrow it through a partnership or other arrangement, or buy it through an acquisition.*

Publish game

"Could you build that capability in Andromeda?" asked Jada.

"Oh gosh, no, not competently anyway," said Suzie. "That is such a different business. We are a technology business. That is a marketing and distribution business. Remember when Disney bought Pixar to own Pixar's cutting-edge animation technology? Disney then didn't ask Pixar to open theme parks. Disney had a brand marketing genius and an entertainment distribution empire. Pixar made amazing high-tech animated films. Two totally different kinds of companies and competencies, but very complementary to each other. I think, like Pixar, it would make no sense for us to be our own publisher."

"So that leads us to a strategy with the second B," said Jada. "You *borrow* that capability in the value chain."

"In a manner of speaking," answered Suzie. "We contract for it with a publisher."

"And what about the third B?" asked Jada. "If you could *buy* and control the publisher, would you give yourself—your gaming studio—better terms than you currently get?"

"For sure!" said Suzie. "But it usually goes the other way. Rather than game studios buying game publishers, over the past few years we've seen the publishers come back down the value chain—and buy game studios to own and control the terms and conditions of the relationship."

"What about the tech companies that make the consoles and computers?" asked Alexis. "I pay the bills for my teenagers, and the invoices all come from Sony or Microsoft. It looks to me like those equipment makers are integrating forward *and* backward, given they own the console *and* the subscription service to it. And Microsoft just bought one of the big publishers and the game studios owned by that publisher."

"It's been the wild west in our industry for sure," said Suzie.

"Great observations," said Conrad. "What you are seeing is somebody else's corporate strategy at work—combinations of capability building, integrations, acquisitions, mergers, divestments, and much more—but all with a strategic aim in mind: to position the firm in a place of sustainable competitive advantage in a dynamic industry. Every industry goes through it, not just electronic gaming."

"If there is a strategy for vertical integration, there must also be one for horizontal integration?" asked Kurt.

> *In a dynamic industry, firms will use combinations of capability building, integrations, acquisitions, mergers, divestments, and much more as part of their corporate strategy. But always with the strategic aim in mind of positioning the firm in a place of sustainable competitive advantage.*

"For sure," said Jada. "If vertical refers to integration along the value chain, horizontal refers to expanding one activity in that chain. So, in Suzie's case, it could mean gaining the capability to control other gaming studios so that Andromeda would be able to produce three or four different kinds of blockbusters a year from different studios, not just the home-grown one."

Kurt and Suzie shared a glance. "Um, what do you mean by gaining the capability?" asked Suzie. "What's that involve?"

"Well, do you agree, Suzie, that the horizontal integration strategy Jada outlined might, in theory, make sense for strengthening your competitive advantage?"

"Yes, in theory," offered Suzie cautiously. "Presuming that these new studios doing different kinds of games were all still supporting our AI-enhanced gaming."

"Fair enough," said Conrad. "So, the next question would be, what is the best way to 'gain the capability' to advance that strategy? Would it be best to *build* those new studios yourself, *borrow* the work of already existing studios through licensing arrangements, or *buy* them outright and control them?"

"As an investment professional, my answer would be 'it depends,'" said Kurt. "Suzie and I would want to see the numbers and the models for cost, degree of difficulty, how long it would take with each option, terms and conditions and all that before answering the question."

"*It depends* is always a safe answer in strategy," said Jada, "because it's true. In this scenario we're kicking around, if Andromeda were to *build* two or three more studios from scratch to make additional games, it could take a long time. *Borrowing* those two or three new games per year to sell through Andromeda by licensing them from other studios that developed the games could work—but who knows if you'll get the quality control you want or if you'll end up paying more than had you done it yourself?"

"What about buying?" asked Suzie, glancing again at Kurt and this time holding her gaze long enough to suggest she was gauging his approval.

Jada looked at Conrad. *What is this body language about?* they both wondered.

"Well, a little earlier you raised the Disney–Pixar merger," said Jada. "Before Disney bought Pixar outright, they essentially *borrowed* the Pixar movies by signing an agreement with Pixar that would allow Disney to distribute Pixar films. Over time, this arrangement became so expensive for Disney that they ultimately concluded that buying and controlling Pixar was a more cost-effective alternative to continued licensing. So, a *buy* option would depend on a lot of questions, but cost is certainly foremost among them."

Thinking about mergers and acquisitions (M&As)

Suzie was taking notes with uncharacteristic energy. Without looking up, she asked, "What are the other considerations someone should think about with the buy option?"

Conrad was at the board and put down his marker. "Okay you two, what are all the sidelong glances about? This is not Jada's or my first rodeo. You're asking these questions not just to learn but because something else is happening, right?"

Suzie and Kurt looked again at each other. *Should we put all our cards on the table?* they were both thinking.

"We are under a non-disclosure agreement," said Conrad. "What are you up to? It's easier for us if you have a backstory, and you tell us what it is."

Kurt shifted forward in his seat, and said in earnest, "Here's the deal. We're contemplating an acquisition *for* Andromeda, maybe more of a merger. On the other side of the ledger, we've received offers to buy Andromeda! We're not sure right now if we're buyers, sellers, or neither!"

Conrad smiled. "Here's how a strategic thinker views that dilemma: you are always buying, and as far as your competition is concerned, you are always selling. As an attitude, that gives you strategic optionality."

"An attitude?" repeated Kurt. "But we're looking for a strategy."

"The best strategic thinkers start with attitude," said Conrad, "because it communicates that you understand that some kinds of big corporate moves—a merger, an acquisition, a divestment, a strategic partnership, a joint venture, whatever—are simply a *means to the end* of your strategy. Don't confuse the goals of your strategy with ways to get there."

"That makes sense to me," said Suzie. "And our strategic objective is to be the leader in AI-enhanced video games and triple our market share of the gaming marketplace. But it's hard to see how to build that quickly without some deals—mergers and acquisitions."

"Well, now is a great time to drill down on that," said Jada. "The corporate level, and your corporate strategy, is almost always the level at which M&A activity or any other complex deal is considered. Not the least because that is where the capital for a deal resides."

"Well, you are in our NDA cone of secrecy now," said Kurt. "And you too, Alexis," who made a zipper motion across her lips. "So, we're more than ready for you to reveal the playbook on how to consider these M&A options."

Kurt grabbed his briefcase and drew out a set of folders. "We've got these possible deals in front of us, and it would be great if you could—"

Jada held up both hands. "Let's not get ahead of ourselves. Why don't we spend a little time on thinking strategically about M&A before digging into deal details."

Kurt looked disappointed. "Okay, yes, that makes sense."

"Deal fever!" laughed Conrad. "It's infectious. The sense of urgency can get the better of anyone."

"What's most important, versus most urgent," Jada added, "is under-standing *how* to think through mergers, acquisitions, strategic partnerships, or other corporate deals *before* we look at specific ones. The thinking may shed new light on how to process the offers you have made or are getting."

> Many corporate moves—a merger, an acquisition, a divestment, a strategic partnership, a joint venture—are simply a means to the end of the strategy. Don't confuse the ultimate purpose of the strategy with the ways to achieve it.

"More important than doing a deal," said Conrad, "is looking at the *why* of alternatives versus the *what*. And truly understanding the challenges that accompany inorganic growth."

"Inorganic growth?" asked Alexis. "Deal fever and inorganic growth— we've switched to talking about medical conditions, right?"

"Very funny," smiled Jada. "Excuse the lingo. We're distinguishing growth via a deal that brings in outside resources or business you did not develop—inorganic—versus growth you achieve by developing your business on its own—organic growth."

"Ah, okay," Alexis smiled. "So what usually prompts a deal—this desire for inorganic growth?"

"Most of the time," answered Conrad, "the chief rationale for doing a deal is because buying it is faster, less painful, more certain, and perhaps cheaper, than trying to build it yourself. Especially if it entails an area in which the firm is not that experienced or talented."

"Well, I'm all for avoiding the pain of building things we're not good at," said Suzie. "There are a dozen things I want to make to add to Andromeda's capabilities and market reach, but when we looked at trying to grow them all from scratch it would not only take forever, but we stood a fair chance of messing it up along the way."

"That's a fair bet," agreed Jada, "if we are to believe the experience of others. Let's return to the Disney–Pixar deal. Disney could have just copied and built a more tech-advanced animation studio like Pixar. They could have even started that process by poaching Pixar's best people, the insiders who knew the secret sauce. But it would have been a slow process. They might have missed an ingredient. The *build* option looked difficult and uncertain."

"I thought they were partners?" asked Alexis. "That was my impression from watching Disney–Pixar movies."

"They were … until they weren't," said Jada. "Since the build option was off the table, Disney used *borrow*—a series of agreements over 15 years to fund, own the rights to, coproduce, or distribute Pixar films. But as Pixar got better and better, the agreements got worse and worse for Disney. Steve Jobs at Pixar did a great job of understanding the shifting balance of power in their relationship and kept concluding better terms and conditions for Pixar. So, to Disney, *borrow* looked less attractive over time."

"Thus, the buy," said Suzie.

"$7.4 billion worth," added Conrad. "Now, corporate strategy often requires big investment. So, to justify this cost to shareholders and them-selves, Disney would have done the analysis and calculations to prove that this expensive inorganic move was the best way for them to get what they needed to grow strategically—which was owning and controlling a world-class, high-tech animation studio with an amazing track record of success."

"Would that be a horizontal integration play?" asked Kurt. "Disney already had its own animation studio—shoot, Disney *invented* animated movies."

"Yes, in a way," said Jada. "And if the Pixar deal had not come through there were other horizontal integration deals to be had—by buying DreamWorks studios, for instance."

"From Pixar's perspective, it would look like a vertical integration, I suppose," offered Suzie. "They were moving forward toward the customer by being part of the world's best distribution and merchandise-licensing company in the entertainment industry—all the stuff closest to the end user."

"Shrewd observation," agreed Conrad as he went to the board again. "Our larger point, though, is that there is always pretty much the same grand rationale everywhere for doing a deal—it advances a firm's strategic position and competitiveness. But underneath that, there are various general strategic reasons for looking at the build, borrow, or buy calculation." He wrote:

1. Vertical integration—buy in the value chain

2. Horizontal integration—buy competitors

3. Product extension—complementary products

4. Market extension—complementary markets

5. Conglomerate buy—diversified businesses with a common parent

"That doesn't seem too complex," said Suzie. "Each one is a general corporate-strategy move? Just need to work the build, borrow, or buy calculations and see which one is best?"

"That's a good first step if you know this is the strategic direction you want to take," answered Jada. "In many scenarios, the time and ability to build or borrow a new capability may not be available, so the calculations will ultimately default to buying."

"I used to do some of this as a banker," offered Kurt. "Financial modeling, execution risk analysis, return on invested capital calculations, and all that jazz. There was always a price at which a deal made sense—it was just a matter of getting there in negotiations."

Conrad laughed. "Yes, Kurt, that is indeed the way a banker has to think. But what we try to think about as strategists is the strategic rationale—particularly for the buy option. M&A is often expensive and risky. It is essential to explore the buyer's rationale before an investment."

Suzie was taking notes furiously. "What are some common rationales you two have seen in M&A?"

Jada started a list on the board.[2]

- *Improve the target company's performance*
- *Consolidate to remove capacity from the industry*
- *Accelerate market access for their or our products*
- *Get skills or technologies faster or at a lower cost than they can be built*
- *Exploit a business's industry-specific scalability*
- *Get in early, on the ground floor, to develop this new business*
- *Consolidate to improve competitive position*
- *Integrate horizontally in a geographic roll-up*
- *Use M&A as an R&D plan*
- *Buy because it's too cheap to ignore*
- *Transform ourselves with a merger as the means*

"Now, those last two," said Jada, "are probably the riskiest, but in some cases worth considering."

"Seems to me that if you have the money, the buy option is always quicker," said Kurt. "Add money and stir—instant new business!"

"And maybe instant turmoil, too?" asked Alexis. "I've heard that more than half of all M&A deals fail."

"More than seventy percent, according to some analyses," said Conrad. "I'm not sure that's true—nobody defines success or failure the same way. But M&A is very risky. A deal can go south for many reasons—culture clashes, employee resistance, customer alienation, and operational disagreements. Many are financial disasters. Look at Microsoft and Nokia, Google and Motorola, AOL and Time Warner, Sprint and Nextel—they all bombed."

Kurt, looking a bit washed out, had hoped for a cheerier message. "But it's such a tempting strategy for fast growth. We march into new markets—or muscle-up with a new capability—overnight!"

"True," said Jada. "But if you see value in your target, others probably do, too, so you stand to lose much of that value in a bidding war. Or suffer as the value dissipates while you struggle to integrate the businesses."

"Culture wars, technology clashes, alienated people—I can definitely see those things happening with an acquisition in my industry space," said Suzie. "So how do we think through whether the deal is a winner or not—and whether to take the risk and spend money?"

"More frameworks!" said Jada. She winked. "I know you're surprised."
Everyone grinned.

"Before I introduce a way to assess whether a deal is a good 'fit,' let's look at the question from the opposite side. We've talked about all the benefits you might get from an acquisition. What about what you can give to an acquisition?"

"Give?" said Kurt. "I thought we were talking about taking advantage of an opportunity—buying a company that will help our competitive advantage."

"For sure. But ultimately, the deal's value will flow from *mutual* benefit," said Jada. "You want to be a giver, not just a taker. You can only suck so much value out of a target you prey on. In the best deals, you make the target company better—not just exploit its assets."

"Let's look at the firm you're considering buying," said Conrad. "Suzie, what do you bring to the table on this deal?"[3]

> Ultimately, a deal's value will flow from mutual benefit between the acquiring company and the acquiree. In the best deals, the buyer makes the target company better and does not just exploit its assets.

Suzie explained that she and Kurt were evaluating a gaming studio focused exclusively on producing slightly AI-enhanced games for phones. That market is one in which Andromeda has little expertise. The target company is young and has only launched one full game. From Andromeda, the young company would get experienced management and infrastructure for building key relationships in the gaming industry. It would also get Andromeda's AI engine, a resource that would cost a fortune to buy themselves.

"So, you would be a good parent to this new child," said Jada. "You would bring them all kinds of advantages they couldn't get if they were raising themselves?"

Suzie and Alexis, both mothers, raised their eyebrows at the parenting metaphor. *Let's not bring the family in*, they both thought.

Jada smiled as the two grimaced. "Well, in truth, it's not my way of thinking about it, but it usually sparks insights. It is a business concept called parenting advantage. What is yours?"

"Hmm," said Suzie. "Okay, I can do that analysis, but if we compare this to my family, I can only go so far. I know my kids, but sometimes I don't know whether my effect on them is neutral, positive … or worse."

"I hear you," said Jada with a smile. "Still, if you understand Andromeda and you understand your acquisition target, then you can ask yourself where you can add value and improve the business if you are its new parent."[4]

"Corporate parenting," said Suzie, reflecting. "So, what kind of corporate parent would we be to this business?"

"Exactly," said Jada. "We've already established that you have a corporate portfolio of different businesses, so how are you being a corporate parent to those businesses now? This might give you some insights about adopting a new child, so to speak."

"Here is another way to assess this Parenting Advantage framework," she said, drawing again.

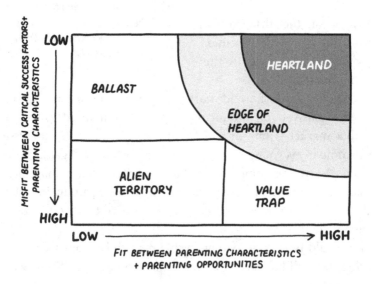

Figure 7.7 Parenting Advantage framework for mergers and acquisitions

(Source: Used with permission of Wiley & Sons, from Goold, M., Campbell, A., & Alexander, M. (1994). *Corporate-Level Strategy: Creating Value in the Multibusiness Company.* Hoboken, NJ: John Wiley & Sons, p. 341; permission conveyed through Copyright Clearance Center, Inc.)

"What you can see is that in Campbell, Goold and Alexander's research, they found that the farther away the target is from the acquirer's core business and core expertise, the harder the 'fit' might be during the 'adoption.'"

Jada pointed in turn to different parts of the diagram. "As you can see on the vertical axis, we want to assess the critical success factors of an acquisition and whether they fit with us as a parent. If, for instance, a critical success factor is the ability of the acquisition to experiment freely and fail often, and yet Andromeda has a zero-tolerance culture for failure, there would be a misfit."

"Or," Suzie offered, "since using AI enhancement is a critical success factor, if they didn't want to develop mobile games with AI, that would be a misfit."

"Totally," said Jada. "The same goes for many other measurements of fit versus key success factors."

"The horizontal axis is a bit more general," said Jada. "It looks at how well you might match what you have as a parent versus what they need or the opportunities they present. As you can see, the framework's developers advise staying in or near what they call the 'heartland' of your business for the most successful fit."

"So, the closer you are to matching these things up with your 'heartland'—the business area you know really well—the better the chance of success with the acquisition?" asked Alexis.

"In this schema, yes," answered Conrad. "But no guarantees. Some of the biggest M&A busts of all time were companies conceivably in the same business and very complementary to each other—Daimler-Benz and Chrysler or Sprint and Nextel, for instance. Other failures were more obviously outside the 'heartland' area— like Google and Motorola, or Microsoft and Nokia."

Another aspect that can separate corporate strategy from business-unit strategy is the level of difficulty and degree of risk and stakeholder involvement.

"I'm not in love with this family terminology," said Kurt. "But I understand how it aids strategic thinking. And I suppose someone seeking to acquire Andromeda would think that way?"

"I would hope so," said Jada. "The idea of 'fit' should be at the top of their minds if they want to be your new parent and add value, not just extract it. From your end of things, you can flip the model on its head and evaluate fit for you as the target."

The room was silent as everyone digested the concepts. "Feels like the big leagues," breathed Alexis. "Complicated stuff."

"And risky," agreed Conrad. "Another thing that can separate corporate strategy from business-unit strategy is the level of difficulty and degree of risk and stakeholder involvement. I always say that you can tell the discussion is about corporate strategy depending on how many lawyers and bankers are in the room."

Kurt laughed. "It wouldn't be so funny if it weren't so true, Conrad. So, have we got what we need to start sorting this out for Suzie?"

"Let's leave you with one more thought to help you," said Jada. "No matter which end you come from in M&A, you'll get more insights if you apply a few big 'tests' to any deal—and not just M&A but a strategic partnership, a joint venture, a divestment, or any other corporate move."

She wrote on the board:[5]

- **The Better Off test**
- **The Ownership test**
- **The Organization test**

"So, Suzie," Jada continued, "Let's apply the 'better off' test to your situation. From a pure performance standpoint, what would the mobile gaming studio you might buy have to prove to you so you would be better off performing together than alone?"

"Ah, I dream about this," said Suzie. "We would have to share technology, expertise, best practices and processes, and we would have to produce things together that neither of us could have on our own. That is the proof point—that the total effect of our joint efforts would be more than the simple sum of the two companies under one roof."

"And at lower costs," said Kurt. "We would have to realize some cost synergies from not running two separate companies and, in turn, could spin off cash to invest in new game builds."

"And you would want to drill down on those synergies in some detail in your analysis," said Jada.

"What about the second test?" said Conrad. "The 'ownership' test. Do you actually need to *own* this company to capture the value they create? Have you looked at a partnership, a licensing deal, or some exclusivity?"

"Not really," answered Kurt. "I guess we could. The target company needs capital to fund their game development at the next level. If we fund it through a leasing-type agreement, we might as well own it, don't you think?"

Jada shrugged. "I don't know. But you've heard our standard answer for strategic thinking: *it depends*. Rent or buy a home? Lease or own a car? All similar decisions. You need to model the likely terms and conditions for each scenario and return to the question of the best way to get the value you want to accomplish your strategic objectives. That is the end goal. Whether you buy or borrow that value, you're looking for a means to your end. So weigh it fairly. Don't let deal fever distort your view of what each thing weighs."

"And the 'organization' test?" asked Alexis. "Is that similar to the Parenting Advantage framework?"

"It touches the same points," said Conrad. "With this test, the key question is: can Suzie organize the combined businesses in such a way that they work well together? Disney and Pixar had very different cultures, processes, and approaches to the market. What about you and the target company?"

> In deciding between licensing, partnering, joint venturing, and acquiring, the firm should model the likely terms and conditions for each scenario and return to the question of the best way to get the value it wants to accomplish its strategic objectives. That is the end goal. Whether it buys or borrows that value, it simply seeks a means to an end. Weigh the options fairly. Don't let deal fever distort your view of what each option weighs.

Suzie rubbed her eyes with fatigue. "I feel like they are Andromeda about five years ago: a similar culture, similar outlook, less mature. I need to get inside their head to know them better."

"Indeed," said Conrad. "At the end of the day, if you do the deal, you will have to make big decisions about how much autonomy they should have—or how little. Modeling the combined organization is key."

"Right," nodded Suzie. "If I push too much Andromeda on them too fast, especially if they see processes and outlooks as alien, I could end up killing the goose before it lays its golden eggs."

"Exactly," said Jada. "People, culture, and customers. Messing those up in an integration can overshadow all the advantages of the supposed fit you identify in the Parenting Advantage framework. You can't see 'fit' as just a financial or engineering issue. The so-called 'soft' fit often ends up being the hard one in many acquisitions."

"Enough for today," said Conrad, now sitting down, placing his hands on the table. "We've come a long way. Business strategy isn't corporate strategy. Corporate strategy isn't just about integration—vertical or horizontal. And integration isn't just about organic growth. Inorganic growth—after a buy/borrow/build assessment that includes the potential for deals—has to play a part, too."

Conrad and Jada's key takeaways

Corporate strategy deals with how different businesses or units within a corporation may or may not work together and how they fit into the corporate portfolio and strategy as a whole.

- How many businesses are you in as a corporation?

- How do those businesses relate to one another?

- How many strategies do you need and how many should be shared?

Corporate strategy is almost always the level at which **M&A activity** is considered and conducted, not least because that is where the investment capital for it is.

Corporate strategy often revolves around **adding new capabilities (or discarding current ones)**. This often prompts a decision to **build, borrow, or buy.**

Some **common forms of corporate strategies** include:

- Vertical integration
- Horizontal integration
- Product extension
- Market extension
- Conglomerate/unrelated

Six common **rationales for doing an acquisition:**

- We will improve the target company's performance.
- We will consolidate to remove capacity from the industry.
- We will accelerate market access for their or our products.
- We will get skills or technologies faster or at lower cost than they can be built.
- We can exploit a business's industry-specific scalability.
- We will get in on the ground floor of something early and help develop that new business.

Too many companies tend to look at acquisitions simply as a way of obtaining value for themselves—they are "takers." A firm can combat this phenomenon by **adding value,** not just looking to take it. You've got to be a "giver"—what do you bring to the table that gives advantage to the target?

The **big three M&A tests:**

- The Ownership test
- The Better Off test
- The Organization test

In M&A, a firm cannot afford to see "fit" as just a financial, strategic, or engineering issue. The so-called **"soft" fit issues**— such as culture—can be decisive.

Works cited and recommendations for further study

Books

De Kluyver, C. A., and Pearce, J. A. (2009). *Strategy: A View from the Top (an Executive Perspective)*. Old Tappan, NJ: Prentice Hall.

Editors of Harvard Business Review (1999). *HBR On Corporate Strategy*. Boston, MA: Harvard Business Review Press.

Frankel, M. E. S. (2017). *Mergers and Acquisitions Basics: The Key Steps of Acquisitions, Divestitures, and Investments*. 2nd ed. Hoboken, NJ: John Wiley & Sons.

Gaughan, P. A. (2005). *Mergers: What Can Go Wrong and How to Prevent It*. Hoboken, NJ: John Wiley & Sons.

Goedhart, M., Koller, T., and Wessels, D. (2015). *Valuation: Measuring and Managing the Value of Companies*. Hoboken, NJ: John Wiley & Sons.

Haspeslagh, P. C., and Jemison, D. B. (1991). *Managing Acquisitions: Creating Value through Corporate Renewal*. New York, NY: The Free Press.

Articles

Anand, B. N. (2012). Corporate strategy. *Harvard Business School Module Note* 713-415. Boston, MA: Harvard Business Publishing.

Bower, J. L. (2001). Not all M&As are alike—and that matters. *Harvard Business Review, 79*(3), 92-101.

Brueller, N. N., Carmeli, A., and Drori, I. (2014). How do different types of mergers and acquisitions facilitate strategic agility? *California Management Review, 56*(3), 39-57.

Campbell, A., Goold, M., and Alexander, M. (1995). Corporate strategy: The quest for parenting advantage. *Harvard Business Review, 73*(2), 120-132.

Cliffe, S. (1999). Can this merger be saved? *Harvard Business Review, 77*(1), 28-44.

Collis, D. J., and Montgomery, C. A. (1998). Creating corporate advantage. *Harvard Business Review, 76*(3), 70–83.

Goedhart, M., Koller, T., and Wessels, D. (2017). The six types of successful acquisitions. McKinsey & Company. https://www.mckinsey.com/capabilities/strategy-and-corporate-finance/our-insights/the-six-types-of-successful-acquisitions, published May 10, 2017, accessed September 18, 2024.

Harding, D., Rovit, S., and Corbett, A. (2004). Avoid merger meltdown: Lessons from mergers and acquisitions leaders. *Strategy & Innovation*, September 15, 2004, 3–5.

Kanter, R. M. (2009). Mergers that stick. *Harvard Business Review, 87*(10), 121–125.

Marks, M. L., Mirvis, P., and Ashkenas R. (2017). Surviving M&A. *Harvard Business Review, 95*(2), 145–149.

Martin, R. (2023). The whether/how distinction. A system for navigating corporate strategy. https://rogermartin.medium.com/the-whether-how-distinction-69c13f8816d, published May 22, 2023, accessed September 17, 2024.

Martin, R. L. (2016). M&A: The one thing you need to get right. *Harvard Business Review, 94*(6), 42–48.

Piskorski, M. J. (2005). Note on corporate strategy. *Harvard Business School Background Note* 705-449, January 2005 (revised February 2006).

Notes for Chapter 7

1 As well as the many foundational works on corporate strategy listed above, see also Professor David Kryscynski's video on corporate vs. business strategy: https://youtu.be/X50pXorhtjY?si=LLxBB-zL-n6lKnnaY, published January 31, 2020, accessed September 19, 2024.
2 Bower, J. L. (2001). Not all M&As are alike—and that matters. *Harvard Business Review, 79*(3), 92–101; Goedhart, M., Koller, T., and Wessels, D. (2017). The six types of successful acquisitions. McKinsey & Company. https://www.mckinsey.com/capabilities/strategy-and-corporate-finance/our-insights/the-six-types-of-successful-acquisitions, published May 10, 2017, accessed September 18, 2024.
3 See especially Martin, R. L. (2016). M&A: The one thing you need to get right. *Harvard Business Review, 94*(6), 42–48.
4 Campbell, A., Goold, M., and Alexander, M. (1995). Corporate strategy: The quest for parenting advantage. *Harvard Business Review, 73*(2), 120–132.
5 Anand, B. N. (2012). Corporate strategy. *Harvard Business School Module Note* 713-415. Boston, MA: Harvard Business Publishing; Piskorski, M. J. (2005). Note on corporate strategy. *Harvard Business School Background Note* 705-449, January 2005 (revised February 2006).

Chapter 8

Seeking Foreign Pastures:
A Dialogue on International Business Strategy

"There are no foreign lands. It is the traveler only who is foreign."

—ROBERT LOUIS STEVENSON

···

Most businesses start as national businesses, but with economic globalization, it is not long before the opportunities of international business present themselves. Several of the CEOs in the Argo Ventures family are considering going global in some way. Derrick (Creativia Playsets), Liz (Healthy Family Foodstuffs), and Steve (Secure Home Suite) are exploring international expansion as part of their overall corporate strategy—but they have three very different perspectives on having an international element to their strategy. In their session with Conrad and Jada, they learn how to use an expanded PESTEL framework to understand global business environments' diverse settings and challenges. They also familiarize themselves with a framework that allows them to distinguish different types of international strategies and different ways to enter international markets. Finally, they learn how to measure "distance" differently than on a map and how that helps them make nuanced decisions about international business ventures.

···

Thinking through going global

Liz Fiscella came into the room brimming with enthusiasm. She and her team had settled on a market expansion strategy that fit every aspect of strategic thinking Conrad and Jada had advised. Because Healthy Family Foodstuffs had started in the Pacific Northwest and had expanded east to the Great Lakes region, her team had identified the next best areas for expansion as being just over the border in Canada.

Her team had conducted an analysis which revealed specific locations that fit the company's demographic target market. They'd considered population density, income distribution, family size, the competitive environment, real estate prices, and supply chain costs. They had looked at all the right criteria. And the size and growth rates of nearby Canadian markets made the targeted locations more than tempting.

"We can thrive there," said Liz, almost giddy with the thought of the opportunity. "Just over the border from our Seattle stores, we can plant our flag in Vancouver, British Columbia. Over from Detroit, we can move into Windsor, Ontario. Just across from Buffalo, we can open up in Toronto."

"So near yet so far," observed Conrad.

"So far?" said Liz, quizzically. "We know these cities personally, much more than other distant markets in the US. They're so close—*literally* adjacent."

"Adjacent, yet a million miles away."

"You're kidding, right?"

"Not kidding." Conrad paused as he tried to sense how serious Liz was. "Why are you even thinking about those markets?"

"Because they're already part of our regional economic zone. We live in an integrated economic neighborhood."

Liz did not like Conrad's doubts about her thinking right from the start. *Am I getting caught in one of his intellectual snares?* she wondered. Her back stiffened. She looked around the room for affirmation. Kurt Amery was on hand today, as were two other CEOs Kurt had asked to join: Steve Adlar, CEO of Secure Home Suite, and Derrick Jouet, CEO of Creativia Playsets. All of the CEOs were attending because they aspired to expand into international markets.

Liz's eyes narrowed. She was uneasy—and irritated. "For goodness' sake, Conrad, you're the one who led us in this direction. We used your suggested market assessment and industry analysis tools, and they showed us that most of our market is 'out there'—beyond the US's borders."

Steve looked for a way to ease the tension. "For a former military guy, Conrad, you're not so hot with maps. The cities Liz mentioned are more or less sister suburbs to her current markets."

"Sisters, yes," said Conrad, "separated at birth by an international border."

"Separated, true," said Liz, "but by the least bordery border I know of!"

"Come on, Conrad," said Kurt. "Outside the US is where the vast majority of potential customers are. The US and Canada are each other's biggest trading partners. That border is economically meaningless. It's one market."

"If only that were true," said Conrad. "The world and its markets are not as 'flat' as advertised."

"But this is Canada, not Uzbekistan!" said Liz. "We can take a freeway across the border."

"Perhaps the freeway exit in Canada does not remotely resemble the roads in your home market," replied Conrad. "And the potholes you hit along the way can make for a bumpy cross-border ride."

Conrad then agreed that the potential in such international markets was, *in theory*, vast. More than ninety-five percent of global customers are not Americans, and almost eighty percent are not even English speakers. To reach those people, however, a company had to address a thicket of complexity—different tax regimes, regulatory constraints, trade policies, politics, environmental rules, employment procedures, competitive laws, cultural habits, and more.

"The border is not just a geographic line," said Conrad. "It is a dividing line—and it divides more winners from losers than you think."

"I guess there may be more things for us to check out than we thought," said Liz, deferring to Conrad, yet still piqued by how he was making an example out of her.

"The point is that there may be more distance between these markets than you think."

"I suppose, but why wouldn't we consider such a rich prospect?"

"You might, but you'll want to measure the distance you have to travel with more than your car's odometer," said Conrad. "Few businesses can drive over the border without a few fender benders or crashes—or at least some time-consuming detours to navigate 'crazy' drivers and hidden barriers."

> *The economic globalization in recent years has been one of the biggest economic phenomena in history. But for most firms, the world and its markets are not as "flat" as advertised.*

"You'll often find," he added, "that the potential for crashes and detours will change your conception of what 'distance' means, whether the country is adjacent or abroad, connected by ship traffic or truck traffic. You may have to recalibrate your expectations, too."

"So near yet so far," said Jada, echoing Conrad's point. "Beware the temptation to think that picking fruit across the line in your next-door neighbor's field will be a cinch. Cultural, administrative, and regulatory differences can fence you out."

Liz folded her arms and looked defiant.

"Look—it's not a hard no—I mean, there is a market out there, no doubt. It's a matter of managing a different kind of strategic risk—this has a level of difficulty not present with domestic expansion," said Conrad. "Getting those risks wrong can stymie your expansion plans and increase costs."

"Okay," said Liz. "Good. We definitely know how to use risk-management tools. With every big decision we make, we go through an analysis and decision-making drill about whether the gain is worth it."

Jada nodded. "Okay, let's look at the right tools for that drill. Rather than jump right into your plan, let's pull the lens back a bit and look at how to approach the whole 'go global' question. It's time to advance your strategic-thinking skills to yet another level."

Decisions of a firm considering going global

Jada had learned from Kurt beforehand that Liz, Steve, and Derrick all wanted to tap international markets but had not used a systematic approach to formulate their strategies. She guessed that none of them—in such different businesses—could be thinking of the same approach.

"Liz," she said, "I think we've got your basic idea on the table: to expand to adjacent markets nearby your areas of strength—but they happen to be in another country?"

"Yes," said Liz, still feeling bruised.

"Okay," said Jada. "So the basic idea is a common one: to advance into more of the same market—a pure expansion of the current concept of Healthy Family Foodstuffs to a new geography."

"Exactly, the same playbook for all our stores," replied Liz.

"So this opportunity is driven by demand? Or at least latent demand that your team believes it can bring to the surface?"

"Yes, that's right. We're not breaking new ground. We have a track record in this target market—growing families devoted to healthy lifestyles but with a sharp eye on their budget."

"So, for the sake of our analysis," said Jada, "your plan fits into the first of three time-tested international expansion strategies." She went to the board and wrote three large capital A's.

"Our conversation today will start with a tool called the Three A's.[1] Our first step is to help each of you characterize your emerging international strategy. As we do that, you'll see how that puts us in a good position to discuss each strategy's pros and cons."

She spelled out the first A on the board:

Aggregation

"Aggregation?" asked Kurt.

"Stick with me," said Jada. "You'll see how the terminology will advance our understanding. In Liz's case, her strategy is to *aggregate* market demand using her standard store playbook in a new geography. In other words, build on where there is new natural demand for the value proposition she currently offers in the US."

Jada explained that the Three A's tool came from a well-known framework based on a wealth of research. It would help structure everyone's understanding of their unique challenges in going international.

"Okay, I get that for Liz's business," said Kurt. "What about your idea, Steve?"

"We've coalesced around a general concept based on prompts from overseas parties," said Steve. "It turns out that our simple and agile office enterprise suite, which was built for home and mobile businesses, has broad appeal worldwide. People from all over the world have reached out to us saying that they want to license our software in their home country. That's how we know we might have an international market."

"Okay, so you're thinking of selling your software as is?" asked Conrad. "International sales done from your home turf in the US? That's a very basic kind of international strategy—same product, non-American customers. Drop and ship internationally."

"Well, that was our first thought," said Steve. "That would be easy. But it turns out the most promising offers were from non-American software companies that wanted the source code so they could put out variations for their local markets and customer demands."

"And you're wondering about how to think about that?"

"Yes—how to think about everything involved, from pricing to controlling the business. And if there is a market there, we're wondering why wouldn't we establish the business there ourselves? Why sell the baseline code and permission to improvise in the code to an Indian company when we can launch our own Indian Secure Home Suite and retain all the value?"

"Whoa, whoa," said Conrad. "A lot is going on there. We'll have to pull that apart. But it sounds like you have a version of the second A for now." He went to the board and wrote "'Adaptation,'" and Jada added the company names:

Aggregation: Healthy Family Foodstuffs

Adaptation: Secure Home Suite

"You're overwhelming me with the strategy lingo," said Steve. "What's the strategic meaning behind this second A?"

"If Liz's *aggregation* strategy is built on the assumption of *similarities* between her national market and some international ones," said Conrad, "your *adaptation* thinking seems to be built on *differences* between the US market and the ones overseas."

"Ah, yes," said Steve. "The discussions of these overseas opportunities revolve around how best to get value in adapting our basic enterprise suite to different needs and requirements in different countries. So, that label makes sense."

"I hope so. Let's not force fit a label," said Conrad. "Our goal here is simply to get you thinking strategically. In this setting, out loud, and with colleagues—even better."

"Your turn, Derrick," said Jada. "I'm guessing the strategy for your business may fit our third A."

"Do I win a prize if so?" said Derrick, feigning excitement.

"You'll win a prize from me," said Kurt, "if you figure out how to go abroad and fatten up that bottom line."

"I'm in," said Derrick, flashing a thumbs-up. "It's not complicated. Our international question is whether we can outsource the manufacturing of our physical playsets to much cheaper overseas locations or third-party manufacturers."

"Thirty years too late!" said Kurt, clearly teasing. "The boom in outsourced manufacturing started fading years ago."

"Not so!" replied Derrick. "Thirty years and still hot! Our research shows we can have our sets manufactured in about four overseas locations for less than half the cost of producing them here—and with no drop in quality."

"Ah ha," said Conrad, "but which of the four, I wonder? Remind me to circle back to that. The point here is that you have a strategy of ..." he grabbed his marker and wrote:

Arbitrage

"More translation needed!" said Kurt.

"It's the third common international business strategy," said Jada. "It's aimed at capturing efficiencies in different markets by saving on costs—raw materials, manufacturing, R&D, labor, and so on. If you can take advantage, you have an arbitrage opportunity. You move some functions to a cheaper location or outsource it internationally altogether."

"Don't tell me, Derrick," smiled Kurt, "are you finally going to stop using expensive Californian artisans to make your physical playsets?"

Derrick teased him back, "Anything to make you happy, Kurt."

Jada, enjoying the banter, added to the board the final A:

Aggregation: Healthy Family Foodstuffs

Adaptation: Secure Home Suite

Arbitrage: Creativia Playsets

"You know, Steve," said Kurt, "I think you have some arbitrage opportunities as well, given how much software development is done globally now."

"Yes. We looked at using software developers in India for some of our development work," said Steve. "They had amazing skills and were about one quarter the cost of a US developer."

"So you considered an arbitrage strategy for labor costs?"

"We couldn't avoid the idea."

"If that were the essence of your international strategy—and a core feature of how you went to market—that's something you *couldn't* avoid."

"Alright, I guess I would then get two of the A's instead of one?"

"Sort of," said Conrad. "That said, we're trying to identify your signature strategy today. Sounds to me like the main thrust of your possible international strategy is creating variations of your product for different international markets. So that pushes you more toward adaptation. Perhaps there is some arbitrage thrown in too."

"But as with any framework," said Jada, clarifying, "we're not doing this as a pin-the-label-on-the-strategy game. Instead, it's another framework to organize our thinking. In this case, classifying and comparing categories forces us to think through options and alternatives and how they differ—or overlap."

"Still," said Liz, "Steve raises a good question. Is it better for a company to look at several international options or stick with one of the three strategies?"

"It depends!" said Conrad. "Our old refrain. The international business guru, Pankaj Ghemawat, who studied this and developed the Three A's approach, found that companies don't always pursue just one strategy or only one at a time. Some emphasize different A's at different points in their evolution as global enterprises."[2]

Three common reasons to go global include wanting to aggregate demand, adapt to new market conditions, and take advantage of cost arbitrage. Companies don't always pursue just one strategy or only one at a time. Some emphasize different A's at different points in their evolution as global enterprises.

"I can see that happening with both Healthy Family Foodstuffs and Secure Home Suite," said Kurt.

"Perhaps Liz might need to adapt to local tastes and local buying habits with some international stores—moving on from the standard store plan. And based on the economics and the difficulty, Steve could flex from simply licensing his brand for exclusive development in each foreign country right on up to planting his flag and opening his own operations."

"The variations are endless," agreed Jada.

Variation in the global business model

"A word of caution, though," said Conrad. "The variations can be your undoing if you're not careful. The more international strategies you have, the more difficult their execution. Overseeing a lot of variation in the business model based on different jurisdictions gets even more complicated. Most global firms ultimately have to decide if they have one global strategy they can manage centrally or multiple domestic strategies varied by geography."

"Yeah, thinking through it," offered Liz, "I wonder how our business would change if I stopped using standardized and centralized sourcing? What if I gave some stores out of the country the autonomy to experiment with products and supply chains? Would that give them advantages specific to their locales?"

"Good questions," said Jada. "You're pointing to one of the most basic strategic questions when looking at international opportunities: how might you change your basic business model—perhaps even your value proposition—to account for different business climates? Whatever competitive advantage you enjoy may not translate to success in another country, even if it looks or feels 'familiar.' It's hard to find more successful American ventures than Walmart, Home Depot or the NFL, but all three have struggled internationally. Or, coming the other way, British grocer Tesco failed in the US."

"But there have to be some common reasons for failure," suggested Kurt. "Some lessons learned with hindsight?"

"Each one was unique to its markets, strategy, and timing," Conrad answered. "But one lesson would be that you have to do the hard strategic thinking early on to clarify what we've discussed so far—international strategy and putting into place the plans and systems to carry that out."

"If you don't know where you are going, any road will get you there," quipped Kurt. "Something my Irish grandfather used to say."

"True enough," agreed Jada. "But strategic clarity is just a starting point. A second lesson would be that you have to do the operational thinking to adapt your hard-earned value proposition. How does that proposition affect the appearance of your products or services, the materials, processing, production, packaging, marketing, sales, style, brand, and more? I mean, at McDonald's in Canada, you can get poutine, and in India you can order a Chicken Maharaja Mac. That's a lot of variation for a company whose business-model breakthrough was fast-food standardization and efficiency."

> The most basic strategic question when looking at international opportunities is how you might need to change your basic business model—perhaps even your value proposition—to account for different business climates. Whatever competitive advantage you enjoy may not translate to success in another country even if it looks or feels "familiar."

"So, I guess that is just a cost-of-doing-business calculation, eh—determining the total expenses and pains associated with entering a new market and operating your business there?" said Steve. "If so much adaptation is required, the costs of conforming to the new market could negate the profit of the opportunity it seems. Then it's just a go or no-go decision?"

"You can model those results," said Conrad, "although in the experience of most international expanders, the best data comes after you take the plunge."

"And even if you have perfect information in advance," added Jada, "there is always a degree of modification required. You don't want to downplay the heavy lifting needed to conform to different government regulations, political stability, tax regimes, new competition, geographic and climatic conditions, commercial infrastructure rules, buyer preferences, product guarantees, packaging guidelines, standards of living, and much more."

"Whew," breathed Derrick. "I don't know if we have enough hands to deal with all those things. And it sounds like a lot of lawyers and consultants."

"It comes with the new territory," smiled Jada. "One famous study called it 'the liability of foreignness.'[3] No matter how smart and analytical you are, you will be at least somewhat unfamiliar with the new environment's cultural, political, and economic wrinkles—and possibly the discriminatory treatment by local officials."

She looked around to see if anyone's enthusiasm had faded. What she saw instead was determination. *It's time to bring out more tools!* she thought. "The good news," she said, "is that it's all figure-outable!"

Conrad decided it was time for some encouragement as well. "There are thousands of amazing international expansion success stories—just look at IKEA. A small, odd, out-of-the-way Swedish furniture store conquers the world. Amazing but true. So don't let the complications stop you from becoming an international strategic thinker."

Analytic frameworks for managing the risk of going global

When the group had settled back into the conference room, Derrick raised his hand as Conrad started drawing on the whiteboard.

"Whatcha got, Derrick?" asked Jada.

"If you are about to walk us through a framework to analyze the conditions on the ground of where we might expand to, why didn't we just start there and save some time?"

"Fair question," conceded Jada. "And you could be right—as we discussed a few weeks ago, the correct order of a strategic-thinking process is less important than just making sure you have all the pieces in there somewhere. However, try this on for size."

Derrick folded his arms and looked skeptical.

Conrad and Jada now understood the lay of the land for each CEO. Liz and her people saw an opportunity in similar Canadian markets close to their current geographies. Steve saw promise in brand licensing prompted by inquiries from overseas companies. Derrick was eyeing offshore manufacturing because it could double his margins.

Jada said to Derrick, "Now that we know what your international strategies might be—store expansion, a variation of local products, and outsourced production—we can target specific geographies in our analysis and their likely complications. That will add to your strategic-thinking powers."

"Okay," said Derrick. "Time to drill down. But does that analysis, factored into our cost-benefit work, give us a go or no-go decision? Or several? A yes to, say, Mexico and Vietnam, but a no to China, for instance?"

"Sounds like you're looking for magical thinking again," said Jada. She scanned the faces around the table. "Nice try, folks!"

She laughed with everyone.

"Insights, just insights," said Derrick. "No magic answers. Forgive me. You can't pull any single lever and have the right answer pop out."

"Forgiven and forgotten," said Jada. "Conrad and I still haven't found that fantasy machine. Wish we had!"

"Still," said Conrad, "what thinking through the frameworks will reveal is that you are likely to have many options for expanding—think back to our build, borrow, or buy framework for corporate strategy. You'll have many ways to crack the international code."

Conrad went back to drawing at the board. "*But!*" he said. "We are getting ahead of ourselves. Behold, the PESTEL framework."

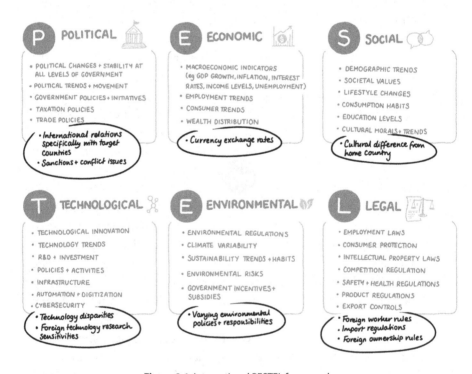

Figure 8.1 International PESTEL framework

"Again?" said Liz. "You dropped that on us when we analyzed our external environment."

"Just so," said Conrad. "But we're now applying it to international markets, and in this case, some of the categories have new subcategories that can be global expansion killers. So, think of this as PESTEL super-charged."

"Can you point to the key ones?" asked Liz. "It's quite an eye chart up there."

Conrad twirled his finger as if beckoning a simple answer. Then he pointed to the board. "Let's look under 'P' for the political category. If we weren't going international, we might think about changes in a local, state, or federal administration, regional policies, or some regulatory trends or laws. But internationally, we also need to consider government stability, national rules for foreign companies, global trade regulations, and the state of relations with our country. My old strategy professors would tell you that war and conflict are normal affairs abroad, and peace is abnormal. Domestically, of course, we don't think that way."

"A messy business," said Steve. "Look at the past few years of trade with the EU and Asia—suddenly, tariffs are everywhere."

"Just so," said Conrad. "If you import goods made elsewhere, that can be a huge factor for you. But in the big picture, not only have trade wars heated up, actual wars have too. Even cold wars. American manufacturers flocked to China in the early 2000s. Since then, they have been looking for alternatives due to political tensions between the US and China. No region of the world—and no business in those regions—is unaffected by political turmoil."

"Political risk analysis," Jada added, "is much more complicated when hopping from country to country—India versus South Africa versus Venezuela versus Romania—than making the same judgments for Denver, Kansas City, Dallas, and Houston ... or London, Manchester, and Birmingham."

"Today's headlines tell that story," agreed Kurt. "But how about the 'E' for economic? What might be unique about that category, unrelated to geopolitics and local political movements?"

"Exchange rates, for one thing," said Jada. "We've seen international expansion plans where the margins needed for success were blown away simply by currency fluctuations."

"But you'll need to consider much more else as well," said Conrad. "Credit accessibility, inflation and unemployment rates, interest rates, and more."

"And how about the 'S' for social?" said Kurt.

"I lived in Europe for years," offered Liz. "Unlike Canada, I would say that culture is the make-or-break social factor there. I found it easy to underestimate how different people are on a cultural level—and how it drives their lifestyle and consumer choices."

"Very true," said Jada. "As the saying goes, 'Culture eats strategy for breakfast.' If culture includes values, systems of belief, and patterns of behavior, who wouldn't fail if they didn't understand that about a potential new market?"[4]

"And the same is true of all the PESTEL factors," said Conrad. "Legal, environmental, technological—they can all eat strategy for breakfast."

"And lunch and dinner," added Jada. "Think of the profound trends shaping our world. In one gulp, they can swallow the most pragmatic of strategies."

"I get that," said Steve. "The PESTEL trends vary from place to place. However, many global trends transcend boundaries. Don't they affect every company on the globe similarly in some respects?"

"Sure," agreed Conrad. "But what we have seen in international business that matters is not so much that there is a global trend—let's say rapidly diminishing birth rates in northeast Asia or rapid urbanization in Africa—but rather what governments are doing about it. That can differ tremendously from jurisdiction to jurisdiction. So, technology trends may be one thing—technology policies are quite another. Look at how the EU treats Apple's and Google's dominant market positions differently than in the US."

"Creativia is looking at a few different places to put our offshore manufacturing facility," Derrick said. "Even our early look shows a wide variety of regulations for the environment, local employment, power usage, taxes, and a dozen other things. All the geographies we're considering are similar economically. But the environmental rules and regulations are so different."

"Circling back to the political category," said Kurt, "I bet you're weighing various incentives that local officials are offering—or not offering—to get Creativia's facility?"

"All so tempting," replied Derrick. "But our lawyers gave us a twenty-page brief on what a legal incentive for companies is versus what a violation of US bribery laws is. It's not like you can assume everything you learned in grade school applies elsewhere."

"Right—and here we are back at social and cultural elements," said Jada. "What we might consider illegal payoffs—'baksheesh' in some of the world—are a customary part of business in some regions. US companies regularly get into trouble for crossing that line."

"What about intellectual property protection?" said Steve. "We're worried about getting ripped off by licensing our brand to a foreign company to create its own variation of Secure Home Suite. I was talking with Suzie, and she said Andromeda eGaming's best anti-tamper software still doesn't stop rampant illegal IP copying."

"We think about intellectual property differently than in many other parts of the world," replied Jada. "And our laws—and theirs—reflect that. In some more communitarian cultures, people scoff at the idea of an individual owning an idea, or other kinds of property. Ideas about what is corruption, what is good conduct—these are things you can't assume are the same worldwide."

"Knowing what you're getting into is the best advice we can leave you with here, I think," said Conrad.

Steve spoke up. "You two mentioned something earlier this morning about measuring distance. But in your usual fashion, you seemed to be speaking figuratively, not literally. What were you getting at?"

Jada smiled at him. "What!?" she said in mock horror. "Strategists thinking figuratively or in analogies? Shocking."

When the laughter settled down, Jada explained the concept.

"Naturally, when it comes to distance, it's typical to first think about geographic distance, as Liz did with Canada. But distance can be measured in other ways that can profoundly impact your business plans. How do you weigh them all? One way is with the CAGE Distance framework."[5]

Conrad was drawing on the board as she spoke.

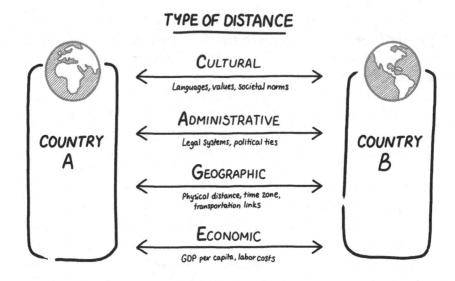

TYPE OF DISTANCE

CULTURAL
Languages, values, societal norms

ADMINISTRATIVE
Legal systems, political ties

GEOGRAPHIC
Physical distance, time zone, transportation links

ECONOMIC
GDP per capita, labor costs

COUNTRY A

COUNTRY B

Figure 8.2 CAGE Distance framework

(Source: Inspired by ideas in Ghemawat, P. (2001). Distance still matters: The hard reality of global expansion. *Harvard Business Review, 79*(8), pp. 137–147.)

"In this framework, we look at distance other than pure geography," said Conrad. "We also include cultural, administrative, and economic distance."

"Is distance here really just another way of saying differences?" asked Liz.

"Yes, I think so," said Jada. "The more different they are from you, the further the distance from you, so to speak. So, Liz, which is closer to your headquarters in Portland, Oregon—China or India?"

"Geographically, China is I suppose," observed Liz. "I know from looking at supply chains that a ship steaming from Mumbai to Portland goes 2,000 more miles than one from Shanghai."

"But administratively, India might be closer to you than China," said Jada. "The Indian legal and administrative system, because of the country's unique history, is based on English law and civil administration traditions. So, too, the American system, because of the US's unique history. Both countries have put their own twist on these somewhat common points of origin, but both have far more in common with each other administratively than either do with the same systems in China."

"Thus, India is 'closer,' administratively," said Liz.

"Yep."

"This could be a good parlor game," quipped Derrick.

"Or a good test of your analysis of different possible international moves," said Conrad. "In the end, all four kinds of distance matter. You need to measure them, and stress test your strategies against them."

"One study," said Jada, "found that countries that are not 'distant' from each other in key ways—even if they are distant geographically—will trade twenty-nine times more with each other than countries that don't share such commonality that brings them 'closer.'"[6]

More than one way to skin the cat

"You've both laid out the things we need to think about pretty clearly," said Liz. "Here I thought it was all easy because I was only talking about Canada."

"Going global is not something you want to screw up by just jumping on the first lead," said Conrad. "That's for sure. But it's very doable, especially if you don't put too much pressure on yourself to reinvent your corporate wheel singlehandedly."

Conrad then explained that Liz, Steve, and Derrick could adopt various approaches to executing an international expansion. Many of these approaches involved partnerships with others, giving them options for entering a new market in different ways. He listed them from least to most complicated.

He went to the board and wrote:

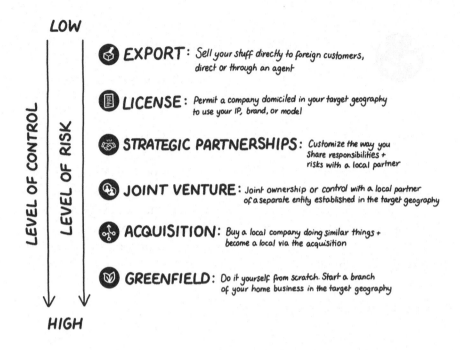

LOW

EXPORT: Sell your stuff directly to foreign customers, direct or through an agent

LICENSE: Permit a company domiciled in your target geography to use your IP, brand, or model

STRATEGIC PARTNERSHIPS: Customize the way you share responsibilities + risks with a local partner

JOINT VENTURE: Joint ownership or control with a local partner of a separate entity established in the target geography

ACQUISITION: Buy a local company doing similar things + become a local via the acquisition

GREENFIELD: Do it yourself from scratch. Start a branch of your home business in the target geography

LEVEL OF CONTROL

LEVEL OF RISK

HIGH

Figure 8.3 Modes of market entry in international business

"Where does my offshoring set of decisions fit?" asked Derrick.

Jada replied, "Well, you know that it is cheaper offshore, and there are different risk profiles in different geographies thanks to the PESTEL and CAGE frameworks, but you then have to think through some mode-of-entry choices."

Derrick thought for a moment. "I guess I see some options. We could contract with an offshore manufacturing shop to do the job and get charged by the pound, so to speak. Or we could partner with a local manufacturer who requires some investment from us. We might have to buy the machine tools, for instance. Alternatively, we could buy an offshore manufacturer in a similar business and own it outright. And finally, we could flat out build our own overseas plant from scratch."

"The whole spectrum is open to you," said Jada. "And like the general model Conrad drew up, you can see that your degree of control ranges from less to more. And so does the risk."

Kurt smiled. "Another session with no magic answers and lots of homework."

"But you do know how to do the homework and get to the answers that might work for you, yes?" said Conrad.

"Yes, that's a relief," said Liz. "For my part, I'm going to relook at this Canadian expansion idea from my team and subject it to these frameworks for analysis and decision-making. Maybe we jumped the gun. We were excited because it seemed close and felt familiar."

"And it might be!" said Jada. "But familiarity with the market attractiveness alone can mask the complications of going global. There are a lot of decisions about the degree to which you need to adapt your value proposition, the modifications you might need to make to your business model to deal with operating in a foreign environment, the particular risks of 'distance' as we defined it, and the different modes of entry you can choose from based on all that. But don't give up on the market idea until you work through that."

"Yes, it is very possible that HFF could do well in those nearby Canadian markets," agreed Conrad. "But remember that great phrase you heard earlier, the 'liability of foreignness,' which is from global business expert Juan Alcácer.[7] He would warn that even if you established a very local competitive advantage in some markets in Canada, you might still be challenged by unfamiliarity with environmental, cultural, political, and economic differences, geographic distance, discriminatory treatment by local governments, and so on. As Walmart and the NFL learned, among others, it is not easy to replicate what works in one place with what works somewhere else."

"Fair warning," replied Liz. "We now have some ways to get out ahead of that in our thinking so whatever decision we make it will be an informed one."

Conrad and Jada's key takeaways

Key factors in measuring an **international market's attractiveness:**

- The market's size and growth rate
- PESTEL considerations
- The competitive environment
- Distance (CAGE framework)

Three basic strategies to compete on the global stage:

- **Aggregation**—achieving economies of scale by standardizing regional or global operations.
- **Adaptation**—boosting market share by customizing processes and offering to meet the unique needs of local markets.
- **Arbitrage**—exploiting the differences in markets.

CAGE framework for measuring "distance" (differences):

- Cultural distance
- Administrative distance
- Geographic distance
- Economic distance

Key decisions of a firm when globalizing:

- Value proposition adaptation decisions—adapting the company's basic value proposition/business model for a new global market/new customers.
- Quality and appearance of products/services, materials, processing, production, packaging, marketing, sales, style, brand, etc.
- Degree of modification required to conform to government regulations, competition, geographic and climatic conditions, commercial infrastructure, buyer preferences, product guarantees, packaging design, standard of living, and target market purchasing power.

Options for **modes of entry** into international markets:

- Exporting
- Licensing
- Strategic alliances and joint ventures
- Direct investment—acquisitions and greenfields

Works cited and recommendations for further study

Books

DeKluyver, C. A. (2010). *Fundamentals of Global Strategy: A Business Model Approach.* Hampton, NJ: Business Expert Press.

DeKluyver, C. A., and Pearce, J. A. (2015). *Strategic Management: An Executive Perspective.* Hampton, NJ: Business Expert Press, chapters 8 and 9.

Ghemawat, P. (2007). *Redefining Global Strategy: Crossing Borders in a World Where Differences Still Matter.* Boston, MA: Harvard Business School Press.

Ghemawat, P., and Jones, G. (2017). Globalization in historical perspective. In Ghemawat, P. (ed.), *The Laws of Globalization and Business Applications* (pp. 56–81). New York, NY: Cambridge University Press.

Hamel, G., and Prahalad, C. K. (2018). Do you really have a global strategy? In Buckley, P. J. (ed.), *International Business* (pp. 285–94). London: Routledge.

Jones, G. (1996). *The Evolution of International Business.* London: Routledge.

Articles

Alcácer, J. (2014). Competing globally. *Harvard Business School Course Overview Note* 713-422, March 2014.

Carr, C., and Collis, D. (2011). Should you have a global strategy? *MIT Sloan Management Review.* https://sloanreview.mit.edu/article/should-you-have-a-global-strategy/, published September 21, 2011, accessed September 17, 2024.

Ghemawat, P. (2007). Managing differences: The central challenge of global strategy. *Harvard Business Review, 85*(3), 58-68.

Hout, T., Porter, M., and Rudden, E. (1982). How global companies win out. *Harvard Business Review, 60*(5), 98-108.

Notes for Chapter 8

1   Ghemawat, P. (2007). Managing differences: The central challenge of global strategy. *Harvard Business Review, 85*(3), 58–68 for the three A's framework.

2   Ibid.

3   See Alcácer, J. (2014). Competing globally. *Harvard Business School Course Overview Note* 713-422, March 2014.

4   A definition drawn from Edgar Schein. See Schein, E. H. (2010). *Organizational Culture and Leadership.* 4th ed. San Francisco, CA: Jossey-Bass.

5   Ghemawat, P. (2007). *Redefining Global Strategy: Crossing Borders in a World Where Differences Still Matter.* Boston, MA: Harvard Business School Press.

6   DeKluyver, C. A. (2010). *Fundamentals of Global Strategy: A Business Model Approach.* Hampton, NJ: Business Expert Press.

7   Alcácer, J. (2014). Competing globally. *Harvard Business School Course Overview Note* 713-422, March 2014.

Chapter 9

Creating a Plan and Keeping Score:
A Dialogue on Strategic Planning and Execution

"The most successful strategies are visions, not plans."
—*Strategy professor* HENRY MINTZBERG

Alexis Chapman, the CEO of Celar Logistics, has committed to a new strategic direction for her company and is anxious to get started. In considering how to implement the strategy and track its execution, Alexis, along with Kurt and Derrick, learn that strategic thinking and strategic planning are not only different things but in the corporate world are often even opposites. Instead of treating the strategy-implementation process as a rote-planning exercise or annual budget drill, Alexis discovers how to make strategic planning useful and cognizant of strategic thinking. She is also able to pick a strategic-planning method that best fits her company and situation. At the end of the conversation, the team is left with a series of frameworks to track the most common foibles that prevent companies from successfully realizing their strategy, how to avoid those traps, and how to track progress.

Strategic planning and strategic thinking are two different things

Alexis Chapman rubbed her hands together briskly, as if trying to start a fire. "Alrighty, now," she exclaimed, "it's time to stop thinking and start working!" Like Kurt and Derrick, who were on hand for today's conversation, she was itching to implement her strategic ideas.

She was teasing Conrad and Jada with this comment, poking fun at their love of thought before action. She raised her eyebrows and laughed to show that she was just ribbing the consultants.

Jada laughed and she felt sympathetic toward Alexis. Executives always longed to turn from the armchair-like, intellectual path of strategic thinking to the freeway of strategic implementation. What could be more natural? A bias toward action was good in a leader.

"Sorry to tease, but I'm an operator," said Alexis proudly. "I've spent my career as a logistics planner and operator—for the Air Force and now in my own company. I like putting steps on paper and assigning tasks to people. I'm ready to roll out this strategy like clockwork."

"Understood," said Conrad. "You're paid for producing real outcomes, not just having strategic thoughts. Time to put shoulders to the strategic implementation wheel."

"To the wheel!" said Alexis, agreeably. "And at Celar Logistics, we've jumped right to it. I've got the outlines of a plan with all the steps we need to take, who takes charge of what, when they should finish."

Conrad and Jada looked at each other.

Alexis kept talking, not noticing the consultants' doubtful faces. "Heck, yes," she went on, "in a company full of people with project-management certifications, developing a strategic plan is not hard."

"Not hard, eh?" said Conrad, pausing. "Well, maybe that can be true sometimes."

Alexis's eyes narrowed. "Don't be throwing some new voodoo into the room now, Conrad, right when we're crouched at the starting line and ready to run—and based on your guidance."

"No voodoo," Conrad said in a soft voice. "I'm just not sure that was our guidance."

Alexis rolled her eyes. "We followed your guidance to a T."

Conrad didn't want to get the day's conversation off on the wrong foot. He knew from experience that at this point in his strategic-thinking work, executives assumed they had grasped the whole picture. Alexis was not the only one in the room today who assumed as much. So did Kurt and the other executive joining, Derrick. Talented executives knew plenty about strategic implementation and didn't think they needed to learn much from consultants.

And yet Conrad and Jada did have more guidance to share. The story of how to become a complete strategic thinker didn't end with international expansion. It continued with how to take all that earlier thinking through to implementation. The handoff was not as straightforward and predictable as executives thought.

"What if I told you that strategic planning and strategic thinking are not the same thing?" Conrad said.

Alexis crossed her arms. "I'd say I don't know what you're talking about."

"And what if I told you they can even work at cross purposes to each other?"

Alexis was silent.

Jada leaned into the silence and said diplomatically, "Look, we're all on the same sheet of paper. The next step in thinking strategically is to discuss planning and implementation so that your vision happens—and the plan genuinely executes your strategy."

Alexis said stiffly, "It's hard to disagree with that. But I do execution year in and year out and make a lot of money while I'm at it. No brag, just fact: I'm an expert at planning and execution."

> *Strategic planning and strategic thinking are not necessarily the same thing and can even work at cross purposes to each other.*

Conrad and Jada appreciated that Kurt, Alexis, and Derrick were experts. They also understood that the executives had tired from traveling a long road with them and were eager to jump to execution. At this point, that road had taken them through deep dives into changing markets to understand their forces of competition, turned the mirror on themselves and dug out their hard-to-match core competencies, identified strategic initiatives to position themselves for greater advantage in the market, and honed business models to make their preferred strategic initiatives profitable.

And yet Conrad and Jada knew from the failures they had seen before that the no-brag-just-fact executives would still trip up if they didn't connect thinking and implementing in one smooth operation. "You're an expert, yes," said Conrad. "The question, though, is how to make sure you apply your expertise in implementation in such a way that it's driven by your new expertise in strategic thinking."

Conrad looked to Jada, and she could tell he was ready to hand off the conversation to her fully.

"Let's talk about the outlines of the plan you've put together," Jada said. "How did you do that? Or better yet, let's back up. How has Celar done its strategic planning in the past?"

"Annually, in the early fall," Alexis said. "We start planning for the new calendar year around September—each department rolling up its budgets and plans for the new year, including wish lists for improvements and new initiatives. My management team and I rack and stack the departmental plans, layer some corporate initiatives on top, and negotiate to get to a final strategic plan for the new year."

"So," said Jada, "it sounds like your annual budget drill doubles as your strategic-planning process."

"I suppose so," said Alexis. "But I have no problem with that. We run a tight ship and always seek to improve and advance. Our process makes sure we don't overdrive our headlights."

"Right ... okay," said Jada. "But if the baseline for that planning process is always the past year's performance, you're directing your thinking back in time."

"Sure—but what's wrong with that?" said Alexis. "Back to the past where we have data we can rely on to gauge forward motion."

"Because going back to past data can drag your thinking backward. And that creates a disconnect. You want to look forward as a strategic thinker and not backward as a strategic planner. The landscape may look entirely different depending on which way you're facing."[1]

"You know," said Derrick, joining the conversation, "we do an annual planning and budget drill too—I don't know many companies who don't. There's no way to implement without it."

"True, true," said Jada. "And there's nothing wrong with that. But remember the difference between such necessary planning—mistakenly called 'strategic' in our minds—and true strategic thinking, the kind you have done with us over the past few weeks."

"Strategic thinking," continued Jada, "is constantly thinking about the economic ecosystem in which your business exists and how it might change. Suppose your strategic planning is driven by the calendar or the budget, by the known and processed, by familiar objectives known to be accomplishable. In that case, it tends not to have a forward-looking strategic perspective—or at least not very far forward."

Strategic thinking is about envisioning a future that has not yet happened and ideal outcomes in it.

"Okay," said Derrick, "so maybe sometimes we adopt a backward gaze as demanded by 'the drill.'"

"And you should," said Conrad. "But a caution: remember the study we discussed weeks ago showing that only a few executives naturally use a strategic 'action' logic?"

"Yes—it showed that executives who are good at getting things done tend not to think long-term and big-picture to make their case," said Derrick.[2]

"That's right," said Conrad.

"I guess I'm a bit guilty of that," said Alexis. "And I remember you saying that most executives—the great majority—are more oriented toward short-term achievements and using data-driven expertise to make their decisions."

"That's just what the study says," said Jada. "So-called 'achievers' and 'experts' make up two thirds of the executive population, strategists only four percent."

"And that's normal," said Conrad reassuringly.

"More than normal in a company like mine," admitted Alexis. "Our culture worships the time-budget-schedule trinity. We are oriented toward action and hitting our logistical goals. We are engineers, supply chain experts, operations management gurus, logisticians."

"Achievers and experts?" asked Jada.

Strategic thinkers focus constantly on the economic ecosystem in which the business exists and how it might be changing. If strategic planning is driven by the calendar or the budget, by the known data, and by familiar objectives known to be accomplishable, it tends not to have a forward-looking strategic perspective.

"I guess that's the case. We get the job done. But I think of that as a strength, and you're saying it's a problem?"

"Not a problem in the right context," said Conrad. "But it comes with a downside. If you remain in the mode of an achiever or expert as you do your strategic plan, you might end up with a list of things people know they can do because they've done it before."

"Your strategy," said Jada, "on which you've worked really hard, shows how you might shape your future to your advantage. But, suppose you plan based on what you know now and what is accomplishable today. In that case, you risk dragging your planning backward into the comfort of the known past—not forward into the ambiguity of the unknown future."

"Okay, I'm getting it," said Alexis. "Our implementation becomes orphaned from our thinking. It doesn't carry our strategic insights forward."

Conrad stood up. "That's the risk."

"Okay," said Derrick, "I'm also getting what you mean. But how big a risk is it?"

"Let me throw up some of the differences between thinking and planning on the flipcharts to see if that adds some clarity."[3]

Conrad knew he had a hard sell on his hands. Executives like Alexis and Derrick had delivered stellar results for Kurt for years based on their execution skills. He wasn't surprised, as he finished at the flipcharts, that he was meeting resistance.

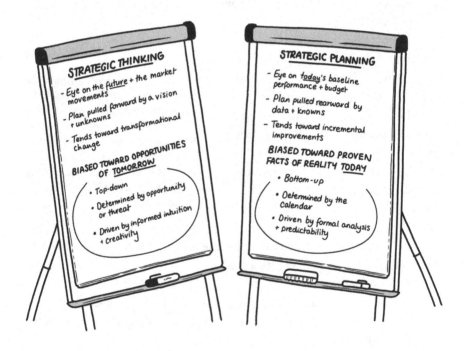

Figure 9.1 Comparing strategic thinking and corporate planning

"But aren't you exaggerating the distinction," said Derrick, "so you can make your case? It feels … well, a little forced."

Conrad looked at him thoughtfully. "It's a bold characterization, I agree. But the distinction holds—and matters. If you engage in corporate planning—and call it strategic planning—you tend to root strategy implementation in the known past instead of freeing yourself to tackle the unknowns of the future."

Derrick wasn't satisfied. "But this makes it seem like strategic thinking is some dreamy exercise divorced from reality, and the type of 'strategic' planning we've done in the past is simply adding five percent better performance to last year's plan. That seems unfair."

"Unfair, perhaps," said Jada, "but your objection is helping us make our point. We're talking about two different methods for moving into the future. One is more likely to produce a vision of a different future, and the other is more likely to offer some modest improvement on past performance."

"Okay," said Derrick. "I actually want both! Change to the new us and improvement of the old us."

"I get it," said Jada. "Admittedly, Conrad's list doesn't completely represent the reality you face daily. But the distinctions he's making are instructive, and they're true enough that you should think of them as lessons from a cautionary tale. Too often companies fail at the strategic transformation because they planned for the modest improvements—even accidentally!"

Alexis leaned in. "I understand what you're saying in my head," she said. "But my heart says that one approach feels airy-fairy and the other feels locked down and rigorous."

"Thinking and implementation are rigorous exercises," argued Conrad. "Good strategic thinking is not 'airy-fairy.' It relentlessly aligns opportunities in the changing market with your capabilities. You then wrap your strategic plan around that."

> Standard corporate planning can sometimes root strategy implementation in the known past, offering modest improvement as progress. True strategic planning should free the firm to tackle the unknowns of the future with new ideas.

"Strategic thinkers always look forward," he added. "They're not trying to get one percent more out of the current company—but rather figuring out what the company needs to be to thrive in the future. As leaders, think of your job as not just running the company you are, but creating the company you *are not*—yet."

"I can tell you that we do the annual budget drill at Argo Ventures," said Kurt. "While we sometimes bat around ideas for change based on the market, our planning process is built of a bottom-up assessment based on last year's numbers and trend lines."

> *Thinking and implementation are rigorous exercises, not just academic exercises. Good strategic thinking relentlessly aligns opportunities in the changing market with your capabilities.*

"That puts you in the company of ninety percent of firms," said Jada. "We call that strategic *programming*. If you're only thinking that way—through the known numbers—it is hard to forecast discontinuities or create novel strategies. That method mostly pulls a company toward the details of standard business execution instead of creating a new approach or direction in a dynamic market."

"Okay, okay," said Alexis impatiently. "I get it, I get it. Point made. But I'm still not sure I buy it."

"And what's your hesitation in buying it?" asked Jada.

"It sounds to me like you're saying that strategic planning is a waste of time, and that can't be true."

"You're right—that's not true," said Jada. "Strategic planning is super useful—I can't imagine getting to the future without it."

"The question is," said Conrad, "how do you make sure that strategic thinking flows into strategic planning so you get the best results? How can you be sure that your thoughts about the future inform action in the present? As a start, you want to choose the right tool at the right time and use it in the right way."

"Experience shows," said Jada, "that you can avoid many of the risks if you follow what I call my commandments for strategic planning." She went to the board.

1. **Do your strategic thinking first, then construct your plan around that.**

2. **Make your starting point and your most important strategic metrics customer-, revenue-, market-, or competition-based, not cost-structure- or current-capabilities-based.**

3. Strategies are best formulated outside-in but executed inside-out. Start with the external environment in the analysis and then base execution on internal considerations.

4. Ask the right questions about customers, market dynamics, and competitors—and challenge all assumptions.

5. Make your process and people comfortable with discomfort. Do not turn strategic ideas into problems that can be "solved" with tried-and-tested tools. Everybody loves the knowable, controllable, and predictable, but true innovation and strategic breakthroughs often come from embracing uncertainty and exploring the unknown.

6. Make room in discussion and analysis for intuitive (not definitive) thinking. Combine rigor with creativity. Ask questions like:[4]
   - What would have to be true for this to happen?
   - What would it take to achieve this?

7. Don't let the fact that strategy emerges as events unfold become an excuse to declare the future so volatile that you cannot make choices. Stuff happens—lean into that.

8. Keep it simple.

9. Embrace the intelligent unknown; this is not about perfection—but a bet.

10. The process is more important than the plan. As President Dwight Eisenhower said, "Plans are worthless, but planning is everything."[5]

From thinking to action

The group reconvened after a break. Kurt and Alexis had talked privately, and Alexis had come to the conclusion that the distinction between strategic thinking and planning would indeed make life easier for her when implementing a strategic plan at Celar Logistics. Derrick felt the same way, starting to see the value of this new distinction for Creativia Playsets.

"It makes sense to me," said Alexis. "We need to view strategic planning as the extension of all we've learned about strategic thinking—to stay focused on the future, the market, and change."

Conrad and Jada nodded, obviously pleased that Alexis was now on board.

Embrace the intelligent unknown. This is not about perfection—but an educated bet on the future.

"But, given that I'm a loggie," Alexis added, "I still wouldn't mind having a template for the plan I need to create that captures our strategic thinking. Have you got one of those in your kit bag?"

"I'm glad you asked," said Conrad. He stood up and went to the whiteboard and drew a familiar diagram, one the group had looked at in a different context a few weeks earlier. "I hope you see this diagram in a new light."

"An old picture is worth a thousand words you didn't discover the first time," said Alexis. "Yes, it puts strategic planning in its proper place, so to speak."

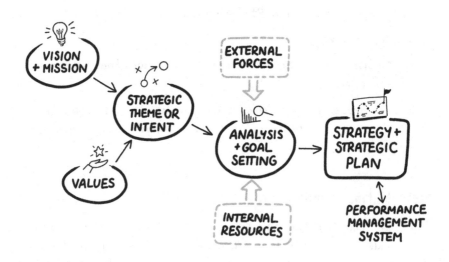

Figure 9.2 Strategic planning as the extension of strategic thinking

"You see how your strategic plan," said Conrad, "really should be an end product of the strategic-thinking process. That way, it can capture all the tough discussions and choices you made about purpose, mission, values, your changing market, your core competencies, and your various strategic choices."

"I do remember that. But what I could really use," said Alexis, "is a rubric which shows the flow of thinking into the plan itself. At a firm like ours with a checklist culture, we like to mark progress by ticking off boxes."

"Sure," Conrad said. "Let me see if I can match Jada's ten commandments with my ten strategic-planning steps, starting with some boxes you've already ticked."[6]

STRATEGIC PLANNING STEPS

1. Analyze external trends.

2. Analyze past strategies (yours and others!).

3. Evaluate the current strategy (especially what competitive advantages it did or did not give you).

4. Analyze internal capabilities (core competencies especially—and resources).

5. Generate new strategic options around your aspirations—an imagined excellent future (this is a creative exercise, while the first four were analytical).

6. Identify actions and resources needed to undertake and realize the options.

7. Analyze/model the risks of each possible option; weigh the pros and cons.

8. Pick an option.

9. Form a project plan to get there.

10. Have a mechanism/system to follow up, check progress, assign accountability, allocate resources, and provide oversight.

"Love it," said Alexis, taking notes. "Cut and dried—no problem."

"Well, yes—and no," replied Conrad. "Let's talk about a few other factors that pose a challenge as you flow from thinking to action. Yes, the resulting plan—step nine—should be simple, not least because it needs to withstand bumping up against reality, which requires some flexibility. Remember what famous strategist and championship boxer Mike Tyson said: 'Everybody has plans until they get hit for the first time.'"[7]

The group laughed. "In the military, we said that no plan survives first contact with the enemy," offered Alexis.

"I would add the KISS principle to steps nine and ten—Keep It Simple, Sister," said Jada. "In a simple plan—*not* simplistic—it will be easier to track execution on the big things that really matter to the changes that you want to make."

Jada looked around the room at the nodding heads. A thought occurred to her.

"You know, gang?" she said. "Let's suspend the execution discussion for just a bit. We should first discuss *how* you plan for the future—there are different methods to think through the planning—and how to stress test your thinking during these ten steps."

Scenario-based and options-led strategic planning

"Uh-oh, more frameworks," said Kurt as Jada started drawing. "I'm running out of notebook!"

"Yes, Kurt," scolded Conrad playfully. "Another one to show you a different way to get to the decisions Alexis is dying to make and implement. Like all our frameworks, it's just a way to organize your thinking and process information coherently, ask the right questions, and spark conversations that surface insights."

"No right or wrong answer, correct?" asked Derrick. "It must have been hard for you two to grade tests in your strategy classes."

Jada turned back around. "No right or wrong answer," she agreed. "Every strategy tool is simply meant to drive you to consider and ultimately make choices—ones that position the firm for future advantage vis-à-vis the competition."

"So ... ta da! Here is another way to think about driving that process of making choices," Jada continued. "We take a common business problem, say, how to gain more market share. If we think about that problem as a strategic choice—with different strategic moves that might bring more market share—we can envision possibilities to solve that problem."

"Like create a new product or service," said Derrick.

"Or go into a new geography," said Alexis. "Or change our business model."

"Or enter into a partnership ... or do some M&A for vertical or horizontal integration," added Kurt.

"Yes—any of those—or a dozen more," agreed Jada.

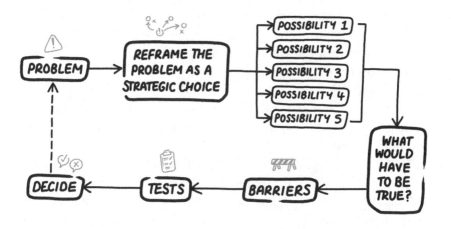

Figure 9.3 Making strategic choices
(Source: © 2013 by Roger L. Martin. Reprinted with kind permission by Roger L. Martin)

"And then we can look at the pros and cons of each possibility?" asked Alexis.

"Yes, but as you can see from the diagram, we still want to keep our minds open, and not let our quest for analysis and data based on the past shut down options that could prove valuable in the future. So we start by asking, 'What would have to be true for this possibility to be viable—and available to us?'"

"And then," said Kurt, pointing to the board, "we can see if what is needed to pursue that option is possible."

"Right," said Jada. "Life experience will tell you 'no' a lot—but go ahead and play out the implications anyway. Don't tell yourself 'no' too early in the process. Ask instead what it would take to get to 'yes'. If you're worried about being too optimistic, you can always test the options later before making a final choice."

"Don't negotiate against yourself, in other words," said Derrick.

"Precisely," agreed Conrad. "And another thing: don't let a preferred option win the day because everyone can understand it, and it's doable."

"Ah, you've been listening to my meetings!" said Alexis, now delighted to be talking through the details of planning.

"Tell us more," said Conrad.

"As you might expect, my firm prioritizes operational excellence. We're not too creative—we do what we know to work, what is proven. Do you know what we call somebody who is too creative in the logistics and delivery business?"

"Can't wait to hear it."

"Lost on their route," she said to laughter. "So, we do math. Engineers, operations managers, loggies—we love math, we love certainty, we love to crunch the data."

"So it's a challenge to generate creativity and keep an open mind in strategic planning," said Conrad.

"That's a fact. So, here's my concern: how can I keep creative options on the table for as long as possible before they are data'd to death by our best analysis?"

"A lot of it is just the rules around the flow of your discussion: the cycles of discussion that happen as you create and examine options," said Conrad. "How you focus those cycles determines the focus of options. For example, strategic-planning guru Jan Rivkin at Harvard said that executives shouldn't allow themselves to get focused on 'What should we do?' They should focus on 'What might we do?'"[8]

"Seemingly small changes in attitude can have a considerable result in practice," said Jada.

"Okay. I can keep the aperture wide open in the beginning," said Alexis, "but my people love to jump in with proof of what will and won't work based on their experience."

"Rivkin would say not to let them say what they believe based on what they know, but rather what they would *have* to believe for this option to work. Then you push the burden of proof into a more creative discussion."

> To keep creative options and discussions open for analysis, executives shouldn't allow themselves to get focused on 'What should we do?'. Instead they should focus on 'What might we do?'.

"It matters, too, who is in the room," said Jada. "Consider breaking up the planning teams to get people with different worldviews and perspectives facing each other. Include people who don't generally work together."

"That will all help," agreed Alexis. "My team and I circled quickly around a preferred direction related to one strategy we came up with. That seemed comfortable at first. But we folded our analysis around that to confirm it as the best direction—and I was worried about early conclusion bias."

"A strong possibility," said Conrad. "Settling on a decision too quickly while ignoring further analysis or alternative options is an easy pitfall."

"That's what I was thinking. I would feel more comfortable if we had several credible options on the table *before* we analyzed them and ultimately made a choice."

"That sounds wise to me," said Conrad. "To help you with that, let me give you one more way to force that kind of creative thinking. It's a good technique to bet on in companies that are culturally similar to yours—relying on precision performance, known data, and operational excellence for their success."

"Forcing creative thinking comes hard to us," said Alexis. "For us, it's about the math, not the artistry."

Conrad smiled. "Just so. One way to force math geniuses to the creative front lines is to use a method known as scenario-based planning. Form three or four cross-functional teams and have each separately examine a totally different—but still credible—*possible* future in which Celar Logistics would have to compete."

"Wouldn't your strategic choice be influenced most by scenarios you think are most likely?" asked Derrick. "The most likely may not be the best."

"Which is why you use scenarios initially to foster creativity and not decision-making," said Conrad. "The point is to remove the impetus to jump directly to one official corporate future. That process is worth doing in and of itself."

"So you play around in the sandbox of different possible futures before building your castle," said Derrick.

"Yes, and on top of that, playing around gets everyone more attuned to shifts in the strategic environment and the patterns of cause and effect in their market. The magic is not usually the accuracy of the scenarios, but the process of learning together to recognize when your castles are 'still in the air.' Using scenario-based planning can help avoid moving quickly to embrace one official corporate future—and spark more creative planning discussions."

> Using scenario-based planning can help avoid moving quickly to embrace one official corporate future—and spark more creative planning discussions.

"Sounds like Jada's tenth commandment in action!" said Kurt.

"Indeed," agreed Conrad, nodding to Jada. "Good scenario analysis can generate rich strategic discussions. It doesn't test who has the most accurate crystal ball showing the future. Ultimately, the winning scenario often combines characteristics from several possible futures. But the imposition of the method—considering very different futures separately—often forces operational-excellence-type firms to confront more than just what they can perfectly understand and control."

"What is to prevent an unequal weighting on these scenario teams," Kurt asked, "where there are a few throwaway scenarios so people can pay lip service to the method and get back to where they were going to start anyway?"

"That happens," conceded Conrad. "We call that the Goldilocks staff method. People prepare options that are clearly too hot, and some too cold, and therefore the one they've liked from the beginning—often the status quo—is just right."

Kurt laughed.

"But," Conrad continued, "credible scenarios, well-formed teams, and objective and unbiased leadership can help for a more honest analysis—and ultimately a decision."

"And once we have settled on a strategic path," asked Alexis, "we put together an implementation plan?"

"Almost. Just one more thing to talk about after lunch," said Jada. "Before you commit to a project plan, we should discuss how to monitor those plans and avoid any air leaking from your new strategy balloon."

"Good idea," agreed Conrad. "Let's do that. For now, to close out this topic, I would advise that you remember principles rather than fill-in-the-box rubrics. Bookshelves groan under the weight of strategic-planning guides and templates—just use one that you think works best for you, like the ones we wrote on the board. Probably the most important thing to remember is that the strategic options you choose should pass three tests for alignment and consistency."[9]

He wrote on the board:

TEST 1: EXTERNAL ALIGNMENT

Your strategic options should confront + address the opportunities + threats in your external environment. No shadow boxing.
Opportunity gaps represent a misalignment between the environment + the strategy.

TEST 2: INTERNAL ALIGNMENT

The internal dimensions of the organization must be congruent. People, skills, values, behaviors, processes, workflows, organization, capital + structure must all be congruent. Performance gaps often represent a misalignment between the strategy + internal alignment of the firm's parts.

TEST 3: DYNAMIC ALIGNMENT

Is the strategy flexible enough to stay aligned with the changing environment in which it will be implemented? No strategy unfolds in a static environment but rather in an atmosphere of constant action + reaction.

Alexis finished taking notes and looked up. "Good, *now* I am ready to put my shoulder to the wheel. I guess I was too eager earlier this morning."

"We loved it," said Jada. "Every good executive should have a bias toward action. But I'm glad we got a chance to put more context and nuance around how you might construct your strategic plan. At the end of the day, especially with the skills on your team, your people will ultimately fill out a good project plan with the right priorities and sequencing to implement your new strategic initiatives. We're not worried about that."

"Most businesses are good at the 'getting-stuff-done' part," said Conrad. "It's the 'thinking-it-through' bit of the process where we come in handy."

"No doubt," said Alexis. "It sure helped me." She rose with everyone else to break for lunch.

"Oh," Alexis turned back to the room and spoke. "You mentioned that before I shoot off into execution mode, you wanted to talk about some common mistakes companies make in executing a strategy."

"Ah yes, the common foibles and pitfalls of getting it done," said Conrad. "Let's grab a bite and come back so we can share the wisdom of the ages with you on that."

"And give you some tools to monitor your path to change as well," added Jada.

Leakage and common problems during execution

Jada was drawing a picture of a large hot-air balloon on the whiteboard when the group filed back into the conference room after lunch. Without stopping, she asked to the room, "Alexis, Derrick, and Kurt, do you all keep score?"

They looked at each other. Kurt volunteered, "Umm … keep score?"

"Right," said Jada, turning around. "Like in sports. At any point in a baseball game, you can look up and see six, seven, or eight categories of measurement. Glancing at the scoreboard lets you know where you are in the game and how it's progressing. All facts! Nobody argues about which inning is being played or the number of strikes against the batter."

"Of course, yes," said Alexis. "We keep score in our own way. I mean, in logistics, it is pretty cut and dried about whether you got the shipment there, when you got it there, where it was in transit at any given time, and all the rest. We use OKRs—objectives and key results pushed down to the lowest levels—to ensure we're tracking whether we're working toward our goals."[10]

"Okay," said Jada. "Good—that is a solid performance management method, if used correctly. What about you, Derrick?"

"We also keep score in our own way," said Derrick. "We mainly rely on the creative ideas of our play design teams and the marketing we do through our channel partners. So, to track and manage performance, we use the 'Balanced Scorecard'—which gives us performance metrics in a handful of categories: financial, business processes, customer relationships, and learning and growth. We outsource some of our manufacturing, but we try to customize our approach to measure what matters for us."[11]

"Okay, good. What about Argo Ventures, Kurt?"

"We measure ourselves against our financial metrics. Ultimately, we're investors, generating returns for our shareholders, so the financials are key, like internal rate of return, multiple on invested capital, market value, and a few others. We set performance goals vis-à-vis our investors' expectations and against some competitive benchmarks."

"Excellent," said Conrad. "All good companies measure what matters, and the best ones adopt performance management metrics and systems that track the areas that matter most to your success."

Everyone nodded.

"So," said Conrad. "How could somebody screw up a good strategic plan? Well, they don't extend that very same keeping-score philosophy to tracking the implementation and effectiveness of their new strategic initiatives. They don't measure the 'new stuff' that represents the strategic vision and plan."

> All good companies measure what matters, and the best ones adopt performance management metrics and systems that track the areas that matter most to their success. Successfully strategies require measuring the new initiatives and changes that represent the strategic vision and plan.

Alexis looked troubled. "Are you saying I might need a whole new strategic-initiative tracking system for the new strategy, in addition to what we use now for current ops?"

"Not really," replied Conrad. "The thinkers who popularized the 'Balanced Scorecard' model of performance management showed how to use the same system to gauge strategic performance and generate strategic change—even transformation.[12] You can map back your strategic goals to your basic business performance categories."

"What about using a dashboard dedicated to what needs to change to accomplish the new strategy?" suggested Derrick.

"I love that idea!" said Jada. "Leaders are the change agents, and if you believe that part of your job is to create the company you want to become, and not just lead the company you are today, then you should be tracking achievements that capture the changes you are making in your strategic initiatives."

"But keep it simple," said Conrad. "You don't want your strategy to get measured to death just because you love data. Pick things that mark demonstrable progress and which clearly propel you to that place of sustainable competitive advantage. Put those big things in your performance management system."

"Sensible enough," said Alexis. She looked up at the whiteboard. "So, why the drawing of the hot-air balloon with holes?"

Jada smiled, "At the risk of admitting that we are not perfect, we wanted to leave you with some other lessons on what could go wrong when implementing a new strategy. The lessons of so-called leakage are probably far more important—and timeless—than the performance management system you choose to use."

"I do like to learn from the mistakes of others," said Alexis. She smiled at Kurt. "Cheaper that way."

"No strategy gets implemented perfectly," said Jada. "No balloon rises to the heavens without leakage. We can measure that leakage, too, not only in terms of performance and outcomes compared to desired objectives but in terms of the causes of reduced performance and outcomes. Anybody want to guess how much 'air' leaks from the average new strategy balloon?"

"Let me get this straight," said Kurt. "You can measure the leakage?"

"Sure," answered Conrad. "Or, at least, a number of researchers have. Looking across hundreds of new strategies, they analyzed actual versus expected financial performance for new strategies. It turns out that, on average, most companies' strategies deliver only sixty-three percent of their promised financial value."[13]

"And the other thirty-seven percent?" asked Derrick.

"Evaporated. Never accomplished. Leaked out!" said Jada, labeling holes in her balloon diagram. "The better question is *why*? What caused the leakage? The researchers dug deep into these experiences and identified the culprits. Let me show you the top five."

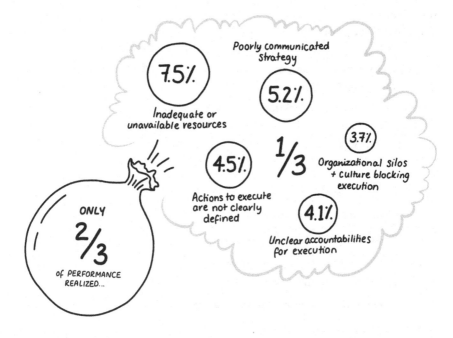

Figure 9.4 The common "leaks" in strategy execution

(Source: Own diagram based on data from Mankins, M. C., & Steele, R. (2005). Turning great strategy into great performance. *Harvard Business Review, 83*(7–8), pp. 56–72, p. 68.)

"I guess I'm surprised and not surprised at the same time," said Alexis. "Getting less than two thirds of performance value out of a new strategy is depressing, especially considering the energy and investment leaders put into it—let alone the upheaval it will cause the firm. On the other hand, these 'culprits' seem to be common management mistakes—and correctible?"

"In hindsight, anyway," said Conrad. "But the challenge is that all this can be invisible to top management until performance deteriorates, and then people pull the wrong levers to turn performance around. But it sure helps if you know the likely pitfalls ahead of time, get ahead of the deterioration curve, and reinforce certain areas before it's too late."

"That's one reason why a performance management system integrated with strategic warning indicators is so important," said Jada.

"I agree," said Kurt with a chuckle. "But do you two always work backward from what not to do to make the point about getting the most bang for your buck out of a new strategy?"

Conrad smiled. "No, we can be positive too—although I think the cautionary tales of human experience are a great way to 'go to school on somebody else's dime,' so to speak."

"So did this research not only point out the culprits but give ways to fix the leaks?" asked Derrick.

"Indeed, yes," said Jada as she drew and labeled repair patches on her balloon:[14]

- *Keep it simple*
- *Challenge assumptions*
- *Speak the same language*
- *Discuss resource deployments early*
- *Identify priorities*
- *Continuously monitor performance*
- *Develop execution ability*

"Such common sense," said Alexis. "And so commonplace. They remind me of how I often spend my day—my leadership life—getting the company to focus on avoiding these mistakes."

"Okay—let's look at another study that highlights other factors for getting maximum strategic performance," said Jada. "The data came from a comprehensive survey of thousands of people in thirty-one companies. The key question was: what are the most important traits for effectively implementing a strategy within an organization?"[15]

Jada put four categories on the board:

- *Information*
- *Decision rights*
- *Motivators*
- *Structure*

"The survey found that most leaders want to reorganize when a strategy starts to fail," said Jada. "But the data shows that issues of organizational structure turn out to be the least important trait of organizational effectiveness when it comes to successfully implementing a new strategy. Structural issues didn't even rank in the top ten of success factors."

"What ended up mattering the most?" asked Kurt.

"The first two categories," answered Jada. "Clarity over who has what information and who gets to make what kinds of decisions. Who knows what? And who decides what? Issues in those two categories were the top seven traits that organizations should have to implement a strategy successfully."

"Wow, that survey seems to reinforce, in its way, the balloon leakage data," said Derrick.

"People are people, it turns out," said Conrad. "And most companies are subject to the typical challenges of any human enterprise. We all know this, but we want to give you several frameworks to organize your new strategy efforts in such a way as to be cognizant of all that, and to lead more effectively as a result. Almost all the great strategic success stories aren't the result of some magic formula that appeared from a lab that nobody else could think of. Rather, they involved a concerted strategic thinking and management process that they applied relentlessly to create a new and better future. And in this case, learning from the lessons of others' struggles with effective implementation."

Alexis slammed her notebook shut. "Amen to that. Noooow I can get to work. Sound the charge!" she laughed.

"Hold that bugle for a second," cautioned Jada. "Let's leave you with one more powerful framework to have as a kind of strategy insurance policy. The more you think it through and apply it to yourself, the more likely you are to have strategic success."

She drew a few boxes on the board.

"It is called 'the Congruence model,'"[16] she said. "It's a great framework just to remind yourself of the need for alignment."

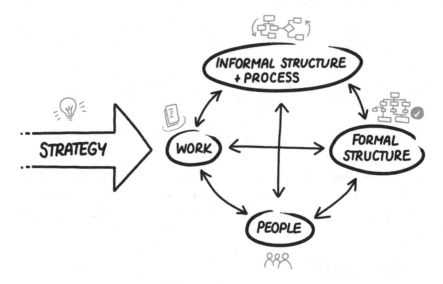

Figure 9.5 The Congruence model

(Source: Used with permission of The Academy of Management, from Nadler, D. A. & Tushman, M. L. (2006). Organizational frame bending: Principles for managing reorganization. *The Academy of Management Executive, 3*(3), pp. 194–204, p. 195; permission conveyed through Copyright Clearance Center, Inc.)

Derrick looked at the four boxes thoughtfully. "Okay, on the one hand it seems pretty simple—make sure all the pieces fit and support each other. But on the other hand, knowing you two, you wouldn't unveil it at the end of this workshop unless it went deeper."

Jada gave a mock look of horror to Conrad. "They're on to us!"

Conrad smiled. "As you know, we like complex ideas explained in simple—*not* simplistic—ways. The Congruence model reminds us of an essential truth in a company: just like a body in motion, all the parts must be aligned and working together to produce the best result."

He pointed to the board. "What we've found is that successfully implementing a strategy depends on the congruence of both the formal and the informal parts of the company. If your strategy calls for a new way to work, based on where you're going in the market, then that needs to be accompanied by supporting changes in the kinds of people and skills you have in the firm, the way the enterprise is organized and how it communicates and makes decisions, and also the values and behaviors that are needed."

"Seems pretty common sense to me," said Kurt.

"Until … it's not," said Jada. "Remember the three alignment tests Conrad put up on the board before our break? You would be amazed at how often this simple principle of alignment and congruence is ignored or not thought of when a firm rolls out a new strategy. Most people focus on closing the gap between where you want to get to in the competitive landscape and where you are now. The starting point of a strategy."

"Nothing wrong with that, correct?" asked Alexis.

"Nope," agreed Conrad. "But you can't do that to the exclusion of closing another potential gap—the execution gap—the one between what you hope to achieve and the actual results. The loss in performance, as we've seen, can often be traced to this lack of internal alignment with the needs of the strategy."

Kurt, Alexis, and Derrick nodded, but Jada could tell they were still only half following the concept.

"Okay, let's learn from real life," she said. "We recently worked with a respected management consulting company that wanted to be more high tech—and provide more original technology solutions to its clients rather than simply consulting services. Well, they put into place a sound strategy to build and acquire these technology capabilities. All good.

"But in implementing the strategy, they layered that new technology work and those new technology skills and those new technology people on top of a structure and a value system that still reflected the old management consulting company's values and behaviors—where all the senior managers in charge of the tech transformation had been employed for decades and decades by this firm as management consultants. I think, as a result, they blunted the impact that their strategic moves might have had—and did not get the max bang for their buck. Not everything was in congruence as they executed the strategy—just some parts."

"You can put a shiny new racing bumper and an airfoil on a reliable old pickup truck," added Conrad. "But unless you change a lot more about how the truck runs, those additions won't make the truck a race car."

"I see why you like this model as a kind of last reminder," said Alexis. "I guess firms trying to transform can be their own worst enemies sometimes."

"Yes, it's built into the difficulty of change," said Conrad. "But if you use these templates and frameworks to organize your thinking, prompt the right discussions with your teams, and stress test your strategic plan, you've got a better chance of getting most of what you want across the finish line."

Conrad and Jada's key takeaways

- **Planning** is about analysis, formalizing steps for almost auto-implementation. Data = The Present. Strategic thinking is about synthesis—involving intuition and creativity.

- **Formal strategic planning** from the bottom up can often simply justify the current reality—an implicit assumption that the world holds still while the plan is being developed and then goes on predictably.

- Make your starting point *and* your most important strategic metrics **customer-, revenue-, market-, or competition-based**—*not* cost-structure- or capabilities-based.

- Make your process and people **comfortable with discomfort**—do not turn strategic ideas into problems that can be "solved" with tried-and-tested tools. Everybody loves the knowable, controllable, and predictable, but needs to learn not to be dependent on it.

- Don't let the fact that strategy emerges as events unfold become an excuse to declare the future so volatile that you cannot make choices. **Stuff happens—lean into that.**

- **Measure what matters.** Pick a performance management system (such as OKRs or the Balanced Scorecard) that tracks the metrics that mark strategic progress and transformation—not just standard operational measurements.

- Beware of **common sources of "leakage"** in the implementation of a strategy—most of which deal with communication, information, decision-making authority, resources, and culture.

- Successfully implementing a strategy depends on the alignment, or **congruence**, of *both* formal and informal parts of the company. The type of work needed to transform the company must be underpinned by the right values and behaviors, the right people and skills, and the right structure and resourcing.

- **Ask:** what needs to change around here to accomplish this strategy?

- **Keep it simple.**

Works cited and recommendations for further study

Books

Covey, S., and McChesney, C. (2023). *The 4 Disciplines of Execution: Achieving Your Wildly Important Goals*. London, England: Simon & Schuster.

Doerr, J. (2018). *Measure What Matters: OKRs—The Simple Idea That Drives 10x Growth*. London, England: Portfolio Penguin.

Kaplan, R. S., and Norton, D. P. (1996). *The Balanced Scorecard: Translating Strategy into Action*. Boston, MA: Harvard Business School Press.

Kaplan, R. S., and Norton, D. P. (2000). *The Strategy-Focused Organization: How Balanced Scorecard Companies Thrive in the New Business Environment*. Boston, MA: Harvard Business School Press.

Kaplan, R. S., and Norton, D. P. (2004). *Strategy Maps: Converting Intangible Assets into Tangible Outcomes*. Boston, MA: Harvard Business School Press.

Lafley, A. G., and Martin, R. L. (2013). *Playing to Win: How Strategy Really Works*. Boston, MA: Harvard Business Review Press.

Mintzberg, H.(1994). *The Rise and Fall of Strategic Planning*. New York, NY: Free Press.

Nadler, D. A., and Tushman, M. L. (1997). *Competing by Design: The Power of Organizational Architecture*. New York, NY: Oxford University Press.

Rivkin, J., and Siggelkow, N. (2009). Organizational design: Balancing search and stability in strategic decision making. In Kleindorfer, P. R., and Wind, Y. (eds.), *The Network Challenge: Strategy, Profit, and Risk in an Interlinked World* (pp. 185-206). Upper Saddle River, NJ: Wharton School Publishing.

Rumelt, R. (2011). *Good Strategy Bad Strategy*. New York, NY: Crown Business.

Articles

Bourgeois, L. J. III. (2013). Developing a strategy. *Darden School of Business Technical Note* S-0232, published November 6, 2013. Charlottesville, VA: Darden School of Business.

Christense, C., Allworth, J., and Dillon, K. (2013). Is your strategy what you say it is? *Rotman Management Magazine*, August 2013.

Hamermesh, R. G. (1986). Making planning strategic. *Harvard Business Review,* 64(4), 115–120.

Hiatt, S. R., and Weber, J. (2012). Congruence model note. *Harvard Business School Technical Note* 413-037, August 2012 (revised October 2012). Boston, MA: Harvard Business Publishing.

Hillen, J. (2017). Are you a strategic thinker or just a planner? https://www.washingtontechnology.com/opinion/2016/08/are-you-a-strategic-thinker-or-just-a-planner/321804/, published August 16, 2016, accessed September 17, 2024.

Kaplan, R. S., and Norton, D. P. (1996). Using the balanced scorecard as a strategic management system. *Harvard Business Review, 74*(1), 75-85.

Kaplan, R. S., and Norton, D. P. (2000). Having trouble with your strategy? Then map it. *Harvard Business Review, 78*(5), 167-76.

Kenny, G. (2016). Strategic plans are less important than strategic planning. *Harvard Business Review Online.* https://hbr.org/2016/06/strategic-plans-are-less-important-than-strategic-planning, published June 21, 2016, accessed September 17, 2024.

Mankins, M. C, and Steele, R. (2005). Turning great strategy into great performance. *Harvard Business Review, 83*(7-8), 64-72.

Martin, R. L. (2014). The big lie of strategic planning. *Harvard Business Review, 92*(1-2), 78-84.

Mercer Delta Consulting, LLC (2004). The congruence model: A roadmap for understanding organizational performance. New York, NY: Mercer Delta Consulting, LLC.

Mintzberg, H. (1994). The fall and rise of strategic planning. *Harvard Business Review, 72*(1), 107-14.

Neilson, G. L., Martin, K. L., and Powers, E. (2008). The secrets to successful strategy execution. *Harvard Business Review, 86*(6), 60-70.

Reeves, M., Love, C., and Tillmanns, P. (2012). Your strategy needs a strategy. *Harvard Business Review, 90*(9), 76-83.

Rivkin, J. W. (2001). An options-led approach to making strategic choices. *Harvard Business School Background Note* 702-433, December 2001 (revised February 2006). Boston, MA: Harvard Business Publishing.

Simons, R. (2010). Stress-test your strategy: The 7 questions to ask. *Harvard Business Review, 88*(11), 93–100.

Notes for Chapter 9

1 See Mintzberg, H. (1994). The fall and rise of strategic planning. *Harvard Business Review, 72*(1), 107-14.
2 Rooke, D., and Torbert, W. R. (2005). 7 transformations of leadership. *Harvard Business Review, 83*(4), 66-76.
3 See especially the well-founded critiques of traditional corporate planning from Henry Mintzberg and Roger Martin in the bibliography for this chapter.
4 Martin, R. L. (2014). A simple nuance that produces great strategy discussions. *Harvard Business Review*. https://hbr.org/2014/05/a-simple-nuance-that-produces-great-strategy-discussions, published May 8, 2014, accessed September 17, 2024.
5 Amalgamated from the references in this chapter, but see especially Mintzberg, H. (1994). The fall and rise of strategic planning. *Harvard Business Review, 72*(1), 107-14; and Martin, R. L. (2014). The big lie of strategic planning. *Harvard Business Review, 92*(1-2), 78-84.
6 Adapted and revised from a number of standard planning approaches, including, Bourgeois, L. J. III. (2013). Developing a strategy. *Darden School of Business Technical Note* S-0232, published November 6, 2013. Charlottesville, VA: Darden School of Business.
7 As quoted in Warner, R. (1987). Biggs has plans for Tyson. *The Times and Democrat*, Orangeburg, South Carolina, August 19, p. 7.
8 Rivkin, J. W. (2001). An options-led approach to making strategic choices. *Harvard Business School Background Note* 702-433, December 2001 (revised February 2006). Boston, MA: Harvard Business Publishing.
9 Hiatt, S. R., and Weber, J. (2012). Congruence model note. *Harvard Business School Technical Note* 413-037, August 2012 (revised October 2012). Boston, MA: Harvard Business Publishing.
10 For this performance management method, see especially Doerr, J. (2018). *Measure What Matters: OKRs—The Simple Idea That Drives 10x Growth*. London, England: Portfolio Penguin.
11 Kaplan, R. S., and Norton, D. P. (2000). *The Strategy-Focused Organization: How Balanced Scorecard Companies Thrive in the New Business Environment*. Boston, MA: Harvard Business School Press; and the other related works on this from Kaplan and Norton (see the bibliography for this chapter).
12 Kaplan, R. S., and Norton, D. P. (2000). Having trouble with your strategy? Then map it. *Harvard Business Review, 78*(5), 167-76.
13 Mankins, M. C, and Steele, R. (2005). Turning great strategy into great performance. *Harvard Business Review, 83*(7-8), 64-72.
14 Ibid.
15 Neilson, G. L., Martin, K. L., and Powers, E. (2008). The secrets to successful strategy execution. *Harvard Business Review, 86*(6), 60-70.
16 Nadler, D. A., and Tushman, M. L. (1997). *Competing by Design: The Power of Organizational Architecture*. New York, NY: Oxford University Press.

Chapter 10

Conclusion: A Dialogue About Questions That Give You Strategic Answers

"A prudent question is one half of wisdom."

—Francis Bacon

Jada looked around the room at Kurt and the six company leaders that she and Conrad had been working with for months.

"I'm gonna miss you all," she said a bit wistfully. "You've been about as open-minded a group of leaders as we've seen in a while. Usually, successful leaders who run good outfits think that our method is perhaps too drawn out and contingent for them to add to their enormous pile of day-to-day responsibilities."

"Drawn out, for sure!" laughed Alexis Chapman. "I was chomping at the bit to get going and you made me think for weeks before I could be my usual action super-hero self."

Ian Driscoll laughed with her. "Me too. Drawn out I get now, but contingent?"

"Contingent!" Conrad said with emphasis. "What you do strategically is *contingent* on other things. Your choices—even your strategic approach—may simply be contingent on the way you ask questions at the beginning of your strategic process. How you start your strategic thinking will definitely shape the outcomes you might consider."

"Thus no magic answers that we all desperately wanted to save time," chimed in Liz Fiscella. "A part of me still yearns for the 'strategy machine'—if there was such a thing—to spit out the right answer."

"A natural impulse," agreed Jada. "Especially for busy people trying to wrestle with a mountain of data and changing market conditions in order to plot a path to the future."

"And I want to get to the future ahead of all my competition," said Suzie Nguyen. "But as I reflect on it, you two gave us something more long-lasting than tomorrow's strategy answer—you helped us learn *how* to think strategically, not *what* to think strategically."

Conrad nodded. "Yes, we're not smart enough to tell you exactly what move to make next for your business. But we can definitely tell you about how to think through the most fundamental purpose of a strategy: to help your firm be in a position of sustainable competitive advantage. Like that TV show, you want to live in 'The Good Place.' A sound strategic method can help you figure out what that 'good place' is, why it's so good, and how to move there."

"It was a super helpful couple of months, for sure," said Derrick Jouet. "And we've all worked through this strategic process you taught us to come up with good options for our own strategies. So, we're at the end. Why is the final exam you gave us for homework about questions, then, and not the possible answers we've labored to produce in this process?"

Kurt Amery looked at Conrad and Jada. "Yeah, I'm on the same sheet of paper as Derrick. At your final presentation shouldn't you be pulling back a curtain to reveal some amazing sculpture or painting that we've all been working on? The dramatic final answer? Instead, your last piece of homework for us was to come in with one question we should be asking to stress test our strategic thinking and our strategies."

> *It is a natural impulse to seek immediate answers to questions of strategy and where to go in the future. But it is more important to learn how to think strategically, not what to think strategically.*

Jada looked at him thoughtfully. "Yeah, I guess some consultants think that the big prize at the end will make you feel like you got your money's worth. But we just want to make sure your heads are in the right place—the strategic place, that is."

Conrad nodded. "Look, gang, you will all ultimately produce the strategic answers you need by yourselves—I guarantee you. Steve will launch a new product or into a new market, Liz will expand, Suzie will do a deal … or three! Ian will figure out how to make money, and so on. That is on you! Our final exam for you is to make sure that you can ask the questions of your strategy that prompt the right discussions among your people—questions that lead you to explore your options with the right tools and then ultimately launch into decision mode. If you don't get into the process the right way, you won't come out with anything good."

Steve Adlar looked around the room and chuckled. "Nice try," he said to his colleagues with a smile.

Jada was up at the whiteboard drawing and turned around to smile at him. "Okay, now that we've reaffirmed that we're all about the method and not your specific answers, let's look at the exam. We asked each of you to come to our final session with one question you might ask your strategy team that would prompt the right conversations and the right process for a sound strategic method. Remember this?" She wrote:[1]

> *Asking the right questions ... →*
>
> *Leads to knowing what analytical frameworks to use ... →*
>
> *Which might give us insights about our challenges and opportunities ... →*
>
> *Which will allow us to develop and analyze possible choices ... →*
>
> *Which should inform our ultimate decision about which way to go.*

Jada put down her marker. So, this is why we end with questions in our final session. Think of it like an orbit around a planet—if you enter it successfully, you can stay in it. Let's get your spaceship in the strategy orbit with the questions as your rocket boosters."

Conrad went to a different patch of board. "Instead of going around the room, let's try and go in order of when you think a strategic question should be asked. Who thinks they are there at the beginning, so to speak?"

Derrick tentatively raised his hand.

"Give it to us, Derrick," said Conrad, his marker poised.

"Well," said Derrick. "You said that one of the primary roles of the leader was to define reality for their followers, and strategy moves you from now to the future, so here's my question."

> *Where are we now?*

"Great," said Conrad. "Just so. And of course, to have a good definition of what 'now' is, you and your team would have to agree about what metrics make sense to measure your current state."

Steve reached into his bag and pulled out a few pages from his Map of Paris exercise. "I pinned my market map up on the wall and circled which neighborhood we live in right now so my people could see it visually."

Conrad and Jada nodded with satisfaction.

Liz spoke up. "Okay, that is a good starting point. Then I think my strategic question naturally follows." She looked sheepish. "I snuck in a double question."

Where do we go and what do we do when we're there?

"Makes sense to me," said Jada, as Conrad wrote it up. "Those go together. If a strategy changes you, you want to define the new destination by more than just a new location on the competitive landscape. Perhaps your scope of activities and market reach has changed as well."

"I am guessing," added Kurt, "that, underneath, that simple question will cause a huge discussion and debate about why such a move was made. The goals to be achieved and the competitive environment in which that happens—and how those interact with each other?"

"Absolutely," agreed Conrad. "You'd be well-served in wrestling with this question to use the frameworks we discussed for external market and internal competency analysis. The great strategist Roger Martin called those questions "defining your winning aspiration" and deciding "where you will play."[2]

Ian Driscoll spoke up. "I'm guessing my question points to the explanation that needs to accompany a suggested move to a new position in the market."

Why does such a move make sense?

Ian continued. "If someone lays out the need to change from what-is-now to what-is-a-better-future, I want to know exactly what it brings us, why that is important, how the competitive landscape looks different once we are there, and if we can realistically pull it off."

"I guess my question is sort of in that vein, but perhaps not?" said Suzie. "Mine is linked to our discussion about core competencies, value disciplines, and the dominant gene in our DNA concept."

What unique value do we bring, and how do we sustain it?

"I thought this was the most important question I could think of because if it turns out there is a 'good place' in a changing market, won't everybody else see it, too? There are not many secret markets. I just figured many other firms in our space are working toward similar goals," she finished.

"Shrewd thinking, Suzie," agreed Jada. "Roger Martin called this the 'How will we win where we have chosen to play?' question, which is at the heart of competitive strategy. In our experience, it is also the question where companies can be the *least* honest with themselves. They can fool themselves into not taking this question seriously, like the evil queen in Snow White being lied to by her mirror."

"I've been waiting to see this sequence unfold and I think my question is next," said Steve. "This came up in my own strategy review after agreement on where to go and why. We then got into a pretty heated discussion about this."

How will we do it and what do we need?

"It turns out we had many different options in that discussion," Steve continued. "We could use some generic strategies or some more innovative and disruptive strategies to move in the market. As you will remember, we were even playing with foreign outsourcing options, joint ventures, or acquisitions as part of the 'how.' Dozens of different ways to possibly get to the same destination."

Jada nodded. "Yes, and they all need to be analyzed and weighed—costs, risks, timing, and much else. The good news is it sounded like you drilled down on the last of Roger Martin's questions: the capabilities you would need to make the move, and the systems to support that."

"At the risk of sounding like I'm charging you fees by the number of frameworks I cite," Conrad said with a smile, "That question drives much of the work we did to understand basic and advanced strategic moves, differences in business models, and the complicated world of M&A and going global."

"There were a lot of frameworks in there for sure," said Kurt. "My take-away was that the key was to know which one to use and how to use it. It helped me to organize all the data I had, let alone all the thoughts in my head."

"Alright you big-brained strategy geeks," said Alexis with a wink to the group. "It won't surprise you to know that I am still focused on execution!" she said to knowing laughter. "So my question's to do with this."

How will we know when we get there?

"I have this nightmare scenario in my head where we decide all these things about how to be well positioned in a changing competitive land-scape," she explained. "People get excited about it and run off and make all kinds of investments and prompt changes, and yet we might not have an accurate way to measure progress or achievement in all the goals accompanying that strategy."

"Nobody likes nightmares," said Jada. "But if you must have one, that's a constructive one because it's risky if you don't measure what matters—strategically, that is. It's critical that you adopt a strategic management system that can take you from planning to measuring performance. You need to keep score and know your progress. A good plan can also help you prioritize things, align goals, set out the sequencing of action, identify dependencies, appoint the responsible parties, hold people accountable, and much else."

Alexis raised an eyebrow dramatically. "Oh ... you like strategic planning now?"

Jada smiled at her. "Look, I realize we gave you a *massive* caveat about the misuse of strategic planning and spent a bunch of time on how not to use it. You cannot let conventional corporate programming drag your strategic process entirely to the known past and rob you of any creative thinking about the future. But we all know that it would be suicide to launch into a strategy without a plan."

"And," added Derrick, "I want to remember why the air usually leaks out of the balloon of a new strategy. I was struck by those similar points of 'leakage' in many strategies—common-sense things that cause a new strategy to deliver less than it promises."

"Good reminder," said Jada. "Simple things can really undercut a good strategy and the impact you hoped for. But knowing what those are likely to be in advance helps you get ahead of that challenge."

"So, these questions you've written up," asked Kurt. "Are we to ask them at the beginning of the strategy process? During? Afterwards as a kind of preflight checklist, like pilots before the plane takes off?"

Conrad looked at him. "Yes, yes, and ... umm ... yes!"

Kurt looked embarrassed.

"The point I'm making, of course," said Conrad, "is that a good strategist is constantly asking questions like these and many more. Moreover, you don't *do* strategy in a static environment. Strategy is performed in a live, dynamic, changing environment. Things need to be constantly measured and reassessed. Changes in the market might cause us to reprioritize our goals and methods. So, these questions force us to have a process for recognizing those external changes, and for analyzing, deciding, and adjusting.

"Similarly, what needs to change about our internal resources, organizational framework, people, processes, or policies to get these things done may shift as we implement the strategy. The question of what needs to change around here to accomplish this strategy must be regularly asked ... and answered."

> *Strategy is performed in a live, dynamic, changing environment. Plans and assumptions need to be constantly measured and reassessed.*

"You've seen the questions we use to keep the strategic process on track," Jada added. "And we told you about Roger Martin's questions. There are other methods including ones you will develop yourself if you are thinking strategically.[3] It's not that important what particular method you use or specific questions you ask. The goal is to use stress-test questions that always give you a strategic dialogue with your leaders so that those common problems in executing strategy are headed off at the pass."

The team in the room nodded their heads.

"Great stuff—well done!" said Jada, putting a huge checkmark and explanation point next to their list of questions on the board. "This list will keep you out of a lot of trouble."

Conrad nodded. "Let me close this out with a thought," he said. "You are all strategic leaders—you were before we met you, even if you didn't think of yourselves that way. Strategy is noble work that exists at a level *above* the day-to-day running of your company. When you work with your team to formulate a new strategy, you give them a renewed sense of purpose, a plan that captures the essence of winning for you far into the future.[4] It can be a real superpower for you if you engage in it, but you have to do it the right way. It is not a magic spell to be cast. Don't use it like some leaders do—portraying it as all about having a brilliant insight and then—boom!"

He paused. "Well, if that worked for a handful of leaders, they are one-in-a-million types. The rest of us get to good strategies by using a disciplined thought process, and some tools and frameworks to organize our thinking. That prompts a discussion … and some analysis … and probably a healthy amount of debate … about what to do, why, when, and how to do it. At the end of the day, we get some options to be weighed or tried, and some choices to be made."

He wrote on the board:

Commit to the process, don't leap to an answer!

"That is what we think strategy is about. We know that you can all think strategically, lead that endeavor, and, in doing so, frame a great future for your firms. Good luck!"

Conrad and Jada's key takeaways

Key questions to ask of your strategy:

- **Where are we now?** What metrics are best to measure our current state?

- **Where do we go?** What goal should we strive for?

- **What do we do when we're there?** What is the scope of our activities and competitive reach?

- **Why does that make sense?** Does achieving that goal advance our strategic intent? Does it serve our mission?

- **What unique value do we bring and how do we sustain it?** Many other companies are out there working toward similar goals. How do we set ourselves apart?

- **How will we do it and what do we need?** Who in our company should "own" this and how will they drive it? What resources, systems, and people are needed?

- **How will we know we get there?** Do we have an accurate way to measure progress or achievement in each goal?

Notes for Chapter 10

1 Kryscynski, D. (2019). "Questions mindset". YouTube video. https://youtu.be/9eTaesblopQ?si=RV-jTq7ACeb0l-0nW, published November 13, 2019, accessed September 22, 2024.
2 Martin, R. (2010). Five questions to build a strategy. *Harvard Business Review*. https://hbr.org/2010/05/the-five-questions-of-strategy, published May 26, 2010, accessed September 22, 2024.
3 See, for instance, Simons, R. (2010). Stress-test your strategy: The 7 questions to ask. *Harvard Business Review*, 88(11), 92–100.
4 Hamel, G., and Prahalad, C. K. (2005). Strategic intent. *Harvard Business Review*, 83(7–8), 148–161.

Acknowledgements

One of the most fortunate circumstances in my career was meeting, working closely with, and learning from two of the great strategic minds of our time: Professors Sir Michael Howard and Sir Lawrence Freedman. Widely considered the most eminent strategists of the age, they understood and taught strategy in its traditional form—its application in the political-military realm and the great turning of history that results.

This is a book on business strategy (about which Freedman has written a bit) and not the grand strategy field in which these two mentors and friends made their name. However, the strategic mindset and the understanding of strategy at its basic science level flow from its original definition: *strategos*—the art of the General. Business strategy is the "applied science" of strategy and the strategic mindset in a different setting than a theater of military operations or a grand diplomatic conference.

From those two men, I learned what strategy and thinking strategically truly means. I was then able to take that into my own work as a soldier, a diplomat, and a CEO. When I told another famous strategist about working with Michael and Lawry for years as a student and board member in the UK, he remarked, "Ah … you were kissed by the gods." Just so. Michael passed away in 2020; nonetheless, here I must say, thank you, Michael and Lawry.

I also want to recognize and thank the working business strategists I have encountered over the years of running businesses and consulting on strategy. Chief among them is Ron Jones, who combines the strategic acumen and cunning of Niccolò Machiavelli with the style of Tony Soprano in an entertaining, insightful, and terrifically effective way. I learned much from working with Ron.

Ron is among the first-class business minds with whom I've worked who I asked to give this manuscript an early read. The others were my partner and the co-author of my last book, Dr. Mark Nevins, my friend and fellow board member Sid Fuchs, and the best strategy student

I ever taught, Kyle Brumby. Many thanks to them for their insights. I incorporated all I could—the omissions or mistakes here are entirely on me.

My publisher, fellow strategy professor, and friend Dietmar Sternad never flagged in his support for this project. Dietmar "got it"—the need for the book, its style, and what I hope it achieves with its readers. We started finishing each other's sentences by the end of our first video call, and we've had a Vulcan mind-meld throughout the project.

My writing coach Bill Birchard looked at the early drafts and provided invaluable feedback and suggestions on engaging business writing (see his book *Writing for Impact*). The talented Amber Anderson did the cover, the illustrations and "whiteboards" in the book. I was lucky to have them on the team for this project.

In my teaching career, I have been fortunate to teach some variation of strategy at various institutions. At George Mason University's Costello College of Business, I taught, and still occasionally teach, the core strategy course in the MBA program. I teach strategic leadership in American institutions and US Grand Strategy at historic Hampden-Sydney College. At Duke University, my alma mater, I teach a course focused on strategic thinking and leadership for graduate students involved in national security. It seems cliché to say that I learned more from my students than they did from me over the years in the classroom, but in my case, it is entirely accurate. Thus, this book's dedication. Thank you also to the university deans, college presidents, program directors, administrators, and fellow faculty who made that teaching possible.

Finally, to my close friends and family; by writing this book in the middle of all my other activities, I stole time away from what should matter most: building and maintaining close relationships. Aristotle reminded us that close friendships and relationships are one of the great purposes of human existence, and without them, happiness is not possible. Writing a book challenges the energy available for that—there are only so many hours in a day—but the support and understanding of my closest friends and family of that reality was crucial. Thank you, dear ones!

Index

About the Author

The Honorable Dr. John Hillen is a Board Chairman, Director, and College Professor. In addition to chairing two corporate boards in the defense technology sector, Hillen serves as the James C. Wheat Jr. Professor at historic Hampden-Sydney College. He also teaches strategy and leadership at Duke University and in the MBA program at George Mason University, where he has been selected three times by the students as the outstanding faculty member in the MBA program. A former public company CEO who has built and sold four mid-sized companies, he is also an award-winning leadership author, a former senior US government official, a decorated combat veteran, an experienced company director, and an executive coach.

Over the past twenty years, John has served as CEO, President, or COO of several different companies—both public and private—in different industries. He has been a director on over a dozen corporate boards (public and private) and a trustee or director in many non-profit enterprises. He took one of his companies public in one of the few successful IPOs in the American economy in 2009.

His last book, *What Happens Now? Reinvent Yourself as a Leader Before Your Business Out-runs You* (co-authored with Mark Nevins), was named one of the top 30 business books of 2018, and is in its third printing. He has published countless articles on strategy in publications such as *Forbes*, *The New York Times*, and *The Wall Street Journal*.

Unanimously confirmed by the Senate in 2005, Hillen served as the Assistant Secretary of State for Political-Military Affairs in the second half of the Bush administration. He served for twelve years as an Army reconnaissance officer and paratrooper. He is a recipient of the US Army Bronze Star for actions in combat, the US Navy's Meritorious Public Service Award, and numerous other awards and decorations.

Dr. Hillen graduated from Duke University with degrees in public policy studies and history and was awarded a Fulbright Scholarship after graduation. He holds a master's degree in war studies from King's College London, a doctorate in international relations from Oxford University, and an MBA from the Johnson School of Management at Cornell University.

Engage John Hillen
in exploring your strategy

Strategy formation & strategic thinking

John can lead your team through one or a series of strategic thinking workshops such as those portrayed in this book. An experienced facilitator who has worked with organizations ranging from large international public companies to small entrepreneurial teams, John uses original and creative exercises to help leaders and organizations develop or refine their strategy. Working together, John helps leadership teams frame their journey to position their enterprise for competitive advantage and achieve great outcomes.

Consulting on specific strategic challenges

Using his strategic expertise working with many kinds of organizations, John can help evaluate business models, aid in plans for organizational transformation, assess mergers and acquisitions, structure market and internal analysis, and implement performance management tools.

Keynote speaking engagements

An experienced speaker in many settings, you can contact John for an inspirational talk on how executives and organizations can develop their strategic thinking 'muscles.'

You can contact John directly or through his speaker's bureau at

https://www.leadingauthorities.com/speakers/john-hillen

Find more out at *www.johnhillen.com*

Boost your confidence, inspire others, become a better leader!

Whether you are new to a leadership role or want to take your existing leadership competencies to a higher level—here's the most practical guide for you. With **50 skill-building exercises** that will help you grow as a leader right away … and with heartwarming illustrations that will allow you to 'feel' what effective leadership really means.

Develop Your Leadership Superpowers: 50 Key Skills You Need to Succeed as a Leader by Dietmar Sternad and Eva Kobin is available wherever good books and ebooks are sold.